phac

D1447298

FEB - - 2025

Praise for *Born Into Loss*

"This compelling book illuminates the challenging life experiences of replacement children and the significance of a loss that echoes across generations. The authors weave together dozens of interviews to uncover the texture of family grief and how it reverberates for children born after the loss of a child. *Born Into Loss* is an invaluable resource for parents who have suffered the loss of a child and for the subsequent children who may identify with the replacement child condition."

—Judy L. Mandel, *New York Times* bestselling author of *Replacement Child: A Memoir* and *White Flag*

"This book offers critical insights about the lived experiences of subsequent children and also explores some of the parallel themes faced by children who are born after a sibling with severe special needs. I was grateful for the attention paid to this often-overlooked group of children. The authors provide a priceless resource for special needs families and for the clinicians and early childhood professionals who work with them."

—Jolene Pearson, PhD, IMH-E® (IV), associate professor emerita of early childhood education, Bethel University

"Vollmann and O'Leary draw from their decades of clinical experience and research to clarify the experience of being born after loss. Their book is a sensitive and critical resource for bereaved parents, healthcare workers, extended family, and all who interface with grieving families and replacement children. It is a much-needed gift for all who are born after loss, offering insight, compassion, and hope. I can't recommend this book enough."

—Rita J. Battat, co-author of *Replacement Children: The Unconscious Script*

"The thousands of children born after loss every year have suddenly acquired allies, in the form of the authors of *Born Into Loss*. They speak for this child in a way rarely seen in the literature. This book is a gift to families who have suffered loss, of course, but it is especially a gift to the children who come after."

—Michael Trout and Mary Koloroutis, authors of *See Me as a Person: Creating Therapeutic Relationships with Patients and Their Families*

"The experiences of children born after a sibling with severe special needs rarely have been understood or explored. This book provides glimpses into the lives, minds, and hearts of these children and offers testimony to the potent and life-shaping influence of their disabled sibling. It provides valuable lessons to families, educators, and practitioners."

—Jean Mendenhall, special education early intervention teacher

"This comprehensive book offers hope to replacement children and support to bereaved parents. Sensitive and encouraging, Sarah Vollmann and Joann O'Leary look at the consequences of sibling loss in a family. This book is a must-read and a gift, offering professional insight on how to identify and support replacement children as well as an in-depth understanding and words of wisdom."

—Kristina Schellinski, author of *Individuation for Adult Replacement Children: Ways of Coming into Being*; co-founder of Replacement Child Forum and Replacement Child Professionals

BORN INTO LOSS

BORN INTO LOSS

LOSS

SHADOWS OF DECEASED SIBLINGS

AND

FAMILY JOURNEYS OF GRIEF

SARAH REED VOLLMANN

AND JOANN M. O'LEARY

ROWMAN & LITTLEFIELD
Lanham • Boulder • New York • London

Published by Rowman & Littlefield
An imprint of The Rowman & Littlefield Publishing Group, Inc.
4501 Forbes Boulevard, Suite 200, Lanham, Maryland 20706
www.rowman.com

86-90 Paul Street, London EC2A 4NE

Copyright © 2025 by Sarah Reed Vollmann and Joann M. O'Leary

All rights reserved. No part of this book may be reproduced in any form or by any electronic or mechanical means, including information storage and retrieval systems, without written permission from the publisher, except by a reviewer who may quote passages in a review.

British Library Cataloguing in Publication Information Available

Library of Congress Cataloging-in-Publication Data

Names: Vollmann, Sarah Reed, 1970- author. | O'Leary, Joann, author.
Title: Born into loss : shadows of deceased siblings and family journeys
   of grief / Sarah Reed Vollmann and Joann M. O'Leary.
Description: Lanham : Rowman & Littlefield, [2025] | Includes
   bibliographical references and index.
Identifiers: LCCN 2024018356 (print) | LCCN 2024018357 (ebook) |
   ISBN 9781538172162 (cloth ; alk. paper) | ISBN 9781538172179
   (ebook)
Subjects: LCSH: Siblings. | Siblings--Death--Psychological aspects.
   | Subsequent pregnancy--Psychological aspects. | Parental grief. |
   Parenting--Psychological aspects.
Classification: LCC BF723.S43 V65 2025 (print) | LCC BF723.S43
   (ebook) | DDC 155.9/37--dc23/eng/20240703
LC record available at https://lccn.loc.gov/2024018356
LC ebook record available at https://lccn.loc.gov/2024018357

♾️™ The paper used in this publication meets the minimum requirements of American National Standard for Information Sciences—Permanence of Paper for Printed Library Materials, ANSI/NISO Z39.48-1992.

For my parents, in loving memory. —Sarah

For my three beautiful daughters, Annie, Michelle, and Erin, and my husband, John Sommerville, who have supported my career with families experiencing an unexpected outcome of pregnancy. —Joann

Contents

Acknowledgments

Sarah's Acknowledgments

I am grateful to the many people who supported me and this book. Thanks must go first to the subsequent siblings and families who shared their stories, and to the team at Rowman & Littlefield, including our insightful and patient editor, Jacqueline Flynn; assistant editors, Joanna Wattenberg and Victoria Shi; and our talented cover designer, Chloe Batch. I am thankful for my co-author, Joann O'Leary, who was excessively kind when my concussion symptoms delayed the book, and whose expertise about pregnancy, infant loss, and early attachment added so much. She is brilliant and kind, and I was honored to write with her.

I want to thank Kell Julliard, who introduced me to the world of research and who was incredibly generous with his advice. My initial research about subsequent children would not have been possible without his guidance. Many individuals helped me with my writing over the years, perhaps even reading early snippets of this book, and I am thankful; they include my beloved high school English teacher, Janet MacBeth; Bill O'Hanlon; Nancy Slonim Aronie and the Chilmark Writing Workshop; and my Buckingham Browne & Nichols School writing group, Candie Sanderson, Josh Walker, and Zoe Balaconis.

I also want to acknowledge several mentors who have informed my work with grief and loss, including Arthur Robbins, who I miss, and whose teachings and spark will always be a guiding influence; Jodie Wigren, who listened beautifully and wisely, and who is also missed; and Ilo Milton, whose expertise and creativity have inspired me throughout the years. I am indebted to many people in the field of bereavement, including Ken Doka and his teachings on disenfranchised loss; Jack Jordan, who invited me to speak about my experiences as a subsequent sibling on his "Our Work, Ourselves" Association for Death Education and Counseling panel; and the International Work Group's brilliant "Family Group" members, who were so welcoming to me in Halifax. I am beyond grateful to my wise and beloved Portland Institute for Loss and Transition colleagues, including Robert Neimeyer, whose teachings on meaning reconstruction are foundational in my understanding of grief; Sharon Strouse, who is a joy to collaborate with and a huge source of inspiration; and Carolyn Ng, Barbara Thompson, and Lara Krawchuk.

Additional colleagues who must be deeply thanked include my Replacement Child Forum colleagues and fellow subsequent siblings, authors Kristina Schellinski, Judy Mandel, and Rita Battat; the Buckingham Browne & Nichols School faculty who supported my growth and work toward this book, including Kim Gold, Jen Price, and Karina Baum; Assumpta Mugiraneza and Kayumba Cyitatire, who supported my exploration of the experiences of second-generation genocide survivors in Rwanda; and my adored colleagues and research partners from The Young Widowhood Project, Liza Barros Lane, who has taught me so much, Lucas Sanchez, and Kelley Ellis.

I also want to express my gratitude to my much-loved family of origin, including my surviving siblings, Bill and Ann. I am grateful for the ways in which our family was resilient and recognize that all members of the family have their own story of loss to tell. And finally, my gratitude and love for my husband and son, Barry and Thomas, are endless, and have no bounds.

Joann's Acknowledgments

No one goes through life without walking alongside others for support and learning. There are many people to thank for this book, most especially the parents whom I have had the honor of working with over the last forty years. They were my teachers during their subsequent pregnancies. Their stories of grief for their much-loved deceased babies and their struggles to attach to the children who followed are powerful. Their fears of also losing their subsequent babies are a huge impediment. My experiences with them, in collaboration with my nursing colleagues Lynnda Parker and Clare Thorwick, led us to develop an interdisciplinary prenatal attachment-based parenting model of intervention, which was integrated into the medical model of care.

I would like to acknowledge my many mentors over the years, including Janet Thayer, Jean Mendenhall, Marie Grimsgard, and James Judd. They worked alongside me in early intervention with families of special needs children. Delphie Fredlund and Dr. Bob ten Bensel were my advisors for my master's degree in public health. Special thanks go to the Minneapolis Rotary Club who, with the support of Dr. Donald Skyes, sponsored my second master's degree in psychology from Queens University in Belfast, Northern Ireland. My PhD was guided by Dr. Ruth Thomas, funded by the Bush Foundation in St. Paul, Minnesota. They sent me to Australia where I met Dr. Jane Warland, a bereaved mother of Emma and subsequent child Sara. Her perspective was valuable.

I am deeply thankful for all the support from my faithful friends and colleagues over many years, including Jolene Pearson, Roberta Hunt, Jacquie Kelley, and Cecilie Gaziano. I also want to acknowledge my colleagues in the field of pre- and perinatal psychology and health, most especially the founders of the Association for Prenatal and Perinatal Psychology and Health, David Chamberlain and Thomas Verny. Along with Willian Emerson and others in our organization, they carry the message forward that one's prenatal environment matters.

Special acknowledgments belong to the deceased children, the siblings who followed, and those whose stories are in the chapter on children with special needs, especially Matthew Pohlad and Christopher and Blake Engstrom, whose parents provide the funding for our first manual written on "Pregnancy After Loss."

I am thankful for my ongoing connection and work with the Star Legacy Foundation. I am equally thankful to my co-author

Sarah. With her excellent editing skills, she built on our interdisciplinary collaboration of research with the children born after a loss, to augment and bring this book to fruition.

One final note: the names of the deceased babies in this book were not changed with permission from their parents. The parents need to hear their deceased babies' names as they did exist and are still very much a part of their families.

Foreword

In the several decades in which I have been practicing as a psychotherapist, I've encountered many clients, of all ages, who were born sometime after the death of a sibling. Interestingly, only rarely were they seeking grief therapy regarding the loss of their brother or sister—although that loss often emerged as significant as they were addressing another, more contemporary loss of a friend or family member. More frequently, they were struggling with vexing issues of perfectionism, difficulties expressing their own needs or desires, a sense of insufficiency to meet the expectations of others, a feeling of "invisibility" in important relationships, turbulent family patterns, or "co-dependency" with or entrenched resentments toward an overprotective parent. Only as we looked into their "origin stories" did we discover the common experience of growing up in the shadow of a sibling's death, and its role in explaining the personal and relational patterns that developed in its wake. With that, the seemingly problematic patterns achieved a new coherence, and conscious, self-compassionate efforts to address them in the present became possible, often including attention to the client's disenfranchised grief for a sibling they had never known.

In *Born Into Loss*, authors Sarah Vollmann, herself born in the shadow of a sister's dying, and Joann O'Leary, a specialist in pregnancy after loss, offer the most complete, most nuanced, and most compassionate coverage of this experience yet published. Drawing on deep-going interviews into the experiences of over one hundred subsequent children, the authors artfully tease out the common strands in their narratives: the lingering grief of their parents, their own vague sense of guilt, the pressure of attempting to fill an impossible void or to measure up to a haunting and idealized ghost, and their striving for acceptance as the unique people they were or as the super-children they attempted to be. Likewise, they explicate the fears of bereaved parents contemplating another pregnancy, their fears in bonding to another child who might also die, the anatomy of replacement dynamics, the complex attachment patterns that often result, and the contradiction of mourning a previous child while parenting a subsequent one. What emerges is an uncommonly intimate portrayal of understudied and typically unconscious family processes that can complicate the lives of later children in a way that follows them into their adult lives.

If readers expect that a project of such scope and depth can only be written in a turgid academic style, they are in for a pleasant surprise. Vollmann and O'Leary, like the subsequent children they frequently quote, speak in an accessible and engaging conversational style, never drawing attention to itself, but clearly and compellingly exploring an experience that is as complex as it is captivating. I found myself fascinated, as the siblings' stories carried me forward to more fully grasp both their struggles and their resilience. The book more than rewarded the reading, sharpening my clinical and more broadly human understanding of lives shaped by grief for someone the subjects never knew. In bravely attempting, often eloquently, to make sense of their own experience, the book's interviewees help the reader find sense and significance in it as well. I recommend it to all parents considering pregnancy after loss of a child, to all subsequent children seeking an intelligent and compassionate mirror of their own developmental challenges, and all those other siblings, family members, and professionals who seek to understand and support them in leading lives in which they feel valued for the unique persons they are.

Robert A. Neimeyer, PhD
Director, Portland Institute for Loss and Transition
Editor, *New Techniques of Grief Therapy:*
Bereavement and Beyond

Preface

We, the two authors, met by chance at a professional conference. Joann approached with a question, and after reading her nametag Sarah exclaimed "I know you! I quoted your work in my article about subsequent children!" We sat together and launched into a lengthy discussion about our shared focus. We were both independently in the early phases of writing books about subsequent children, replacement dynamics, and parental grief. After an hour together, Joann suggested that perhaps we should combine forces, and the story of this book began.

We use the terms "subsequent child" and "subsequent sibling" interchangeably throughout the book to refer to an individual who was born after the death of a sibling. Our drive to research and write about subsequent children was fueled by a dire lack of information. Little has been written or understood regarding the experiences of those who are born after the death of a sibling. There is often an assumption that subsequent children will be untouched by the loss because they did not meet their deceased sibling, and they were not present when the death occurred. If we step back to examine the larger picture, however, we will recognize the enduring grief and trauma of families who lose a child. Subsequent children are born into a drastically altered familial landscape that has been shaped and redefined by grief.

Subsequent siblings frequently face many repercussions that are tied to their role. In some families, subsequent children are conceived, consciously or unconsciously, to replace the deceased sibling and to fill the void. A lot of the clinical literature accordingly refers to subsequent children as "replacement children." We prefer a more nuanced understanding and believe that "replace-ment dynamics" are a more accurate way to understand the var-ied ways that replacement wishes or pressures may be enacted in families.[1]

This book weaves together our cumulative research and interviews of more than one hundred subsequent siblings, with the goal of giving voice to a group that has rarely been heard. We include additional interviews with bereaved parents and siblings who were alive at the time of their sibling's death, whom we refer to as "surviving siblings," for a holistic view upon grieving families and the aftershocks of the loss of a child. All partici-pants gave us their consent to share their stories, and we are very thankful for their important, brave, and generous contributions.

We have both published articles pertaining to subsequent children, but they are housed in clinical journals and primarily read by professionals in the field of grief, loss, and mental health. We hope that this book will be accessible to all, and that it can expand our collective understanding of the common experiences and stories of subsequent children. Many of the subsequent sib-lings whom we interviewed said that they had rarely been given the opportunity to speak about the loss of their sibling or the impact upon them and their families. They often expressed inter-est in the other research participants and wondered aloud if their thoughts or responses were "normal." This book was written for them and for all subsequent siblings. We hope that it will allow subsequent children to examine, normalize, and gain insights about their experiences, and to make meaning, as they wish, of their role and its impact.

This book was also written as a resource for any family that has lost a child, including individuals who parent a subsequent child and those who plan to do so. We hope that it will provide support and insight for parents who contemplate a pregnancy after loss. Bereaved parents are often surprised by the grief and anxiety that can surface during a subsequent pregnancy and the parenting of a subsequent child. Thoughtful and preven-tative measures can be taken if grieving parents are aware of their own needs for support and of the common risks, including replacement dynamics, of the subsequent child role. Finally, we additionally aimed to provide a helpful resource for clinicians, educators, and healthcare workers who work with subsequent children and bereaved families, to heighten awareness and tailor appropriate interventions and support.

While we have both specialized in researching and working with subsequent children and grieving families, we have differing vantage points, life experiences, and professional backgrounds that inform these pages. Sarah is an art therapist and licensed clinical social worker who specializes in working with grief and loss, and she is also a subsequent child. She was invested in writing a book that was grounded in the vantage point of a family as a system, and she was mindful of a need to balance empathy and care for bereaved parents with the vital task of airing subsequent sibling voices. The needs and feelings of subsequent children are sometimes hushed or minimized within a bereaved family to protect and care for grieving parents, because bereaved parents are often identified as the primary mourners with the most devastating loss. In this book she aimed to write with tenderness and care for grieving parents while centering the voices of subsequent children, because they have often been disenfranchised, and they need to be heard. Joann is an infant mental health specialist with expertise in working with parents after pregnancy loss. Her background includes work as a licensed practical nurse in a newborn intensive care unit and in the field of early childhood education. She is passionate about her work with bereaved and pregnant parents, families and infants, and families with children who have special needs. She wrote with a lens upon helping to prevent disrupted attachments during pregnancy and in infancy, and, like Sarah, a deep interest in attachment after loss, and the effects of grief and loss upon a family system over time and across generations.

We will each share our backstory, as our professional and personal journeys provided a bedrock for this book.

Sarah

My sister died in the month of August. She was six years old but almost seven when she drowned in a New Hampshire lake. As with most accidents, a series of events went wrong. The lifeguard had gone off duty moments before, and the adults had briefly stepped away. My sister waded in a shallow spot with a sharp drop-off and suddenly found herself in deep water. She was searched for and found, but not quickly enough.

My family was upended, devastated, and forever changed. After the first agonizing year, they went to Italy for a six-month sabbatical. My parents, who were usually financially cautious, sold the house and cashed in their savings to finance the trip. I think that they were desperate to escape and to try to heal and salvage the family in whatever way that they could. My dad wrote a book, and they lived in the hills of Florence, in an old house surrounded by umbrella pines and Italian cypress trees. He immersed himself in work to cope with his grief. Late one night, when he was up writing and unable to sleep, my mother came downstairs to tell him that she wanted another baby. That would be me. I was born less than two years after my sister died.

What can I tell you about my lost sister? I have fragments of family stories, but not many. Once my dad burned the dinner steak on the grill. The rest of the family refused to eat it, but my sister bravely insisted that it was delicious and gulped it down. Most of the photos of my sister include my brother, because the two of them were inseparable. As a baby she used to coo in her crib, and she was reportedly the easiest baby of all of us. She was buried in a turquoise velvet dress. Her death has stayed with all of us, casting a deep imprint upon our family.

Last year, I traveled to New Hampshire with my mom to put flowers on my sister's grave. We stopped at the florist for our usual pink roses, pale flowers with no smell, bundled with ferns and a spiraling pink ribbon. As per tradition, we also drove by the small house where my family lived when my sister died. Two kids paused in the road as we rounded the block, straddling their bikes before pedaling off in roundabout lines. I always had this view from the car window, this quick sighting from behind glass. As they glanced with neutral eyes at our slow moving car, I thought that they could be my brother and sister, and that my siblings surely rode their bikes in the same pattern on the asphalt that was warmed by the sun. The street sign at the end of the block was weathered and old, and it was surely the same too. It had been there since the start of time, quiet under many snowfalls, and familiar to the smell of rain, tar, and repaved roads.

Construction trucks were parked on the front lawn of my family's former home, and the garage stood gaping open. My mom and I feared that they were ripping down the house. I parked, spoke to the construction workers, and learned that it was simply a renovation. We asked if we could peek inside the house, and they waved us on indifferently.

I was entering this house for the very first time. We walked in quietly. My mother pointed out the living room, and I recognized the cabinets from the Christmas photos of my family from so long ago. We took the small steps upstairs and entered my sister's bedroom.

My mother inhaled. The built-in dresser, where my sister's clothes had been kept, was still there, almost fifty years later. How could this be? I wished secretly that I could steal a knob from the dresser, to have something that my lost sister had touched.

On our drive home, my mom told me that my sister had been a perfect child. This was a familiar and well-worn statement. She explained that many bereaved parents idealize their children after they die, but that my sister was actually perfect. Even her kindergarten teacher said so.

Throughout my childhood, I heard about my perfect sister and knew that I would never measure up. I wondered if I would have even been born if my sister had not died, and worried for my heartbroken parents. I felt the weight of a terrible grief.

My sister's death loomed large for me, but my experience, as the subsequent child born afterwards, was consistently unspoken and strangely set apart. It was simply off the radar. I often looked but was never able to find a book about people who were born after the death of a brother or sister. I eventually became determined to research the topic and to write about it myself. After becoming a therapist who specializes in working with grief and loss, I carried out a qualitative research study, interviewing people who were born after the loss of a sister or brother. As I lived in New York City, my sample was diverse, including people of various nationalities, races, religions, age groups, professions, and backgrounds. The interviews were lengthy, and the participants were excessively generous with their time, spending hours with me to share compelling and emotional stories. Many expressed curiosity about the other participants and hunger for information, because they had never spoken to another subsequent sibling. They frequently stated that our interview was their first invitation or opportunity to discuss and reflect upon their experiences. After completing my research, I published an article in a clinical journal to add to the scant literature and data. My bigger goal was to write this book.

As themes and commonalities emerged from participant interviews, I was interested to learn that subsequent siblings often choose a helping profession. My path fits that mold. I am an art therapist and a clinical social worker with many years of experience working in a range of clinical settings, including mental health clinics, schools, a hospital, a residential treatment facility, and a private practice. I have specialized in working with grief and loss, providing treatment for bereaved children, adolescents, adults, and families. I have also published and presented both nationally and internationally on the topic of bereavement.

Of course, it is not an accident that I have been drawn to working with loss. My sister's death is well processed, and yet it is also a part of me, a part of who I became. I never met my sister, but I am deeply familiar with the void that she left behind.

Joann

It has been over thirty-five years since my nurse colleague, Lynnda Parker, and I began our first pregnancy after loss group. Of the four mothers attending, each had suffered different losses, yet their stories shared common themes: fear and anxiety, mistrust of their body as a safe place for a baby to grow, wanting the pregnancy to be over, and holding back feelings for an unborn baby that might also die. We ended the group by saying "See you in two weeks." They replied, "Two weeks! We need to come every week." When the group ended, we were exhausted. Lynnda, a clinical nurse specialist, turned to me and said: "Did you see all those women with high-risk pregnancies?" She heard the medical implications: mothers who had lost trust in their bodies, putting them at risk for medical complications and preterm labor symptoms they might ignore. As an infant mental health specialist coming from an early childhood background, I replied "Did you see all those babies who may be at risk for attachment disorders?" I visualized babies carried by mothers who were trying to deny the babies within. I understood that these mothers were fearful to attach to a subsequent child and that they were anxiously avoiding a bond. The joy of pregnancy was overshadowed by their anxiety and fear of another loss.

Years later, when my older sister Geraldine was dying, my reasons for being drawn to the feelings of the unborn babies became clear to me. Two days before her death, she looked up at me and said, "You know I never liked you." I replied, yes, that I was aware, but I did not know why. She then said, "I didn't like you even when you were inside mom's belly." Fast forward to her funeral. My uncle, who had lived with us when I was born, said that my sister was so jealous of me that she wouldn't let my mother play with me. When he came home, he noticed I was always in the crib. I remember having nightmares as a child, of going somewhere with my sister and mother and of being left behind. I would always see my sister smirking at my neglect. Now I realize that it was a memory from the crib and wonder about my own prenatal experience.

In presentations around the world, my colleagues and I showed a video we developed, entitled *After Loss: Journey of the Next Pregnancy*. People in the audience repeatedly approached us to say, "I was that child! I heard my parents in the voices of those parents." Some were so emotionally overcome that they could barely speak, and their responses led me to expand my research. In addition to interviewing bereaved parents with subsequent pregnancies, I began to include the adult children who were born after loss, to gain a deeper understanding of the repercussions of loss upon their identities and childhood experiences. In collaboration with my two nurse colleagues, Lynnda and Clare Thorwick, I was also prompted to develop a prenatal parenting intervention to positively influence prenatal attachment. The key messages are that pregnancy is the first stage of parenting[2] and that unborn babies in utero are already here and need attention immediately. Psychoeducation for bereaved and expectant parents can foster understanding that unborn children are, in many ways, attuned to the state of mind and overall well-being of their parents. The months spent in the womb are meaningful and important for a baby's future attachment relationship with their parents. Babies are negatively impacted if they are not fully embraced and welcomed, both during pregnancy and after birth.

Parents who have experienced a loss are more likely to struggle with attachment after a subsequent baby is born. In our many interviews with subsequent siblings, Sarah and I both witnessed ongoing and prevalent themes of replacement dynamics, difficult childhoods, and problematic attachments which stemmed from each family's loss. Our findings validate that attachment issues are as significant as medical issues during a pregnancy following loss.

Like a stone thrown into still water, the loss of a child has a rippling effect in families, impacting parents, surviving siblings, subsequent siblings, attachments, familial roles, and parenting practices. Our combined research explores the profound effects of the death of a child, with a primary focus upon those born after loss. We include the important stories and vantage points of all family members and recognize that the experiences, coping strategies, and resultant roles of bereaved family members are intertwined. The voices of subsequent children have rarely been heard. Their stories are at the heart and center of this book, to illuminate the experiences of replacement dynamics and of being born after loss.

1

The Subsequent Child Experience

Sarah

When I was growing up, I would hesitate when people asked me how many siblings I had. It felt disloyal to omit my sister Julie, who died before I was born, but I did not welcome the reactions that followed when I spoke of her. Most people responded with concern and discomfort upon learning that I had a deceased sister, and with questions about how and when she died. When they learned that she died before I was born, I usually received a dismissive wave, coupled with a big sigh of relief. They essentially withdrew their condolences, not to be unkind, but because my loss did not count in their eyes. They believed that it was not mine to claim and assumed that a death that took place before my birth could not harm or impact me. I quickly learned to avoid mentioning my dead sister.

My later experiences, when I was researching subsequent children and family grief, were often eye-opening. I remember finding one clinical article in which the authors interviewed a bereaved family unit. They sought to deeply understand the workings of family grief after the loss of a child, and to gather all perspectives, including parents and siblings. I was eager to read the article as there was a subsequent sibling in the family. However, the authors chose to interview all of the siblings except for the subsequent child, who was grown and perfectly able to participate. I was dismayed by their omission but not surprised, as subsequent children are so commonly overlooked.

We wrote this book to fill a void. There are many people in the world who were born after the death of a sibling, but they are rarely talked about or included in the literature about sibling loss or family grief. There is clearly an assumption, often held by parents, family members, friends, clinicians, healthcare workers, and educators, that those who are born after the death of a sibling are untouched by their sibling's loss. As a group, subsequent children are usually unseen and unrecognized, in the literature and in their lived experiences. We hope that this book will be a new and needed resource, and that it will shed some light on the subsequent child experience.

There is a little bit of research and clinical literature about subsequent children, but not a lot. The first article about the topic was published in 1964, by Albert Cain, a psychologist, and Barbara Cain, a social worker.[1] They coined the phrase "replacement child" because they noted that bereaved parents sometimes hope that a subsequent child will fill the empty space that was left by the deceased, serving as a replacement. Their study was groundbreaking and critically important for our understanding

of subsequent children. Like all research, it also had a few limitations. The families in their study were generally struggling
more than most. They were referred from therapy settings, as
they were coping with mental health issues and difficult family
dynamics. While the study uncovered vital issues that can arise
for subsequent children, outcomes also vary in each family, and
they are often less severe than those described by Cain and Cain.

The term "replacement child" elicits negative reactions from
some. We agree that it is problematic because it lacks needed
nuance. Rather than viewing all subsequent children as replacement children, or deciding if a subsequent child is, or is not, a
replacement child, we believe that there is a spectrum of replacement dynamics that may be enacted with subsequent children.[2] In
some families, like those in Cain and Cain's study, severe replacement dynamics occur, and parents are deeply invested in having
a subsequent child who serves as a substitute for the deceased.
They describe a set of bereaved parents "who initially went to
adoption agencies after their loss, requesting an eight-year-old,
thin, blue-eyed, blond boy, to replace their eight-year-old, thin,
blue-eyed, blond boy."[3] Other examples of acute replacement
dynamics can include parents who give the subsequent child the
same name as the deceased, or who actively and adamantly push
the subsequent child to mimic the behaviors, interests, or physical presentation of their deceased sibling.

On the opposite end of the spectrum, there are some subsequent children who encounter minimal replacement dynamics
in their families. Their parents are generally able to see them
as unique individuals who are separate from the deceased, and
they are not expected to be substitutes for their lost siblings.
Many subsequent children fall somewhere in the middle of the
spectrum and have evolving experiences. Replacement dynamics are sometimes pronounced with one parent but absent with
the other. They also often shift over time, as families are always
growing and changing.

A few articles and studies have followed Cain and Cain's
work. Some came from single case studies or small samples.[4] They
are valuable additions to our knowledge base but cannot provide

a larger overview to generalize about common subsequent sibling experiences. Other authors wrote about subsequent children with cases derived from the families and offspring of Holocaust survivors.[5] They explored the grief and trauma that is passed down from one generation to the next. Still others interviewed bereaved parents with subsequent children and documented parental vantage points and experiences.[6] Many researchers agreed that "we also need to hear the stories of the [subsequent] siblings."[7] This is the aim of our book.

As you will read in these pages, there are many possible consequences of the subsequent child role, although each person's experience is unique. Those who face higher levels of replacement dynamics are more likely to struggle. They may have low self-esteem, as it is impossible to satisfy a parent's desire for a replacement. They might also have difficulty forming their own, unique identity, because they are encouraged from a young age to be someone else. Fears of another loss might impair a bereaved parent's ability to securely bond to a subsequent child, resulting in a poor attachment experience. As they are born to grieving parents, many subsequent children become caregivers in their families, which is a problematic role reversal. Children need to be parented, rather than assuming worry and responsibility for their parents' needs.

There can also be silver linings to the subsequent child experience. While no one would ever wish for a family's grief and loss, some subsequent children build resilience from their histories and devote themselves to making positive contributions in their families and societies. Many choose helping professions as adults and become highly sensitive and attuned individuals due to their histories of being born after loss. They are often inspired to honor their siblings' memories through service and creative endeavors, and frequently share that their sibling's death provided them with a perspective of gratitude.

In this book, we also share the important stories of grieving parents, surviving siblings, and families. The loss of a child in a family is a shared experience within a family system. While all family members have their own reactions and experiences of the loss, each family member impacts the others. Grief is not a linear process, and significant losses, like the death of a child, are often mourned forever. Most subsequent children are carried in the wombs of grieving mothers, and their parents' bereavement is an essential piece of their origin stories. Children are deeply influenced by their parents' patterns of mourning and their family's coping capacities. We cannot understand a subsequent sibling without understanding the web of their family's grief.

2

The Narratives of Bereaved Parents

The loss of a child is said to cause the most painful grief that one can experience. It defies the natural order. Parents are not supposed to bury their children or leave the hospital without their newborn in their arms. Children are the bearers of the hopes, dreams, and futures of their families, and their parents are tasked to be their protectors. It is fairly rare in today's society for a parent to lose a child of any age. Current statistics of child mortality vary, depending upon the resources, wealth, and overall safety of a child's birthplace, but mortality rates for children have declined significantly. One hundred years ago, mortality rates for children were considerably higher. The death of a child was less surprising, and bereaved parents were likely to have a community of friends, family members, and neighbors who shared in their experience of loss. While our ancestors certainly grieved just as deeply for their lost children as we do today, the experience of child loss has shifted. In today's world, the loss of a child is often experienced as an unexpected, shocking, and unnatural event.

We begin this book with an overview of what parents may experience when their child dies. For subsequent children, their parents' narrative of loss is often a cornerstone that sets the stage for their conception, birth, role, and relationships. The stories of bereaved parents that we share in these pages provide an important context and backstory, allowing us to envision the potential mindset and feelings of grieving parents who face pregnancy and parenting after loss. The loss of a dreamed and planned future with a child is devastating, and a child's death frequently results in lifelong mourning. Parents are changed by losing a child, and their altered identities often include a shift in parenting practices that are rooted in fear, grief, and transformed priorities.

Traumatic and shocking losses, such as the loss of a child, often shatter bereaved parents' worldview and sense of self. Their belief system, sense of safety in the world, and imagined future may dramatically shift. Grieving parents frequently seek meaning as a central part of their mourning process. Many need to redefine themselves, redefine their attachment to their deceased child, and create a new life story for themselves.[1] Bereaved parents benefit from empathetic support, the validation of their needs, and an understanding that they are still parents to a much-loved child, even if that child has died. Rituals also commonly assist bereaved parents, as they foster a continuing bond with the child who died, promote a sense of control, and assist in honoring and memorializing the deceased child.[2] Parents who are well supported and have access to rituals often fare better than those whose grief is unsupported or unrecognized. Likewise, subsequent children usually benefit if their grieving parents are well cared for, and, alternatively, are more likely to encounter adverse family dynamics if their parents' mourning is unsupported or disenfranchised.

As we seek to understand the experiences of bereaved parents from prior generations, it is helpful to consider historical practices concerning infant and child loss. Before the 1970s, most parents received minimal support or resources to make meaning if their child died. Some of the examples shared in this chapter are derived from child losses that occurred in the 1970s, the 1960s, or even earlier, and they shed light upon the hospital practices and bereavement approaches of long ago. They are pertinent, because many adult subsequent siblings and families who read this book may have been impacted by those earlier practices and beliefs. Today, hospitals commonly offer meaningful rituals for bereaved parents who lose an infant, as there is an understanding that the loss of a child of any age or pregnancy stage may cause immense grief. Rituals may include holding and bathing the deceased baby, taking photographs, and dressing the infant, perhaps in clothing that had been chosen for bringing the baby home. Extended family members, such as grandparents, may come to the hospital to provide support, to mourn, and to join the parents in witnessing that the deceased baby existed. Parents often plan and attend funerals. All of these important, more recently offered rituals can help to make meaning of a deceased baby's place in the family and validate the significance of their death.

In earlier times, supportive rituals were rarely offered because the needs of bereaved parents were less understood. Parents may have been told or expected to move forward as if the loss never occurred. A loss that is unseen or invalidated by others commonly causes disenfranchised grief, which is a grief that receives no social recognition, support, or validation, despite the needs and experience of the mourner. Those whose grief is disenfranchised may feel as if they have no right to mourn, as their loss is unrecognized.[3] Grieving parents with disenfranchised grief usually feel isolated and misunderstood, leading to a repressed, hidden, and challenging grieving process.

Hospital Practices of Former Times

Earlier healthcare approaches for bereaved parents, while surely well intentioned, were often disempowering and misguided. The stories shared by participants allow us to glimpse the dynamics that were commonly present for those who lost a child, and to envision the struggles that many parents faced when grieving and approaching subsequent pregnancies and parenthood. In the past it was often considered best practice to shield mothers from unexpected pregnancy outcomes, and mothers were also frequently doubted or dismissed when they expressed concerns about their pregnancies.[4]

Jan's experience, both while pregnant and after giving birth to her deceased baby, illustrates the lack of support and agency that were commonly experienced by bereaved parents. When she was eight months pregnant, Jan went to her doctor with fears about decreased movement from her unborn baby.

> *They told me that sometimes babies don't move around as much when you are this far along in your pregnancy. A week later I went back, and they said the same thing. On my third visit they did x-rays and told me that the baby was dead.* (Jan)

Mothers were frequently anesthetized when giving birth to a baby who died in the womb or who had medical complications, as it was thought to be too traumatic to endure. Jan shared about her birthing experience.

> *They put me out right before he was born. I remember pushing, and then I woke up back in my room. I wasn't offered to see my baby. They told me that he weighed about five pounds, but they were only guessing. I asked what he looked like, and they said that he was blue.* (Jan)

Margie's mother gave birth to a stillborn daughter as her firstborn. Like Jan, she was anesthetized.

> *The resident on call realized that the baby was dead. He had my mother put to sleep. When she woke up, she was told that her baby was dead.* (Margie)

Moms were often deprived of the possibility to see or hold their babies, even when the baby was born alive. Betty never saw her stillborn son, but her husband was able to view him. She refers to her baby as "it," illustrating her lack of connection to the baby.

They did not give it to me to hold. My husband was there and said it looked just like him. He was there for the baptism. (Betty)

Melba's newborn daughter lived for a few hours, but Melba was not allowed to see her.

The major thing that I was so grief-stricken about was that they refused to let me see my baby. The nurse held her for the hour that she lived, and stayed on one side of the glass window while my family was on the other side. Why did they keep the barrier there? (Melba)

Outdated biases about gender informed the practices of healthcare staff in the past. While mothers were commonly excluded, fathers were sometimes allowed to see their dying or deceased babies, although they were sometimes prevented or discouraged from seeing their babies as well. Cap, a bereaved father, was advised against seeing his infant son.

I was told that the disability was awful, and that it would be better not to see my son. I took the doctor at his word. In some ways I regretted it. At the time, I felt that the doctor was right, and that I wouldn't want that memory. I never did see my child. (Cap)

Healthcare staff sometimes encouraged fathers to shield the mothers from loss or upset, causing fathers to feel isolated and alone with their grief. Katherine's older brother was born with special needs, and the doctors urged her father to temporarily withhold the news.

The hospital staff convinced my father not to tell my mom that anything was wrong with my brother for several days after his birth. My brother was born with Down syndrome. My father described walking endlessly on the street, in tears in the rain. I think the worst thing for him was that he had to bear it alone. My mother thought that they had a healthy newborn. The weight was enormous. (Katherine)

Mothers often had longer hospitalizations after giving birth. Some, like Margie's mom, were therefore unable to attend their baby's funeral.

Mom didn't get to go to the funeral, but Dad viewed the baby and went to the funeral. Mom didn't get to do anything to really grieve for her child. That was devastating for her. (Margie)

Some families were unsure of the burial site or outcome, and may not have a grave to visit or the baby's cremated remains. Depending on the religious practices of their church, some parents were unable to bury their babies in "sacred ground," adding to their sorrow and loss. Jan shared her experience.

Our baby wasn't baptized so he had to be buried in unblessed ground. It took a lot of years before we got a marker for him. We have a new priest now. We talked to him, and he didn't understand why the baby would be buried in unblessed ground. That helped put some closure for me. (Jan)

Ongoing Challenges

Our societal understanding of grief is expanding, which has led to some improvements in communal, hospital, and interpersonal practices. Hospitals in many societies have begun to implement more grief- and trauma-informed approaches in their care for bereaved families. However, grieving parents often continue to feel unsupported or misunderstood in various spheres of their lived experiences. Numerous bereaved families from our interviews shared about expectations or behaviors that did not feel attuned, compassionate, or helpful, and that added to their burden of grief. Their feelings and experiences are common for many grieving individuals today.

Guilt and Blame

Parents who lose a child in an accident might feel guilt and anguish about their inability to have prevented their child's death, even if they are blameless. They may also face judgment and blame from other family members, compounding their trauma and grief. Andrew, born after his three-year-old brother drowned, shared that his mother struggled with self-blame.

> *I don't think she ever accepted the fact that it was an accident. It was not something that could have been foreseen. My brother got out through the door, and she turned her back for a minute, apparently. But I think that she went through a lot of beating herself up for it.* (Andrew)

Andrew observed that his paternal grandparents seemed to blame his mother as well.

> *My mother doesn't have a good relationship with my dad's parents. In some ways they blamed her for my brother's death. I think they feel like she should have been a more responsible parent, when in fact I'm sure she was an excellent parent, but [my brother's death] was just a freak thing.* (Andrew)

Kenneth was born after the death of a brother. He was unsure of his brother's diagnosis or cause of death, but he was aware of the blame and anger in his family.

> *My brother started having difficulty breathing. My father rushed him to the hospital, but he died in his arms. My father insisted that my mother should stay in the car, so sometimes,*

when she would get really drunk, my mom would blame my dad for my brother's death. (Kenneth)

A Lack of Social Support or Understanding

Friends and family members do not always understand the significance of a child's death. Some avoid acknowledging or commemorating the loss in a misguided hope of protecting the bereaved. Advice for mourning parents, as described by Jan, is commonly centered upon disregarding the loss and its meaning.

We were told to just forget our loss, and to get on with life. (Jan)

Margie, who was born after a stillborn sister, described her mother's similar narrative.

My mother said that people expected her to snap back. But she carried the grief. (Margie)

Liz was born after her sister died of sudden infant death syndrome. She shared about her mother's experience after the loss.

After my sister's funeral, my mother discovered that her friends had come into the home to take out all of the baby stuff. The crib was taken down, and the baby clothes were taken out of the laundry. I think that everyone was thinking that they should minimize my sister's death, and help my mother avoid thinking about it. (Liz)

A common misconception is that a bereaved parent's mourning should be brief. Andrew revealed that his mother felt unsupported and misunderstood in her grieving process.

My mom went through a period of depression at a time when depression certainly wasn't dealt with through medication. It was a thing that you just had to work through.

*My mom felt pushed by the people around her who thought
"OK, you lost your son a year ago, but you should move on
now." But [your child's death] is not necessarily something
that you move on from.* (Andrew)

Bereaved parents need to speak about their loss as a part
of the healing process, but some, like Melba, describe being discouraged or denied the opportunity to talk about their deceased
children.

*My mother-in-law said that I had not been considerate of my
husband's feelings, and that I needed to support him and not
to talk about our deceased baby. My now ex-husband would
not allow me to talk about our baby. We did not share with
anyone about our grief. It was all bottled up and it stayed
that way.* (Melba)

Parents are sometimes advised by their healthcare provider
to get pregnant again, immediately, as if the deceased child never
existed and can be replaced by another child. Friends and families often encourage a rapid subsequent pregnancy as well. Having a subsequent child is frequently viewed as a solution to fix
and heal families, as described by Kenneth and Marianne.

*The doctors said that my mom should get pregnant right
away because the loss was so great. Having another baby
quickly would be the best thing to do.* (Kenneth)

*She was terrified to have another child and wanted to pro-
tect herself to avoid getting hurt again, but my dad kind of
forced it, and she got pregnant.* (Marianne)

Family and friends frequently hope that the grief of bereaved
parents will diminish once they get pregnant and have a subsequent child. They rarely understand that a new pregnancy often
resurrects or exacerbates a parent's grief for their missing child,
and that a subsequent baby cannot erase their loss. Angelo, who

was born after his three-year-old brother was killed by a drunk driver, shared about his mother's experience.

People would say to my mom, after I was born, that God took one kid but gave her another, and that she should be glad for that. My mom said that was so unfair, and that a new kid can't replace the lost one. (Angelo)

Parents and medical professionals are usually unaware that a previous loss can influence a subsequent pregnancy and birth. Only in her interview, fifty years after her son died, did Betty become conscious of the impact of her son's death upon her labor and birthing experience with her subsequent daughter.

I was fearful when I was pregnant with my daughter but thrilled at the same time. My son died right before birth when he went through the birth canal. So I held on to my daughter in labor for a long three days, because I was afraid of something going wrong during birth. It was all unconscious at the time, but it makes sense to me now. (Betty)

After losing their infant son, Cap and Marie took three years to decide that they would try to have another child. They were anxious and hypervigilant throughout the next pregnancy, despite the doctors' reassurance that the risk of another loss was low. Their fears and worry were not unusual, as "grief brings such a tremendous sense of danger to our lives. It is not so much a sense of impending doom as it is the pervasive sense that we are no longer safe."[5]

In my next pregnancy I watched myself like a hawk. I didn't eat anything wrong. I was very disciplined. (Marie)

When it was time to go to the hospital, I was so nervous that I began doing everything backwards. I had unbuttoned my shirt before this happened and I buttoned it and started unbuttoning it again and doing everything backwards and

*twice until I got my mind organized. We got there fast. I'll
never forget going to the viewing window to see our daughter after she was born. She was lying there, kind of gasping.
I hadn't experienced that before. A nurse told me not to
worry, and that the baby was in fine shape. It was a great
relief when we could bring her home.* (Cap)

Cap died at age ninety-three. His subsequent daughter, Anita,
revealed that her deceased brother was repeatedly referenced as
the family faced Cap's death, demonstrating the significance and
lasting imprint of the loss of a child upon a family.

*During the last weeks of my dad's life, he told his caregiver
that he was so afraid when I was born to find out if I was
healthy or not. He explained that he was afraid because they
lost their first child and shared his sorrow about my sibling's death. After he died, my mom spoke to a medium, who
informed her that my deceased brother was there to greet my
dad when he passed over. It was so comforting for both of us
to hear this.* (Anita)

Conclusion

The death of a child is a devastating and life-altering event, and
bereaved parents may not receive the support or care that they
need. The stories shared by our parent participants provide a
glimpse into the complexity and significance of their losses, while
also furnishing a backdrop for the experiences of subsequent
children. Child loss shapes a parent's reactions, hopes, plans, and
fears, and informs their thoughts and emotions if they choose
to undertake a subsequent pregnancy and parenting role. Many
bereaved parents face painful and complex hurdles as they con-
ceive, give birth, and parent a subsequent child. It is likely that
their experience of loss will deeply influence the life and identity of their subsequent child, who may have been conceived out
of grief, hope, despair, and love. The grief and loss of parents
are often central building blocks in a subsequent child's history,

and may provide an inheritance of challenge, mourning, and resilience.

This poem, written by the parents of a stillborn daughter, demonstrates that attachments can begin before birth, and highlights the significance of prenatal parenting and infant loss.

Dear Madison

Know you were loved from the moment you came into our lives.

Know your dad and I were so excited for you.

Know you brought so much joy to those around you – to your parents, your grandparents, and your aunts and uncles.

As you grew inside of me, we learned so much about you.

You were feisty – moving around at doctor's appointments, making it harder for the doctor to find you.

You were strong – kicking and dancing in your mom's belly.

You loved music – especially when your dad sang to you.

Our time with you was an adventure. We took you all over New York City – from midtown to downtown, to Roosevelt Island, and of course, your namesake – Madison Square Park.

You traveled to Texas, DC, and Delaware. And you were just getting to know New Jersey.

But you weren't ours to keep. We were meant to take care of you for only 38 weeks, even though we would have done anything to keep you for longer.

Our beautiful baby girl Madison, we will miss you and love you always.

Love,

Your mom and dad

(Poem by Christine and Sid, bereaved parents)

3

Pregnancy After Loss

Many of us believe that our lives began at the moment of our birth and imagine that our attachments to our parents developed in the months that followed. While that is true in many respects, we also have intrauterine experiences that impact us. Prenatal care is important for the well-being of a baby. Pregnant mothers are advised to avoid drinking alcohol or smoking, to eat healthy foods, and to get frequent check-ups, as well as regular exercise and sleep. These precautions help to ensure a healthy environment for the fetus. A mother's health and wellness extend beyond doctor visits and diet to include her mental health, self-care, resources, and environment. If a pregnant woman is facing high levels of stress, trauma, and grief, her baby's intrauterine experience might be negatively impacted.[1]

The months that we spend in the womb influence our attachment relationship with our parents and our budding identity. Researchers are aware that our vital, early attachments begin in the womb, and that they impact our future attachments and well-being. "Today we realize that prenatal development—all that happens in the interdependent life of the womb, influenced as we are by so many other factors—has a significant impact on the type of people we become later in life. Even before we are born, we are already embedded in a web of relationships."[2] The intrauterine experiences of subsequent children are worth contemplating, as it is important for the reader to understand their potential significance. Subsequent children are often carried in the wombs of mothers who, along with their partners, are grieving and fear for the safety of their unborn child.

Bereaved Parents in Pregnancy

Bereaved parents often face a torrent of feelings when they become pregnant again. The meaning of pregnancy changed forever for them after their prior loss. Memories of their deceased child coupled with intense fears of another loss may cloud their initial joy. Fears of another loss might be so strong that they shut down all emotions to survive the long months of their pregnancy. It is a common assumption that bereaved parents will rediscover happiness once they become pregnant again, but they may silently struggle with underlying grief and fear. They might be hypervigilant as they wait for the arrival of their subsequent child while also preparing themselves for the possibility of another loss.

Sheri, whose son was stillborn, was very frightened when pregnant with her subsequent daughter. She struggled with her pregnancy and often avoided going out because she did not want to see other pregnant women. She was painfully aware that her mindset and pregnancy experience were drastically different from those who had not experienced a loss.

> It's frustrating to see first-time parents who are pregnant because we can't have that joy anymore. That joy has been taken from us and replaced with fear. We just keep wondering if this baby is going to make it. (Sheri)

Attachment After Loss

Attachment ideally begins during pregnancy and continues after the baby's birth. A healthy attachment consists of a strong, nurturing, and secure bond that is felt by the child and the caregiver;

it is formed when parents are available and attuned to their baby. On the other hand, insecure attachments develop when parents are unable to be attuned, emotionally present, and prepared to bond.[3]

Subsequent children are often at risk for an insecure attachment because bereaved parents may be unable to embrace a subsequent pregnancy.[4] Parents who lose a child experience not only intense grief, but also a traumatic event, which is known to cause horror and a sense of helplessness. Bereaved mothers who are pregnant with a subsequent child, like Audra and Sally, might resist any connection, or avoid the belief that an unborn baby is growing within, because the prospect of another loss is terrifying.

I didn't believe that I was pregnant, even though we had seen and heard the heartbeat. It was still really hard to accept that we were pregnant again. (Audra)

I didn't even want to say how many weeks pregnant I was. I just wanted to avoid thinking that there was a baby inside who could also die. (Sally)

Partners of pregnant spouses often share their trepidation about pregnancy after loss. Although Russ and his wife shared a healthy older child, their loss of an infant caused Russ to be fearful during their subsequent pregnancy.

Just because there is a baby inside doesn't mean it's going to be alright. It's never written in stone that when you get pregnant you're definitely going to have a kid. (Russ)

The anxiety and experiences of bereaved parents facing a subsequent pregnancy are often unrecognized and minimized, despite the gains that we have made as a society in understanding grief. Parents may find that their healthcare providers are dismissive of any voiced concerns. Annette, who fearfully sought comfort and support from her doctor, felt unheard.

The pregnancy was terrifying. I went back to the same doctor [who had witnessed the loss of my first baby] and he simply said that he was not going to let that happen again. It was not helpful at all. If it was preventable, why did he let it happen in the first place? He told me that I wasn't really at high risk and gave me the overall message that I shouldn't talk to him about my concerns. So I didn't, even though I needed to. (Annette)

If parents lose a child during pregnancy or at birth, their pregnancy and birthing plan for their subsequent child may be affected by their prior loss. Becky was definite in her plan for a Cesarean when her subsequent daughter was born. Her first son died at thirty-six weeks, and her second son suffered severe trauma after being stuck in the birth canal. She was adamant about avoiding a vaginal delivery.

I realized that I couldn't feel safe with a vaginal birth, and that I wouldn't feel safe until Katie was born. (Becky)

Like Becky, Marianne's mother was fearful of having another child because of her difficult history. Her first baby was institutionalized as he was born with severe disabilities, and her grief about him was unsupported and repressed.

My mother was terrified the whole time she was pregnant with me, because she hadn't processed any of her emotions about my brother, and never really grieved. (Marianne)

Cumulative Grief and Loss

Bereaved parents sometimes endure additional losses that coincide, in a relatively short time span, with the death of their child. Old losses might resurface for them as well, because new losses often ignite grief from the past. Facing multiple losses can exacerbate a parent's grief, placing a subsequent child at greater risk for an impaired attachment, replacement dynamics, and a home environment of acute mourning. Meghan described her mother's cumulative grief.

> *When my mother was nineteen years old, she lost her mother to breast cancer. Nine years later, when she was pregnant with me, her father died from lung cancer. It was a lot of loss. I was sort of bathed in all of that grief.* (Meghan)

Bal, who was born after the death of a brother, was aware of numerous losses and stressors that his parents faced in the same year as his brother's death.

> *My brother died, and around the same time, my paternal grandmother was diagnosed with terminal cancer. A few months later, while my mother was expecting me, my maternal grandfather passed away.* (Bal)

Susan, who was always aware of her sister Christine's death, eventually learned about a brother who also died before she was born. She reflected on her parents' repeated heartbreak.

> *When I was ten my mother told me about my brother James, their first-born. He had medical issues and died at birth. Due to his severe disabilities, my parents were told that his death was for the best. My mum told me of how she carried his little white coffin to the church altar. Both of my parents were heartbroken.* (Susan)

Grief Repercussions for the Subsequent Baby

Many subsequent children wonder about the repercussions of their parents' grief upon their identity and life story and feel the need to make sense of the circumstances of their conception, intrauterine experience, and birth. Tret, who was conceived only three months after her brother's death, believes that her early experiences made her vulnerable and led her to be the carrier of her mother's physical and emotional issues.

When I was in high school these thoughts and feelings surfaced for me. I have a lot of the illnesses of my mother, and I always attribute it to the fact that I was born out of guilt and out of mourning. My mother was grieving the whole time she carried me, and I think that I carry a lot of her illnesses as a result. (Tret)

Several of the subsequent children who were interviewed revealed that they turned to regression therapy as a part of their exploration and healing process. The approach uses hypnosis and focuses upon the past, with the goal of understanding how past events influence a person's life, identity, needs, and behaviors. Regression therapy may not resonate with everyone, but its widespread use in our sample indicates that many subsequent children are compelled to explore the past and to wonder about the impact of their sibling's death. Many described sessions in which they deliberately revisited or uncovered difficult memories from their early infancy and the womb. The surprisingly numerous reports of subsequent children seeking regression therapy point to a prevailing sense that something was amiss in their early experiences and to a common drive for heightened understanding, meaning making, and healing. Themes of loneliness and a lack of connection were frequent in their described regression therapy experiences. Anita, who was born after a deceased brother, was reminded of a feeling of death, which she connected to the loss of her brother and the grief in her family.

I was drawn into the womb which was this dark, deep, dank pit. It was kind of scary and depressing. It felt like death. It was like being stuck in the muck in the bottom of this dark well, like a horror movie, but I wasn't scared. I came back out and felt relieved. It was almost like being aware of this death thing that was pulling at me, but now being okay with it. (Anita)

Margie, who was born after a stillborn sister, described herself as being alone for most of her childhood. She experienced a sense of loneliness as she imagined herself in the womb.

As we went back into the womb I had a sense of the birth, of being all alone, and being unaccepted. (Margie)

Bereaved parents may engage in "emotional cushioning," protecting themselves by avoiding an attachment to a subsequent baby who might not survive.[5] Liz, who was born after a deceased sister, considered her mom's grief, and its impact upon their attachment. She developed a heightened awareness of the consequences of her mother's grief when she was pregnant with her own children.

What was it really like for me, all those months [in the womb]? Being pregnant again must have produced stress for my mom. So I'm sure that my mom held her emotions inside when she was pregnant with me. What a hostile environment it must have been. (Liz)

When subsequent children contemplate their life stories, early attachment experiences often become a primary focus. Many, like Jenna, expressed a belief that their intrauterine and babyhood experiences were impaired by their parents' grief, angst, and inability to be fully present. They also recognized the enduring impact of their parents' fear and hesitation to attach to them, because a damaged bond became the foundation of the relationship.

My mom and I have a lot of problems, and I think it is because she was not sure that I was going to live. I can imagine that is how anyone would be. If you lose one child, suddenly your whole perspective of life changes. Of course you'd wonder if the next child is going to live. I think that during her whole pregnancy she didn't really bond with me. Her energy was different, and with me, it was more detached. (Jenna)

Many subsequent siblings, like Susan, believe that they were conceived and carried in grief.

My mum was inconsolable when my sister Christine died. At that time my biological father had just been released from prison. I think that it was my mom's grief that led her back to my father, and so I was "accidentally" conceived. Her unplanned pregnancy with me threw my mum's world into further turmoil. (Susan)

In a memoir that explores her life as a subsequent child, author Mary Knight shared that she was carried in the womb of a grieving mother. She wondered about her experience in the womb and the impact of her mother's mourning.

As I continued to unravel the timing of my birth, I realized that my mother conceived me within a year after my brother Rickie died. I was carried in her womb during a time of grief. My mother's description of the year after Rickie died was that she was numb and doesn't remember anything. She may have been beginning to feel again during the time she carried me, and yet I have to ask, "What was she feeling?" (Mary Knight)[6]

One subsequent sibling, Katia, spoke with fervor about the complexities and hardships of being conceived in grief, and shared her worry that bereaved parents do not always understand or consider its repercussions for their subsequent children. In the spirit of prevention, she asked us to use this book to alert and educate bereaved parents.

Tell bereaved parents who have another child that their next child is conceived in grief. I know, because it was my experience as a baby. (Katia)

Support for Parents with a Subsequent Pregnancy

Support, with a lens upon the needs of both the parents and the subsequent child, is frequently advisable for bereaved parents facing a subsequent pregnancy. Bereaved parents need gentleness, time, empathy, and nurturance. When they are pregnant after loss, sensitive and attentive care is often paramount, as illustrated in Ava's story. She described her subsequent pregnancy experiences, which were informed by her grief and loss.

Every new experience with a baby in the doctor's office, even with a baby in the uterus, feels heightened. As a mom you don't want to miss an opportunity to ask questions or follow up on a feeling that you have, because you know what the outcome can be if you don't. Every visit feels heightened. Sometimes that can be good because you're being proactive. It can also be tiring for staff who are seeing one pregnant woman after another. Moms who had a prior loss are triple checking, did we do this, did we cover this, do I have a question about this. Because you have to be persistent to get a live baby. (Ava)

Bereaved parents also often benefit from support groups, where they can share their feelings with others who have lost a child. Support groups are often formed through hospital-based or community-based bereavement programs, and they may be online or in person. They provide a supportive space where parents may process a range of issues, including grief for the deceased child, concerns about their subsequent pregnancy, and fears and ambivalence about attaching to a subsequent unborn baby.[7] Through sharing together, group members usually feel deeply understood and less alone. Many also find meaning in supporting others who share their experiences. Tyler and Marissa, bereaved parents who were expecting a subsequent child, described the benefits that they experienced in their group.

We were trying to derive as much joy as possible from our [subsequent] pregnancy while also battling our fears. It was helpful to talk to others in a group, who also lost a child and were expecting another. When you hear about others who have gone through it you can recognize things that will be helpful in the long run. It's nice to hear other people's perspectives. It also helps to hear about how others explain their feelings, because we struggle to explain it to friends and family. It's hard to articulate what pregnancy after loss is like, as well as our grief about losing Henry. (Tyler and Marissa)

Bereaved parents additionally need psychoeducation.[8] They can be taught that their subsequent child might sense their grief and distress while in the womb, and that fear and mourning can influence the attachment process. Information about the attachment needs of their subsequent baby and the potential risks faced by subsequent children can assist them in becoming more attuned, aware, and purposeful in their parenting. With education and supportive intervention, parents who are pregnant after loss can build attachments to their subsequent babies and welcome them as unique individuals who do not serve as replacements for the deceased.

Conclusion

Bereaved parents facing subsequent pregnancies may struggle to embrace their subsequent baby, as they fear another loss and continue to mourn. A pregnancy after loss is often mired in anxiety, sorrow, and fear, overshadowing the joyful anticipation of parenthood. Positive tasks of pregnancy such as anticipating a fulfilling future with one's child, preparing oneself for parenting, and building a positive bond may feel impossible because of the prior loss. Babies in the womb may also be negatively affected by maternal stress and grief. A prenatal attachment-based model of care, in tandem with medical care, is vital for bereaved parents.

Parental support and psychoeducation are also important preventative measures, and they can positively alter outcomes and experiences for bereaved parents and their future subsequent children. Healing is possible for adult subsequent children as well. They may find it helpful to understand common parental reactions to a pregnancy after loss, and to consider the influence of grief upon their conception and months in the womb. Many subsequent children find value and empowerment in piecing together their stories and origins, and in comprehending how their sibling's death may have shaped their attachments, family dynamics, and identity.

Joann: Advice for Parents about Prenatal Parenting and Attachment

My background as an infant mental health specialist has allowed me to work with pregnant families for many years and to develop a prenatal attachment-based model of care. As seen in the stories of this book, families who are pregnant after a loss need psychosocial intervention just as urgently as they need medical care. Intervention is often lacking, however, as many health providers do not understand the dynamics and complexities of subsequent pregnancies. Appropriate psychosocial care is vital for grieving families because it fosters stability, mental health, and positive attachments.

Parents grieve deeply for their deceased child, and while they may intellectually know that the subsequent child is a different baby, most continue to yearn for the deceased, and to wish for their return. Differentiating the unborn child from the deceased is often a painful and slow process, taking time and nurturing care. Most parents need to hear that their fears and anxieties are normal. Their angst, rather than being caused by a lack of desire for the subsequent baby, is rooted in their deep longing for both their deceased and their subsequent child.

It is important for families who are pregnant after a loss to connect with others who understand their journey. In a support group, they can learn how to navigate grief and attachment together. In my weekly groups, we conclude every meeting with an affirmation for each unborn baby and a description of their development, purposefully promoting parents' attachment to their subsequent baby.

The descriptions provide reminders that the unborn babies are listening as a part of the group, that they are unique individuals who are not replacements, and that they need immediate parental attention. We start with the youngest babies, perhaps at six weeks gestation. The words are directed first to the babies, and then to the parents.

Sweet baby, your world is filled with beautiful sounds to hear and explore.

The ears of your baby are starting to form.

We end with the oldest babies, perhaps at thirty-six weeks gestation.

You are growing so beautifully, little sweetheart. You are perfect in every way.

Your baby is now seventeen to eighteen inches long and weighs about 5½ pounds.

As they begin their journey of parenting a baby that follows a loss, parents can be assisted to envision the subsequent child as a unique individual, not a replacement, while also learning that they can maintain a continuing bond and parenting relationship with the deceased. I encourage those who are pregnant and parenting after loss to reach out for the support and care that they need.

4

Attachment Relationships

Attachments are lasting and meaningful connections formed between human beings. We form important attachments throughout our lives, but many researchers believe that the relationships between infants and their caregivers are uniquely significant, as they impact the baby's social, emotional, and cognitive development, and are a foundation for the infant's healthy development.[1] Children are biologically programmed to seek attachments to their caregivers because their survival, mental health, and development depend upon attachments and care. To securely attach, infants need caregivers who are responsive, attuned to their needs, and reliably accessible.[2] If a secure attachment is developed, the caregiver will serve as a safe, secure base from which the child can explore the world, and a trusted source who provides a growth-enhancing environment. Our earliest attachment experiences are paramount, as they may support or confound our development.

When children receive caregiving that does not provide adequate connection and reassurance, they are generally unable to form a secure attachment and will adopt one of three possible insecure attachment styles. They might acquire an anxious attachment, seeking closeness while preoccupied and fearful of abandonment. They may develop an avoidant attachment, showing ambivalence or emotional distance toward caregivers. Or they might display a disorganized attachment, demonstrating fearful and avoidant behaviors in tandem with a desire for closeness. All insecure attachment styles negatively impact a child's capacity to thrive.[3] Children who are insecurely attached are less able to explore as they lack a sense of safety, and their anxiety, fear, or ambivalence will impede their sense of well-being and connection to others. Subsequent siblings sometimes develop insecure attachments to caregivers because they are born to grieving and emotionally unavailable parents.

The importance of early attachments is additionally supported by the theory that infants, from birth to around eighteen months, face a crucial stage of development, known as trust versus mistrust.[4] Trust is formed when infants experience a secure and nurturing attachment with caregivers who are sufficiently dependable and attuned to their needs. A strong attachment will not form, however, if primary caregivers are unavailable or unreliable; infants will mistrust their caregivers, becoming fearful about the world and unsure that their needs will be met. If infants can develop trust, they learn to believe that their needs will be met, that the world is a safe place, and that they can rely upon their primary caregiver. Infants who successfully form trust are more likely to establish trusting and positive attachments throughout their lives, so their early attachment experiences often have profound impacts upon their future relationships and mental health.

Bereaved Parents and Attachment

If the loss of a child is not adequately mourned, it is likely to undermine a parent's ability to embrace and attach to a subsequent child. Bereaved parents are sometimes haunted by their memories and yearning for their deceased child, and live with "ghosts in the nursery."[5] Some may struggle to attach to a subsequent child because of the trauma of their loss, their longing for the deceased, and their fear of another death.[6] Due to their grief, parents may feel unable to reciprocate and relate to a subsequent child, or to be fully present, physically affectionate, and emotionally attuned.[7]

During a subsequent pregnancy, bereaved parents might consider their subsequent child to be a "maybe baby," as quoted from a young sibling whose family experienced a prior loss. They may therefore avoid the mental and physical preparations that are generally made during pregnancy, such as dreaming of a future with their child, making plans, and adjusting to accommodate their new roles and the new arrival. Janet, who was born after the death of her brother, learned as an adult that her family did not prepare for her birth and arrival, because they were fearful of another loss.

> I know that there was no nursery prepared, and that nothing was done until I came home. Mom allowed no baby showers, no baby gifts prior to my birth. She was not going to have that hardship again. I had no baby book, no memories recorded of my birth, no baby gifts. There was nothing in my room that indicated that my birth was a special event. (Janet)

Grieving parents might be too frightened or ambivalent to contemplate possible names for a subsequent child. Margie, who was born after a deceased sister, learned that her parents only selected boy names before her birth, which illustrated their underlying fears about having or losing another baby girl. Their choice to allow someone else to name her points to their hesitancy to attach.

> The person who named me was my Aunt Pat. She asked my parents what names they had chosen, and they only said Jim. So she suggested Margaret Lynn, and that's my name. (Margie)

Parents' trauma may be reignited during the birth of their subsequent child. Margie's mother requested to be fully awake for Margie's birth, but she was anesthetized, just as she had been during the stillbirth of Margie's sister. Margie learned about her traumatic birth story from her parents, and she believes that it set the stage for her strained relationship with her mother.

> *My mother woke up screaming at my birth, crying out "My baby is dead." I wonder if it didn't set up a dynamic between us, because my birth was so frightening. It was a reminder of what happened to her previous child, and that it could happen again.* (Margie)

While some subsequent children sense their parents' apprehension or ambivalence about bonding from a young age, others do not fully understand the impact of their sibling's death until later in life. When pregnant herself, Mary began to develop a deeper understanding of her own childhood experiences as a subsequent sibling, and to contemplate the circumstances of her birth.

> *I had a brother whom I never had the chance to know, because he died of a brain tumor. I realized that he had died less than two years before I was born, and that I was born into a grieving family. This awareness explained the fact that although I had always known I was loved, I had felt that, as a young child, I was held at arms' length. It also explained why my first memories of my parents' faces were of pain.* (Mary Knight)[8]

Jenna, who was born after a stillborn brother, also shared memories of detached or avoidant parenting.

> *I think that my mom was very hands-off with me at the beginning. She didn't really bond with me when she was pregnant or even after I was born. And now I have a horrible relationship with my mom. She kind of betrayed me when*

I was little. So now I don't trust. I am very wary of being betrayed. (Jenna)

Children who were born after a sibling with acute special needs sometimes face attachment disruptions and issues, like subsequent children. Marianne was born after a disabled brother, who was institutionalized and kept as a family secret. Although Marianne was healthy at birth, her mother feared that she would develop a disability like her sibling. Marianne learned that when she cried as a baby it reminded her mother of her brother. Her mother would lie in her bed frozen with anxiety, leaving her to cry unattended in her crib.

My crying went on day after day after day, until my dad would come home at night. He would hold me. My mom didn't want to connect to me while I was in her womb, and she didn't want to connect to me for my first year of life until she knew I was healthy. I know that my crying reminded her of my brother. She didn't want to get hurt like that again, so to protect herself she didn't open herself to me until I was about one year old. (Marianne)

As an adult, Marianne learned that the early months and years of life have a vital impact upon one's emotional health and development. She went to therapy and eventually confronted her mother about her experience as an infant.

When I talked to my mother about it, and I was angry at that point, she said, "Well, it was only for a year." I said, "A year! That is half of my prime development time! It has taken layers and layers of work to repair. I have spent a lot of time healing from this." (Marianne)

Agnes was born after the death of her sister, who died due to the congenital abnormality of missing an esophagus. Although her digestive system was normal, Agnes suffered from projectile vomiting, symptoms that seemed to mirror her sister's disability. Her mother was too anxious and frightened to care for her.

> *I don't remember being with my mother, except when I got older. She told me that she did not really take care of me when I was a baby. She had an extremely nervous reaction to me, especially when I started projectile vomiting. My dad's sisters evidently took care of me.* (Agnes)

Eric, who was born after a deceased brother, believes that the allergy that he developed to his mother's milk was symbolic of their impaired attachment.

> *I was born three years after my brother died. I became allergic to my mother's milk at four months of age. I have touched on this in regressive therapy, and it feels as if my mother was rejecting me. She and her milk were both embittered.* (Eric)

Eric described a lack of attachment with his father as well.

> *My dad just didn't have the energy for me. I think he bonded less with me than anybody else. He may have avoided connecting to me because he was worried about losing me due to my allergies.* (Eric)

Many subsequent children, including those without health issues, may have experiences with parents who struggle in their parenting role. Natalie, who was born after her three-year-old sister died from drowning, described a mom who could not take care of her during the first year of her life.

> *My mom went back home to her parents after I was born, and my dad took care of me. My mother later said that she regretted missing out on a lot of my babyhood, but she just felt the way that she was feeling. She wasn't able to deal with it.* (Natalie)

Mia was born after the death of a two-year-old sister, who was reportedly very beautiful. She grew up with the belief that she was less attractive than her deceased sister, and with experiences of a distant and aloof mother. As an adult, she learned from extended family that her mother was unavailable and rejecting during her infancy.

> *My uncle told me that the family was very disturbed with my mother when I was a young child, because she didn't pick me up enough or pay enough attention to me. I remember following my mom around with my little carpet sweeper. She was always irritated and busy and preoccupied. My sense of her was that there were more important things and that I had to kind of work my way around what was important. She was never a person I could go to for comfort. She sometimes made things worse. So I think that our bond was pretty disturbed.* (Mia)

Like Mia, many other subsequent siblings described feeling rejected by their parents. Marisol was born after the death of a sibling, but her parents were reticent to discuss their loss, and she was unaware of her sibling's name or gender. She believed that her sibling's death created fear and distrust in her parents, causing them to reject her and avoid attachment.

> *There are no baby pictures of me. When I inquired about it, my mom said it's because I was so skinny, and so tiny, that the camera couldn't pick me up. And she said I was ugly, because my hair was skinny and straight, so they didn't take any pictures of me.* (Marisol)

Sally, who was born after the death of a five-year-old brother, grew up feeling unwelcome and like a disappointment to her parents.

> *My mom was not in love with me as a child.* (Sally)

Dana, who was born after a brother who died at birth, shared a wish for more closeness with her mother and a sense that her brother's death was the cause of their impaired bond.

> *I wonder how we would have been different [if my brother had not died]. Maybe my mom would have talked to me more. Maybe we would have been closer.* (Dana)

Many subsequent children remember undemonstrative parenting. A limited or impaired attachment is sometimes demonstrated through a lack of physical contact or touch. Margie described a mother who withheld comforting behaviors, which seemed to illustrate her mother's fears of closeness and attachment.

> *My mother would talk with me, but she didn't touch me. It is a significant thing, because I really wanted touching, but I knew that it would never happen. It never occurred to me to reach out to her.* (Margie)

Contrasts in Attachments

Some subsequent children, when observing their parents with a younger sibling or grandchild, may witness loving attention that they instinctively know they never received. Janet remembers elaborate preparations for her sister Ginger's birth that were a sharp contrast to her own experience. While Janet was given hand-me-downs from her older siblings, her father built new furniture for Ginger, including a solid walnut toy box. Her recollections were reinforced by her mother, who claimed that Janet's birth was normal but, in contrast, described Ginger's birth as wonderful, and Ginger as a beautiful daughter. Janet's sense of isolation, envy, and sadness are revealed in her memories of her sister's baby shower.

> *I remember very vividly being at a [prenatal] baby shower for my little sister and seeing a bright blue plush bunny sitting*

on the fire box. I couldn't touch it because it was for Ginger. When she was born, I wasn't supposed to touch the gifts or the blue bunny. There was nothing like that for me. (Janet)

All mourning families cope differently, and some bereaved parents feel more ready than others to parent and accept a subsequent child. Chloe's parents actively grieved before Chloe's birth, and they were well supported after her brother's death. The care that they received coupled with their own healthy mourning process helped them to welcome Chloe and to forge a positive bond.

My parents told me that when I was born, they were so happy that they cried, because they loved me so much. (Chloe)

Doris, who had a subsequent son after losing her first child, was similarly able to embrace her subsequent child, both during pregnancy and after his birth.

[When I was pregnant with my son,] I would talk to him. I would read stories to him. I would rub my abdomen. It was a way to communicate with him. I would tell him how eager I was to meet him. After his birth, I held him in his first moments, and said "baruch haba shalom motek sheliy." It means welcome in peace, my baby. I had practiced for weeks. I wanted him to hear Hebrew as the first sounds in his ears. The joy of having him was just so enormous. His cry was so wonderful and enormous to me. (Doris)

One Positive Attachment

Some subsequent children experience one caregiver who is unable to securely bond with them, but another who can provide a steady and loving attachment. Natalie, Jenna, and Margie described disrupted or difficult attachment experiences with their mothers, but they also spoke of present and caring fathers, who played crucial attachment roles.

My dad was the one who took care of me. He took a leave. After I was born, until I was about a year old, he did everything. I don't think I suffered. My dad was very good at taking care of me. (Natalie)

My mom never really bonded to me, and she was not demonstrative. My father is though. There are no problems in my relationship with my dad. We get along really well. My dad and I are more alike. (Jenna)

My dad did not let me be invisible. He used to play with me, singing a special song that went "Hey around the corner, who, who." Wherever I was, when I'd hear him sing I'd run to the kitchen, peek around the corner, and sing back, "who, who." He made me feel special. (Margie)

Childhood attachments are critical to a person's growth and development, but additional, meaningful attachments are often constructed throughout the lifespan. Some subsequent children who feel invisible in their families of origin are resilient enough to build strong attachments as adults. Janet and Mary, both subsequent siblings, described secure and healthy bonds to their life partners.

I have no doubt at all about his love for me. We are happy to be together, and I think that we're closer and have more fun than anybody I know. If I let him know what I need, he is right there. I really feel appreciated for who I am. (Mary)

My husband is my best friend. (Janet)

Preventative Intervention

Grieving parents may struggle to attach to a subsequent child, but stronger and healthier attachment experiences can be created. Bereaved parents can be educated about pregnancy's significance as a beginning stage of parenting and attachment. They can also be supported in forming a continuing bond to their deceased child, while simultaneously embracing their subsequent baby as an individual who is separate from the deceased, not a replacement. Appropriate supports, such as therapists, support groups for grieving parents, attuned and educated healthcare staff, and psychoeducational resources, can assist with their healing process. Preventative measures, which include supportive intervention for parents during a subsequent pregnancy and beyond, can promote healthier family dynamics and heightened coping for all family members.[9]

Conclusion

Those born after loss are at heightened risk for impaired attachments with their primary caregivers. Bereaved parents may struggle to bond with a subsequent child because of their grief, anxiety, and fear of another loss. They may not recognize the needs of their subsequent child because of their mourning and inner turmoil. In some families, bereaved parents feel unable to care for their subsequent child after birth and may temporarily delegate the baby's care to a spouse or relative. In other families, mourning parents who are physically present may be emotionally unavailable or rejecting. As healthy attachments are a building block for one's future mental health, relationships, and coping capacities, a subsequent child's damaged bonding experience may have lifelong implications.

There is a spectrum of possible attachment experiences. Some parents are emotionally available and ready to welcome their subsequent child. In other families, subsequent children may form a strong attachment with one parent or another significant adult. Having one reliable and loving attachment figure can allow children to build trust and resiliency, and promotes their development, well-being, and mental health.

Adult subsequent siblings may recognize subtle or profound ruptures in their early attachment bonds. While difficult dynamics from infancy cannot be altered, it can be profoundly healing to understand them and to frame them in a meaningful context.

Some subsequent siblings may benefit from the exploration of their early attachments with a therapist. Others might attempt to have healing and productive conversations with their primary caregivers. Family relationships are not stagnant, and in some cases more positive bonds can be forged later in the lifespan. A deeper understanding fostered later in life does not replace the attachments that one needed in infancy, but it can sometimes promote heightened wellness, healing, and resiliency.

5

The Inadequate
Replacement Child

Bereaved parents sometimes choose to have a subsequent child in the hopes of lessening their grief. Replacement dynamics are set into motion when parents, consciously or unconsciously, anticipate that a child born after loss will heal the family and fill their void. Subsequent children are often referred to as replacement children because they may be viewed, to varying extents, as replacements for their deceased sibling.[1] It might be more accurate to define them as inadequate replacement children, as it is impossible to truly replace another person or to erase the grief of a mourning parent. Through the lens of grief and longing, parents may remember the deceased as a perfect child, and the subsequent child, who cannot alleviate the family's grief, will be destined to disappoint.

Most studies refer to all subsequent children as replacement children. Recent research has noted, however, that there is a range of possible experiences, and that a framework of replacement dynamics might foster a more thorough understanding of the subsequent child role. A lens of replacement dynamics allows us to acknowledge a nuanced spectrum of lived experiences, rather than simply deciding if a subsequent child is or is not a replacement child.[2] In some families, a subsequent child is viewed as a replacement by one parent, but not by the other. Replacement dynamics are not static, and often shift over time. They may be highly pronounced, moderate, or minimal.

An Unreachable Benchmark

Children become attuned to their parents' cues at an early age and internalize spoken and unspoken parental messages. They intrinsically seek parental approval and love, and try to please their parents in an effort to attach and be cared for. Subsequent siblings often live with an ongoing, arduous sense of being unable to fulfill the wishes and needs of their grieving parents. As illustrated in Justine's story, they may sense their parent's wish for a replacement at an extremely young age, and it can powerfully impact their behavior and budding identity. Justine was given her deceased brother's name, Micah, as a middle name. Their mother, Cheryl, shared Justine's comments as a two-year-old, which illustrate Justine's attempts to step into the shoes of her deceased brother.

> *She was just two years old when she started claiming that she took Micah's place. We named her Justine Micah, but she didn't say "I'm Justine Micah" or "Micah is my name too." She said, "I am Micah." And when we celebrated Micah's birthday, Justine kept talking through the day about how she is my Micah. She said "This is my birthday," claiming it as her own.* (Cheryl)

As they are generally unable to fulfill their parents' hopes, subsequent children are often prone to low self-esteem. Many shared memories of feeling inferior to their deceased sibling as they could not compete with a brother or sister who was perfect and idealized in their parents' eyes. Mia, who was born after the death of a two-year-old sister, shared her sense of being unable to measure up to her deceased sister.

> *I remember my reaction when I saw a photo of my deceased sister that I hadn't seen before. She was in bed in the picture, which was taken a week or so before she died. She had flowing light brown curls. I saw this beautiful child who was adored by my parents, and I remember thinking that I was a burden and not pretty enough. I was just a lousy substitute.* (Mia)

Pierre was born after his eight-year-old sister died of cancer. Like Mia, he felt unable to compete with his sibling.

> *My deceased sister was described as being very smart. My mom kept saying that for someone in second grade, she was very smart, unlike me. My mom called me a moron growing up. She didn't realize. Maybe she said it three times, but it seemed like a hundred.* (Pierre)

Many subsequent children experience subtle or overt comparisons, made by their parents, that favor their deceased sibling. Some participants also believe that their parents used unfavorable comparisons to their deceased sibling to push them toward desired behaviors. Pierre shared about the dynamic in his family.

> *They probably compared me to my sister, and talked about how smart my sister was, to make me try harder in school.* (Pierre)

Natalie, who was born after the death of her three-year-old sister, described a similar dynamic with her mother.

> *My mom talked about my sister's clothes and about how neat she kept her room. She said that my sister didn't want to eat her dessert before her food and that she was very organized. Whereas I was the total opposite.* (Natalie)

In some families, choices and unspoken messages additionally convey that the deceased is more valued and beloved than the subsequent child. In Natalie's home, the allocation of bedrooms felt symbolic of her sister's idealized and preferred status. While her deceased sister's bedroom remained empty and exactly as she kept it, Natalie had to share a bedroom with her brother.

Striving to Satisfy Expectations

In an effort to gain love and acceptance, subsequent children may try to live up to their parent's hopes and to become the replacement that their parent wishes for. Andrew, who was born after the loss of his three-year-old brother, described his ongoing desire to satisfy the hopes and needs of his parents.

> I have this huge need not to disappoint my parents. I always felt the need, not to make up for their loss, but definitely to live up to what my brother's standards would have been. (Andrew)

Some subsequent children are acutely aware, from a young age, that their deceased sibling fulfilled certain parental dreams while they do not. Natalie's deceased sister reportedly had the qualities that their mother wished for and seemed to be following in their mother's footsteps as a dancer. Natalie was a self-described tomboy who refused to dance.

> My sister was exactly the way that my mother would want her little girl to be. She was very feminine and very quiet. My mother had been a dancer and already enrolled her in dance classes. I resented [the comparisons between me and my sister], especially when there was a pull between my mother wanting me to take dance lessons when I was a tomboy. My relationship with my mother got a little combative. (Natalie)

Instead of attempting to become the replacement that her mother wished for, Natalie described a more rebellious stance, which was adaptive; Natalie was resolute to be true to herself and to avoid becoming a replica of her deceased sister.

> *I was very determined, from an early age, not to be anybody else. Even sometimes maybe too much. There was a time that I didn't like certain foods, and my mother would say oh, your sister didn't like that either. So I would force myself to eat it, like really horrible vegetables. I did not want [to be identified with my sister].* (Natalie)

Like Natalie, subsequent children might rebel against replacement pressures, or, more often, they strive to satisfy their families. The pressure to be a "good replacement," which can be spoken or unspoken, conscious or unconscious, often begins at the subsequent child's earliest and most tender age, and is highly impactful upon the subsequent child's developing identity. It is difficult to develop one's authentic identity while being pressured to uphold the traits or promise of someone else. Many subsequent children set very high standards for themselves in the hopes of being good enough and have an enduring need to achieve and to be successful. Andrew described hardworking traits that he embodied to avoid being viewed as an insufficient replacement.

> *Because they lost their first born, I feel like if I am lazy or irresponsible or not hardworking, I would be the son that they never wanted, and they'd wish and think "If only we had that other son [our deceased child], the good son."* (Andrew)

Susan, who was born after the death of a sister, felt as if she never lived up to her mother's standards, despite being a brilliant student.

> *I needed to do well. That's probably what getting the good grades was about. I needed to be the bright one, the clever one, the successful one, the one to stay alive.* (Susan)

Janet, born after her deceased brother, struggled to feel accepted or welcomed in her family. She worked hard to win their love and approval.

I became, in some sense, the perfect child. I was a straight A student. I learned to read when I was three when my mother was teaching my older sister how to read. So at four I was reading at a first- and second-grade level. (Janet)

CR was born after his infant sister died of congenital heart disease. His parents were determined to have another child after their loss, and they went to great lengths to have another baby. CR grew up with a sense of their heavy expectations.

My parents let me know that the only reason I am here is because I am a replacement. I felt like I had to be something big, because I'm the only one left. I felt this internal pressure to make up for this. I couldn't just be an average person. There was so much pressure that was not intentional. There was a spotlight on me for my whole life, and it was suffocating. (CR)

Subsequent children can sometimes pinpoint personality traits in themselves that are seemingly rooted in their replacement role, illustrating its potentially profound and widespread repercussions upon their identity formation. Tret was born after the loss of a brother. She was the only child who was expected to scrub the floors and clean the house, and she was tasked with making the beds of her older brothers. Tret longed to go on fishing trips with her father and brothers but was never invited. She believes that she became a performer and was drawn to the stage because she felt unrecognized as a unique individual in her family.

I'm sure a lot of my need to be a performer connects to being born through grief. It has a lot to do with being okay with myself. It says a lot about my need to be seen. Being on stage

is very much a part of what makes me feel whole and seen.
(Tret)

Andrew believes that he inherited some of his brother's functions and roles in the family.

I am the peacemaker in my family. I think it is probably the role that my brother would have played in my family [if he were alive]. I'm not sure what my role would have been.
(Andrew)

A sense of feeling invisible is commonly reported by subsequent children. Many feel voiceless and describe parents who were oblivious or neglectful of their needs, exacerbating their feelings of invisibility. Margie, born after a stillborn sister, shared her sense of being unseen.

I'd ask myself, "What does a person have to do to get seen in this family?" I felt like I was a disappointment and that I was invisible. I also always felt like my mother and I weren't really connected. I never got upset, never threw a tantrum. That was the cost of feeling invisible in the family. Why would I complain? It didn't do any good.
(Margie)

Mia, born after a deceased sister, felt devalued and unrecognized by her mother.

I think that I quickly realized, growing up, there was not much to be gotten from my mom. My mom was the Boy Scout den mother for both of my brothers, but when I asked her to be a den mother for me, she said that she didn't have time. At another point I needed a coat. At the time my mom was throwing a bridal shower for her best friend's kid. She was spending all of this money on this bridal shower, but told me that we didn't have money to get me a coat. She finally took me to a discount clothing place and bought me

*a ten-dollar coat. Again, it was always the message that my
needs were not paramount.* (Mia)

Margie felt neglected by her mother, as her basic needs were
often overlooked.

*My mother wasn't abusive. It was more like neglect. She just
didn't see me. It was a weird dynamic. For instance, my sister used to show my mother my worn underwear and say
"You have to buy her underwear. These have holes in them."*
(Margie)

Some subsequent children described going to great lengths
to gain their parents' attention to avoid feeling invisible. Susan
recounted hiding in her home, causing her parents intense worry.
In hiding for hours, she created a scenario in which she was
missed and longed for, like her deceased sibling. It may have been
an unconscious means to seek her parents' love and full attention, and to finally be center stage as the beloved child.

*I remember hiding in the cupboard beneath the stairs. My
parents called the police, and the police helicopter was in
the sky looking for me as there was a lake nearby. I curled
up behind a coat listening to their distress and fear. It wasn't
an intentional act designed to cause alarm on my part, but
it was an emerging pattern in my behavior. I think it was
something about drawing attention.* (Susan)

Never Feeling Good Enough

Despite their high achievements, many subsequent children feel
as if they are never good enough. Many feel inadequate and
unable to satisfy their parents, because they grew up with impossible parental hopes and expectations. Subsequent children cannot erase the grief and loss in their families.

*My desire to achieve was and still is insatiable. I never feel
like I've achieved. It has been an impossible task. When I*

got my PhD my mother was quick to dismiss it, pointing out that medical doctors are the only real doctors. I think I look for my mum to be impressed, but I have realized I will never truly impress her. With each achievement I always seem to fall short in some way. (Susan)

I was hospitalized at times during high school because of depression, but I still graduated and excelled. I was in the top academic percentage of my class. When I went back to graduate school, I had seven kids, but I crocheted an Afghan for my father for Christmas and made him a half gallon of his favorite homemade soup. But it didn't matter what I did. It wasn't ever rewarded at home. (Agnes)

In addition to feeling unable to impress or satisfy their parents, subsequent children also often feel unable to acknowledge their own successes or to fully believe in themselves. Susan described having imposter syndrome, as she doubts her own skills and fears being exposed as a fraud.

Even if I was a medical doctor and I was a brain surgeon, I wouldn't be a real one. Everyone would wonder where the real doctors were. (Susan)

Along a similar vein, some subsequent children feel like they never fully belong in their families due to a lack of attachment, connection, or acceptance. Anna, born after a lost sibling, grew up feeling disconnected and misunderstood by her mother.

I felt unseen for who I am. I felt so lonely. I always had the impression that I had no place and was not really welcome. I wondered if I was adopted or something. I knew it was not true, but all my life I felt like I didn't belong to this family. (Anna)

Agnes was born after the loss of her infant sister. She worked hard to please her parents and was successful at school, but she never felt accepted or recognized.

I just didn't fit in the family. All my life it was said to me, "why does it have to be you?" (Agnes)

Marisol, who was born after loss, described a lack of family cohesion and parental care.

I have this dream of hoping that I'll find my real parents [even though I know that my parents are my real parents]. My parents just didn't behave like parents. (Marisol)

Acute Replacement Dynamics

The scope and severity of replacement dynamics varies among families and over time. Weighty replacement dynamics were described by some of the subsequent siblings in our sample. Mia was given the same name as her deceased sister, and Kenneth was regularly called by his deceased brother's name. They were both painfully aware of their role as a substitute and of the heavy hopes held by their mothers that they would fill the void left by their deceased sibling. They struggled to be embraced as themselves or to be recognized as individuals who were separate and distinct from the deceased.

When I was thirteen, I came across my sister's birth certificate. I saw that her name was the same as mine, just with one letter different in the spelling. I felt so cheated and lied to. It would have been helpful to know that my name was recycled and that it had belonged to my sister. My name became a point of deception. (Mia)

Mia also questioned her mother's choice to alter her birth certificate so that she could attend school early. It seemed like another indication that her mother did not accept her as she was, and it forced her to live an untruth that did not align with her true identity. Mia wondered if her mother falsified her age so that she would be closer in age to her deceased sister.

She sent me off to kindergarten, telling me not to tell anyone about my real birthday. She took it one step further and staged birthday parties for me on my fake birthday every year. When I got to high school, I told my mom that I wanted people to know my real birthday. She said that I'd better not tell anybody, because the school might put me back a year. (Mia)

Kenneth's mom suffered from alcoholism and would call Kenneth by his deceased brother's name when she was inebriated. He remembers crying out "No, I'm Kenneth." He felt as if he was a substitute for his brother, and that he was never really loved or accepted as himself.

My mom was in another world filled with grief. She would hold me and call me Ricky, [my brother's name]. I'd just want to get away. It was way too emotional for me. She'd say "You're my little angel, you're my little Ricky. God sent you." It seems like it wasn't my life, it was dealing with the loss that was never dealt with. I feel sad for myself that I wasn't getting the real thing [from my mom], but that it was for somebody else different than me. Going to the grave site, she would hug me more than the other kids. I realized part of me was in the ground and that she was transferring something. I didn't think that she really loved me. It's hard enough having an alcoholic mother, but I also had to go through the sense that she never really loved me, but somebody else. (Kenneth)

It seems meaningful that as an adult Kenneth changed his name to Reggie, which sounds quite similar to Ricky. One can speculate that perhaps he wasn't able to fully form or own his identity as Kenneth, and that his impression of being a replacement for Ricky became a significant part of his sense of self.

Evolving Dynamics

Replacement dynamics are not stagnant. While they often continue throughout a family's lifespan, they also might shift or wane. Comparisons to an idealized deceased sibling sometimes subside after the subsequent children surpass the age of their deceased sibling. Bonds may be forged or strengthened with parents over time, and some subsequent children begin to feel more recognized and embraced in later years. Pierre described an evolving dynamic in his family.

Once I was in third grade, and older than my sister was when she died, it was not possible to compare us anymore. (Pierre)

Despite the very difficult beginnings of their relationship, Natalie and her mother became a bit more connected when Natalie was an adolescent.

My mom and I butted heads for a long, long time. Then my parents separated for three years while I was in high school. My mother and I started talking more, and she needed me. (Natalie)

While Janet's relationship with her mother remained laden with replacement dynamics, she reported a shift in her bond with her father that occurred when he was elderly.

In his older years my dad said "You are the most special daughter to me." It was precious to know this. I worked really hard on our relationship. (Janet)

A Hierarchy of Subsequent Children

When several children are born after a loss, the first subsequent, born closest to the loss, sometimes faces harsher replacement dynamics than the siblings born later. Perhaps the first subsequent children are more likely to be viewed as inadequate replacements because the loss is more recent, and they inaugurate the replacement role. Marilyn was the first subsequent child to be born after the death of a sister. Carolyn was born after Marilyn, and Cathy followed. Cathy, who was the sibling to be interviewed, described stark differences between Marilyn and Carolyn's experiences, and Marilyn's unique struggles as the first subsequent child.

The loss of my mother's first baby affected my oldest sister, Marilyn, very, very, strongly. She has always talked to me about how much she wanted mother's love and never had it, and how sad she was that mother never nurtured her, couldn't hold her, and didn't listen to her. Marilyn just didn't feel loved and cared about. I asked Carolyn if she felt the same way and she said no, and that our mother was always there for her. (Cathy)

Cathy shared a family story that highlights the different mothering experiences of her two sisters and the lack of parental attunement that Marilyn faced as the first subsequent child.

When Marilyn was in first grade, she wet her pants in school and was sent home to have her clothes changed. Our mother got upset with her and was very angry and aloof. She sent her to her room to change her clothes and made her walk back to school to face her classmates alone. Carolyn later had the same thing happen, also wetting her pants at school. She says that when she got home mother picked her up in her lap, wet pants and all, and rocked her in the rocking chair, just holding her, telling her it was all right, and not to be sad. It was a day and night difference. (Cathy)

Invisible into Adulthood

Replacement dynamics do not necessarily end, and they may continue to be severe and enacted when subsequent siblings are adults. For Mia, her parents' decisions about their will reinforced her sense of being unrecognized.

Instead of splitting the inheritance three ways for us, her three children, my mother decided to give each of us one-sixth, so that she could split the other half among the grandchildren. My brothers protested, stating that their children did not need the money and that I deserved one third. My mom initially listened to my brothers and agreed to change the will, but soon after she changed it back to her original plan. (Mia)

As an adult Janet observed a conversation between her mother and a family friend, Nancy, who shared Janet's mother's experience of having a subsequent child after loss. Nancy expressed joy about her subsequent child, but Janet's mother did not. As Janet listened to their contrasting narratives, she felt invisible, both in her recollections of her childhood experiences and in her witnessing of a conversation that omitted any sense of her value.

Forty-two years after Danny's death, I listened to my mom and Nancy talk about the loss of their babies. I listened to my mother talk about her broken heart, and these two women could relate, but I never heard Mom talk about the joy of having a healthy child one year later, while that was Nancy's focus. Nancy made her subsequent baby into the center of her world, but I never felt like I was the center of my mom's world. (Janet)

Throughout her life, Janet continued to endure a lack of empathy from her mother and underlying messages that she was not good enough, as evidenced in her mom's criticisms and expressions of disapproval.

As an adult I've dealt with some medical issues. My mom is aware. When I'm fatigued the left side of my face droops, and it looks like I have Bell's palsy. Once when I was with my mom I was tired and hot, and she asked me why I was holding my mouth like that. I said that I was tired, and that my mouth does that. She said, "It's very unattractive. Don't do that." Nothing I do is ever enough. (Janet)

As an additional consequence of the subsequent child role, some subsequent siblings describe feeling inadequate or unseen in their romantic relationships and families of procreation. It is not surprising, as we often unconsciously re-create problematic patterns from our families of origin when we choose partners and create a new family. We are drawn to what is familiar, and we may have an unconscious drive to master situations and relationships that were difficult for us in our formative years. Unfortunately, we often simply set ourselves up to repeat painful patterns.

> *I made very bad choices about men. I didn't know how to feel important enough or worthy enough, and I always felt like any relationship I had with a man was nothing short of a miracle. I wasn't very savvy. In my relationships with men, it was always more about them than it was about me.* (Margie)

> *My feeling of being a replacement and a booby prize was intensified when I married my husband. I married into an alcoholic abusive family system. I was always left out, and I wrestled with that feeling of not being part of the family. It was painful for me when I was excluded from conversations or when they called me a dummy at a card game. It made me play out some old family dynamics from my childhood when I did not feel good enough.* (Janet)

Looking Back

Many subsequent siblings speak regretfully and mournfully about their fractured families. Those who grew up in inadequate replacement roles often have difficult memories as they reminisce about their childhoods and families of origin.

> *I don't feel like my family was a unit. We were sort of splintered [after my sister's death].* (Natalie)

> *I wish we had been a happy family like everybody else on the block. I didn't want to be a part of our family. I think it was*

a combination of everything: their hard lives, their losing a child, and then not dealing with it. (Kenneth)

The effects of a replacement role are often far-reaching, impacting a subsequent child's identity, relationships, and life experiences. A common fundamental challenge for subsequent children is to become their true and authentic selves, as their growth and identity formation are thwarted by familial pressures to replace another person.[3] When asked if she experienced any ongoing effects of being born after loss, Elena, who was born after her deceased brother, replied with a list of repercussions.

I feel as if I must be perfect and I am never content with what I achieve. I want recognition, but in the end I can't give it to myself, and something stops me from succeeding. I also feel competitive. I replaced a brother, a boy, and feel like I must be better than the boy or the man. But I am not even pursuing ambition or competitiveness because I am forever craving and seeking love. Even in my relationships I am often barking up the wrong tree, risking repeating the rejection and betrayal that I experienced in my family of origin by courting people who do not accept me and trying to win them over. I have spent much of my life seeking transformation, meaning, and a spiritual grounding. The greatest discovery was when I felt and found the words to express that there is a self within, that was repressed and denied, but there is a self that is definitely there! It has been a complex process to access my true self. (Elena)

Conclusion

The stage is set for replacement dynamics when grieving parents hope or believe that their subsequent child will mend their hearts and fill a void of loss. Subsequent children cannot extinguish their parents' loss or grief, and they shoulder impossible hopes and demands when their parents look to them as replacements. Bereaved parents frequently struggle to attach to a subsequent child, and experience disappointment and sorrow when their subsequent child does not provide the relief that they ache for. Many also idealize their deceased child, creating a scenario in which the subsequent child can never measure up and feels like an inadequate replacement.

The meaning and presence of replacement dynamics are often unrecognized in families because they are conscious and unconscious, spoken and unspoken, and they quietly permeate relationships and assigned roles. Parents are generally unaware of the varied impacts of their grief, erroneously assuming that their subsequent children will be untouched by a death that occurred before their birth. When parents are immersed in their own grief, they are commonly unable to be attuned to their subsequent child's needs or to perceive the harm and burden of their replacement wishes.

6

The Gift Child

While replacement dynamics are usually rooted in the idealization of the deceased child, some bereaved parents idealize their subsequent children instead,[1] viewing their birth as a gift and a new beginning.[2] We refer to these children, who are conceived or viewed as idealized replacements, as gift children.[3] There are some advantages in the gift child role, but significant pressures exist as well when children are idealized. Despite being cherished, gift children serve in a role of replacement that has its own burdens. It is complex to grow up on a pedestal and to feel the weight of a grieving family's needs and expectations. Gift children often experience pressure to comfort and protect their bereaved parents, and may fear becoming a disappointing replacement. They are also prone to survivor guilt, as their parents' adoration is rooted in the death of their sibling and their replacement role. Like inadequate replacement children, their identities and family relationships are founded in dynamics of idealization and replacement. They were conceived out of their parent's hope to fill their family's void, and their role as a replacement child frequently becomes a central piece of their identity.

In recent years, a practice of referring to babies born after loss as "rainbow babies" has become relatively common in the United States, and perhaps in some countries abroad as well. This trend began with the understandable goal of comforting bereaved parents and celebrating new beginnings, but it inadvertently sets the stage for gift child dynamics. Instead of being viewed and welcomed as babies with unique identities that are yet to be determined, rainbow babies are named, from conception or from birth, as children that came after loss. Their identities are indelibly and purposefully linked to their deceased siblings and to a role of healing their families. Like a rainbow, which consoles and brings joy after a rainfall, rainbow babies are, by definition, expected to make things better. While rainbow babies are often cherished by their families, there is an underlying weight and cost in the purpose that they are assigned.

Research about gift children is sparse, but it suggests that gift child dynamics may be more likely for subsequent children who are born after the loss of an infant. Deceased infants' identities remain relatively unformed, so perhaps it is more difficult for parents to idealize them or to make comparisons between them and their subsequent children. It is important to note that not all subsequent children born after a deceased infant become gift children, but that it may be a predisposing factor.

A Wish to Replace

Gift children are often aware that their parents conceived them with the intention to replace their deceased sibling. Rebecca, who was born after her nine-month-old sister died of a virus, knew that her role as a replacement was an integral piece of her origin story.

> *My mom was a devout Catholic. She said that after my sister died, she asked God to give her another daughter to replace her, [my deceased] sister. I look just like her, like we are twins. My mother actually believed that I was a gift from God.* (Rebecca)

Liz, who was born after a deceased sister, described her mother's wish to have another daughter who physically resembled the deceased.

> *My mother often told me the story about my birth. While she was pregnant with me, everyone supposedly told her that they hoped that she would have a blond-haired, blue-eyed boy, because [my deceased sister], Mary, had brown hair and brown eyes. But she told them no, that she wanted another brown-haired, brown-eyed girl. And that's what she got with me.* (Liz)

Candace, who was born after the loss of her infant sister, described herself as a beloved replacement child. She believed that she took the place of her deceased sibling.

> *I was the replacement child. I was the child that they wanted, and I replaced the child who was deceased. I was brought up as an only child. They loved me terribly. Cherished me.* (Candace)

An Idealized Status

Gift children are idealized as a part of their role. Their parents often view them as model children and maintain unrealistic and inflated beliefs about their talents and characteristics. Daniel, who was born after the death of an infant brother, shared memories of being adored and admired.

> *I was idealized in some ways. I had all of these people who were showering praise. Even the neighbors would ask their kids why they couldn't behave more like I did. I suspect that my brother's death had something to do with it.* (Daniel)

A Gift and a Miracle

Many gift children describe a birth story in which they were identified as a miracle or as a gift from God. Dorotha, who was born after a deceased brother, shared memories of feeling cherished by her parents. Four additional siblings were born after her, but Dorotha remained the favorite.

> *I know every child thinks that they're the favorite, but I believe I really was. My parents had a loss and couldn't get pregnant again for three years. My name, Dorotha, means gift of God. When I was born my dad said "I don't care if we ever have any more children. This is the miracle."* (Dorotha)

Eric, whose birth followed the death of a brother, believes that his name was chosen to acknowledge his role in the family.

> *I was actually named Eric Theodore, Theodore meaning "gift of God."* (Eric)

Favoritism and Indulgence

Gift children are generally cognizant of the favoritism that they experience in their families, which they equate to their subsequent child role. Edwin, who was born after the loss of his infant brother, was aware of the parental favor that he often received.

> *Because of being born after [my sibling's death], I was pampered a lot. I was so much taken care of, much more than my [surviving and subsequent] brothers and sisters.* (Edwin)

Likewise, Ann grew up with an awareness of being cherished and favored.

> *I know when I came along, that I was extremely wanted. The other kids would say I was the most wanted [of all of the children]. My mom was quite thrilled to have me.* (Ann)

Marie was born after the loss of two siblings, and she was welcomed with joy, relief, and open arms. She believes that she received preferential treatment due to her role.

My mom had stillborn children before having me. I was the miracle baby, because I was the one that made it. I think there was a lot of praying going on when she was pregnant with me, whether my mom knew it or not, from the whole family. I was probably very spoiled. As far as my dad was concerned, if there was anything that I ever wanted or needed I was going to get it. (Marie)

Many gift children describe a special connection with their parents, like Sophie, who was born after the death of a sister.

I was my mom's favorite. She basically told me so. I remember exactly what my mom was doing and where she was standing when she turned to me to say, "You know, I really wanted you." She said it with the emphasis on "you." (Sophie)

Rebecca described a deep connection to her mother.

With my mother, I could sense that there was a special bond between us. She believed that she asked for another child, and that God heard her. So she did have a thing with me. I had a very close relationship with my mom, and I think it probably has to do with that. (Rebecca)

Lana, who was born after the death of her twenty-year-old sister, knew that her father adored her, and that he was comforted by her birth.

I was treated like the apple of my father's eye. I think maybe that he was so taken up with me coming on the scene that it probably dissipated some of his melancholy about losing his [other] daughter. (Lana)

We can speculate that the extra attention that gift children receive is often based in their idealized status and perhaps also in their parents' underlying fear of another loss. Daniel described growing up with parents who were highly attentive and vigilant of his needs.

> *I got all the attention. I was doted upon. I was carefully taken care of. I suspect that there was a lot of attention paid to me so that I'd be healthy.* (Daniel)

Liz, who was born after her sibling died of sudden infant death syndrome, remembered a father who was loving, watchful, and worried about her well-being.

> *I think I had a very loving, special childhood. My father would go into my room at night to make sure I was OK. He'd spend hours watching me, put his hand on my chest just to make sure I was breathing.* (Liz)

Helpers for Their Grieving Parents

Many gift children, like Rebecca, express gladness that they were able to be in a helpful role for their mourning parents and an awareness of their function, as the child born after loss, to provide comfort.

> *I think to a certain extent my mother thought I had replaced her daughter. I was glad that I was helpful to my mom in that way.* (Rebecca)

Johanna was born after her parents lost a baby in utero. She was thankful that she brought her parents some solace.

> *I was happy that I was able to come into their lives. It feels like they chose me and that I chose them. My mom says that God made me for them, and that it was just a wonderful, beautiful thing.* (Johanna)

Embracing the Gift Child Role

In some cases, gift children internalize and welcome their identification as a positive replacement. Rebecca's wish that she had been named after her deceased sister points to her gladness about her gift child role, and to the centrality of the gift child role in her sense of self.

> *Obviously my mom named me something else, [not the same name as my deceased sister]. I would have loved to have been given [my sister's] name instead. That would have been such a nice name for me.* (Rebecca)

Comparisons and Remembrance of the Deceased

Like inadequate replacement children, gift children sometimes experience repeated comparisons to their deceased siblings. Comparisons for gift children are generally favorable, however, as gift children are the ones to be idealized. They usually reinforce the gift's child's status as a positive replacement. For Rebecca, comparisons to her deceased sister were a welcome experience.

> *My mother thought that [my deceased sister] and I looked a lot alike. We are like twins. I didn't mind being compared to her. I was happy about it, because I think that I was well received. Obviously I was wanted. I felt wanted. I felt loved. Being in that role was positive for me.* (Rebecca)

In some families, the comparisons place the deceased in a negative light, illustrating a shift away from idealizing the deceased. Candace was told that she was an easy baby to care for, but her deceased sister was described otherwise.

> *They say that [my deceased sister] cried a lot. She was fussy about what she drank or ate.* (Candace)

In many gift child families, however, there are few comparisons to the deceased because the lost sibling is rarely spoken
of and takes up little space in the family's focus. Rebecca and
Daniel both shared that their deceased siblings were infrequently
referenced in their families.

> *My mother didn't keep pictures of my deceased sister
> around. She had this one picture, and it was in an album. We
> didn't go to the cemetery. I don't know where she is buried. I
> think to a certain extent my mother wanted to put my sister's
> death behind her.* (Rebecca)

> *Because my brother was only a day old and he was so little,
> he was never included. He was not talked about, hardly at
> all. I think my parents probably moved on. There wasn't any
> weeping, there was none of that.* (Daniel)

Some gift children, like Candace, describe their parents'
avoidance of grief and loss, and understand it as an effort to
survive and move forward.

> *I don't know if they ever went to my sister's grave. If they
> ever did grieve, I was shielded completely. They never talked
> about it. As an adult, I equate this with people who lived
> through the Holocaust. People want to make a new life, a
> new beginning, new family, and don't want to talk about the
> past.* (Candace)

Negative Repercussions of the Gift Child Role

Some gift children, like Marie, identify a sense of pressure that
they experienced because of their role.

> *Even from when I was little, hearing that I was the miracle
> baby, I'm sure it put pressure on me to be a really good kid,
> and not to mess up.* (Marie)

Daniel described his role in his family as a "Little Lord Fauntleroy."[4] He was referring to a story in which a young boy is born into poverty, but in a surprising twist of fate he inherits a lordship title and a vast estate because his father and uncles have died. Little Lord Fauntleroy's life and fortune are drastically altered by the death of other family members. Daniel's association to this character hints that he seems to recognize a similar dynamic in his life story.

> *Because I was the only kid on the block, or the only kid in the house, I should say, I was getting perks out of [my role]. There were advantages that were happening.* (Daniel)

We can hypothesize that gift children might have complicated underlying feelings about inadvertently gaining advantages from the death of their sibling and from the replacement dynamics of their gift child experience. While Candace initially described a blissfully happy childhood and family life, she opened up later in her interview with a starkly different vantage point about some of her experiences. Her comment about blame seems meaningful, as blame and guilt are common repercussions of replacement dynamics.

> *The worst thing was that I had no one to play with, and no one to blame. I was lonely and spoiled.* (Candace)

As he considered what life would have been like if his brother had lived, Daniel was initially focused upon negative consequences.

> *I probably wouldn't have gotten nearly the attention [if my brother had lived]. I would have had to do a lot of sharing. There would have been a lot of competition, I suppose, and sharing of attention.* (Daniel)

After his interview concluded, Daniel asked to turn the tape recorder back on, to add a few more thoughts. Like Candace, he expressed a sense that his initial comments about his positive family life might not tell the full story. We can wonder if parents who engage in gift child dynamics often repress their grief and loss, and if their children are taught to do the same.

I avoid sadness and things that aren't pleasant. (Daniel)

The Gift Child Role Over Time

As with all replacement dynamics, gift child dynamics may shift over time and might be enacted by one parent but not the other. Marie described the differing attitudes of her parents.

I don't think that my mom ever put me on a pedestal because I was the child that survived. I think that my dad did, however. (Marie)

Many gift children reported that they continued to be the favorite child in adulthood. Like Sophie, their status as the helper and favored child might lead to caregiving roles when their parents are elderly.

My mom and I had a bond that she didn't have with my other sisters. I know that for a fact. She chose to live in my town in her senior years. I told her that if she ever needed to be with one of us, that she could come to me. I wanted her to come, and she wanted to be with me. (Sophie)

Conclusion

The gift child role has definite advantages over the inadequate replacement child role, because gift children are welcomed and cherished in their families. However, all children deeply need to be seen and accepted as unique individuals. As gift children are idealized and viewed as replacements, they are not fully seen as their true selves, which is harmful for their identity formation and self-esteem. They are often glad to help their parents cope and recover from their loss, but problems arise when children worry and care for the needs of their parents. Roles are reversed when children become their parents' caretakers; the children's evolving needs risk being unseen and unaddressed. Gift children may fear becoming an inadequate replacement child and feel pressure to live up to an expectation that they will provide comfort to their parents and fill the void of loss. They are also at risk for survivor guilt because they recognize that their favored status is caused by the death of their sibling. In many families with gift children, the deceased is rarely spoken of or commemorated, which hints at a possible repressed and unprocessed loss.

Obviously, not all subsequent children who are deeply loved become gift children. Unfortunate gift child dynamics begin when subsequent children are idealized and hopes are placed upon them to heal the family and replace the sibling who was lost. When replacement dynamics begin, the subsequent child's identity becomes entangled with the deceased, and they are unable to be fully seen or understood as a unique individual who is separate from the loss. A key to healthier outcomes for all subsequent children lies in embracing and seeing them for who they truly are, without idealization or replacement expectations.

7

Meaning Making

After a significant loss, we often struggle with a new reality that feels unthinkable and overwhelming. We may need to redefine ourselves and our understanding of the world after losing a loved one,[1] because our prior self-image and beliefs have been shattered. Our identity, sense of purpose, spiritual beliefs, relationships, vision of the world, or imagined future might be irrevocably changed. Because our life stories were derailed by loss, we frequently need to construct a new life narrative. We seek and find meaning in our new narratives. Our reinvented life stories will ideally integrate our pre-loss and post-lost identities and allow our narrative to move forward on a new and unexpected track. Researchers have found that meaning making is a central part of the mourning process.[2] Meaning making may permit us to process grief reactions, address unfinished business, and reorient ourselves in the world, and it is usually essential for our adaptation to a major loss.

Many subsequent children have a deep need to process their sibling's death and to make sense of its repercussions, as their loss may feel unclear and ambiguous. They do not have memories to bolster a continuing bond to their deceased sibling, to define and frame the relationship, or to make sense of who their sibling was as an individual. Their families often believe that they were not impacted by their sibling's death because it happened before their birth. Opportunities to explore the significance of their loss are limited, as they did not have access to rituals or support that may have been offered at the time of their sibling's death. In some cases, their sibling was a secret, and they have minimal information. Subsequent children may question how their family was changed by the loss; how it impacted family relationships, dynamics, and their identity; and who their sibling was. Their need to make meaning mirrors the process of most people who have experienced a significant loss.

Questioning Loss and Suffering

The bereaved frequently question how their loved one could have died and why they are enduring such a painful loss. Denise, who was born after the death of her two-year-old sister, struggled to understand why her family experienced such a tragic loss and how her sister could have died at such a young age.

> *I definitely felt confused. Why did my sister die? She is related to me, and she died? What happened? Why did she die when she was still a baby? It's confusing.* (Denise)

After a loss, it is also common to question why there is so much suffering in the world. Andrew, who was born after his three-year-old brother died in a drowning accident, shared his thinking process as he sought to make meaning of his family's loss. He pondered existential questions about the workings of the world, considered fate, and touched upon the unanswered question of why he lived while his brother did not.

> *September 11th was an interesting day. I was at the World Trade Center. One of the things that rattles around in my mind is why people have to suffer. That probably comes from the suffering that I saw as a child from my mom. The Trade Center really opened that up for me. I often question*

why we have pain in our lives like this. Is it because it makes you stronger, or appreciate your life and the things you have? I can't buy that. Why are some babies born into famine, only to starve to death right after they are born? What is the grand design for that? If there is a merciful God, how can they do this? At the Trade Center on 9/11 I saw people suffering. It makes me question things like fate. I had just finished my walk across the plaza, and I was away from the buildings. But if I had stopped to get a cup of coffee and was coming out of the building at that time I would have died. It was just so random. People behind me on the train may not have survived because things fell on them, or they were burned to death. So much of our life, we can try so hard to be controlled about certain things, and yet so much of it is by chance. So you wonder, why people suffer, and why some people are slated to live and certain people are not. (Andrew)

Spiritual Beliefs or Exploration

Some subsequent children, like Andrew, turn to spirituality or a belief in a higher power as they attempt to make meaning of their sibling's death and their survival.

Because of my brother's death, I was forced to think about something more than just what is here, in front of us. There's something larger out there. I don't consider myself to be spiritual in any way, but I always felt like there was something else. There's more meaning than what we see here, and there's more around us than what we see here. I do believe that there is a spiritual world out there, a place where you may go, where your soul may go. I was always made to believe that [my deceased brother] was in that place, and that he was watching us. (Andrew)

Maria, who was born after the death of two sisters, chose to visit a psychic healer as a part of her quest for meaning.

I didn't tell the healer that I had sisters who died before I was born. I didn't tell her about their initials either. [They both had names that began with the letter A.] Without knowing anything about me she told me that these spirits were around and said that she was seeing an A name with a female spirit. She also said that when I was born the souls of my sisters were with me. So I have my sisters around me. It was interesting and odd at the same time to hear this. (Maria)

Some subsequent siblings, like Charlotte, report experiencing a sighting of their deceased sibling, which points to a need for connection and sense making.

I was getting into my parents' bed in the middle of the night when I was five and I remember telling my mom that I just saw somebody on the stairs who looks like Ethan [my deceased brother]. That always stuck with me, that I had a visit from him. (Charlotte)

Some also rely upon religion and spirituality to anchor their belief of where their sibling is now. Gregory, who was born after his infant brother died of sudden infant death syndrome, believes that his brother is happy and at peace in heaven.

I rejoiced for [my deceased brother's] time on earth because he was baptized when he died, so I think it's up to the mighty God, because I believe in the hereafter. So he got the easy way out. He didn't have to go through suffering and pain. He just came in, left, and went back to God. He was innocent, and he was baptized. So I think he is up there in heaven, partying. (Gregory)

Sheree, who was born after a stillborn sister and several miscarriages, explained that she looks forward to meeting all of her deceased siblings in the afterlife.

I guess I'm connected to all of my siblings in some way. They say that after you die, you get to meet all of the people [who died before you]. Maybe I'll see them. That will be cool. (Sheree)

Spiritual exploration and the seeking of a connection to one's sibling can evolve and occur at any time throughout the lifespan. Liz described her spiritual process and a growing connection to her deceased sister.

As I've gotten older and explored my spirituality in the last couple of years, I've thought more about my [deceased] sister. I can still forge a relationship with her spiritually. (Liz)

The Deceased Sibling as Angel or Guide

Many subsequent children, like Denise, Susan, and Alan, believe that their deceased sibling is an angel and perhaps a guardian and protector. It seems to be a way for some subsequent children to give the deceased an active and positive role in their lives, while also forging a loving connection.

We have this connection that I can't really explain. I think that she is a guardian angel of mine. (Denise)

When I thought of my sister, I imagined her as an angel. It's clear, in the few photographs that we have of her, that she was very pretty in an angelic sense. She looked cherubic, with blonde cascading curls. According to my mum and my grandparents her behavior was angelic too. (Susan)

All my life I have spoken to her, thinking of her as an angel. (Alan)

Subsequent siblings may believe that their deceased brother or sister is a source of ongoing support and guidance, and look to them for help when they need it. CR expressed certainty that his deceased sister is a protector.

> *I definitely feel my sister's presence, like a guardian angel. I firmly believe that she protects me, because I've survived way too many near death experiences. After so many examples I became sure that she is there. No other explanation makes sense.* (CR)

Johanna believes that her deceased brother is present and supportive when she is in need.

> *My [deceased] brother comes to me when I'm hurting, or when I've done something wrong, and I didn't tell my parents. I'll be sleeping and I'll feel him in the room—not physically, but mentally I'll feel him in the room. It feels great. It makes me feel like I am different but I am different in a good way. He encourages me to do the right thing, to tell my parents that I did something wrong.* (Johanna)

Jack and Olivia, two young children who are both subsequent siblings, shared their sense of their deceased brother's helpful presence.

> *Sometimes when I'm walking down the stairs and my balance isn't very good, I lose my balance, I catch myself and [my deceased brother] helps me.* (Jack)

> *Yes, that's what happens to me a lot. I get so scared when I fall back and he helps me. I think, Oh, that was a close one.* (Olivia)

Dorotha, who was born after the death of her brother Michael, took on a caretaking role in her family, both during her childhood and as an adult. While caring for her dying father she sensed Michael's presence.

One day I was driving and praying to myself, hoping that my dad would make it. All of a sudden I had this flash of Michael, like Michael the Archangel. It was a soothing feeling. He said, "I'm going to take care of Dad now. You've had him all these years. Now it's my turn. Don't worry. I'll take care of him." At first I wondered if I was making this up, but I don't think so. It was a definite message from beyond. My brother, who never got to be raised by my dad, was going to be with him as he passed. This strong young man that I never knew was there to help me. (Dorotha)

Reincarnation

As they seek meaning, some subsequent children wonder if they are the reincarnation of their deceased sibling. Andrew described a profound process of reflection.

For a while, maybe when I was a teenager, I was kind of preoccupied with the thought that maybe I was my brother. Because I started to learn about reincarnation. And I thought to myself, I wasn't born when he died, so what if his soul is mine? But that went away, because then I came to realize that I'm my own person. Even if I was him, I'm still my own person. (Andrew)

Lori questioned if she was the reincarnation of her deceased sister. Her mother always told her that she was an exact replication of her lost sister, which may have contributed to her questions and wonderings.

At one time I was wondering. I don't know much about this soul stuff, but maybe her body died but her soul is the same as mine, and her soul got my body. So maybe I am her. Because we look so much alike. I don't guess anybody really knows how any of that stuff works. It was just a thought that I've had. Maybe I am her. (Lori)

Some subsequent siblings, like Tret and Edwin, conclude that they truly are the reincarnation of their deceased sibling, which might feel comforting or helpful as they consider their loss and the workings of the world.

> *When I first started thinking about being a replacement, I had a connection in my brain that I am really Brian [my deceased brother]. I just feel like I'm the same soul as Brian, and that it wasn't his time to live. Maybe Brian wasn't ready to be born, or he was supposed to be a girl. I think I have Brian's middle name because I am Brian, who came back as Tret.* (Tret)

> *My parents thought that it was God's will that my brother died. So my name, in my language, means the will of God. My parents named me the will of God, because they think that I am my brother, the baby who has come back. I think so too. They said he looked exactly like me. They believe that I am the baby that came back again. It actually makes me feel better. It makes me feel better that the baby is back, and that you shouldn't worry about it.* (Edwin)

Reincarnation, and the possibility of being a reincarnated version of the deceased sibling, seems to be a common consideration for subsequent children. Many may question the possibility of reincarnation because they need to make sense of the fact that they are alive while their sibling has died, or as a response to replacement dynamics in their families. Being a reincarnated version of the deceased sibling would, in some ways, allow the subsequent child to be an authentic replacement. Like Edwin, subsequent children might believe that being the reincarnation of their deceased sibling would lessen the blow of loss for their families.

Processing the Loss Over Time

Many subsequent siblings recalled their active attempts, from across their lifespan, to process their sibling's death and integrate their sibling into their life story. Their explorations point to a need for understanding and mastery. For example, during his childhood Jack repeatedly drew his deceased brother as an angel, in an apparent attempt to bring his brother's identity and presence into focus. Jack always depicted his brother at the age that he would be if he were still living, which seemed to foster their ongoing relationship and maintained his sibling's older brother role.

> *I've made many pictures of [my deceased brother] as an angel. I never made pictures of him as a little baby. He's ten, [so I draw him as a ten-year-old].* (Jack)

Charlotte remembers drawing and writing about her deceased sibling at different stages in her life and used creative forums to explore and define, for herself and others, her family's status and story.

> *In one of my early family drawings, I drew him as an angel. Then in first grade I wrote that I had a mom, a dad, and two brothers, but that one was dead. For my college entrance essay, I also wrote about Sebastian [my deceased brother]. I explained that we've always been a family of five, but that most people don't see it.* (Charlotte)

Tallying Siblings in the Family

Subsequent children have the complex decision of how to verbally define their family when asked how many siblings they have. There is obviously no right or wrong answer. Some subsequent siblings may prefer to keep their loss private while others might share more openly about their sibling's death. They are likely to be influenced by their family's approach, which could be anywhere on a spectrum from secrecy to openness. As subsequent children consider how to represent and envision their family's composition, they work toward integrating the loss into their life narrative, in whatever way makes sense and feels right for them. Edwin, who always includes his deceased brother when asked how many siblings he has, pointed out that his deceased brother is absent and yet still present in some ways. This contradiction sums up the struggle of some subsequent children to define their families, for themselves and for others.

> *I always include [my deceased brother] when people ask how many siblings we are. But some people don't like it. Like my uncle will tell me that I shouldn't [include my deceased brother], because somebody dead is dead. But that's not exactly true.* (Edwin)

Andrew also chooses to include his deceased brother when defining his family to others.

> *When people ask how many kids are in your family, I say four [and include my deceased brother]. Because I consider him, in a lot of ways, as still alive.* (Andrew)

When the orthodontist asked six-year-old Charlotte if she had any siblings, Charlotte replied that she had two brothers, one dead and one alive. Charlotte then explained to her mother that she wanted people to be aware of her deceased sibling.

> *Dead or alive, he is still my brother!* (Charlotte)

Other subsequent children, like Dierdre and Rebecca, choose not to include their deceased sibling in their sibling count.

> *[When asked how many siblings I have], I just say one sister. It's really her and me.* (Dierdre)

> *I don't count her. Isn't that sad? If someone asks how many children my mother had, however, I'd include her.* (Rebecca)

Subsequent children may change their answer and thoughts about the question as they grow and evolve with their loss, as described by Dana.

I remember saying that I have two brothers. Now I just say that I have one brother. I am not sure when I made that shift. (Dana)

Subsequent children may also grapple to designate and verbalize birth order roles as they consider their family composition. Kate, a subsequent sibling who lost two brothers, simply described herself to others as the oldest child in the family.

Technically I am not the oldest. I say I'm the oldest when asked though, because it is too hard to explain. There is no need to explain to most people about [my deceased siblings]. (Kate)

Carrying Forward

Subsequent siblings sometimes feel the need to carry their deceased sibling forward. They might try to live fully and productively enough for both themselves and their deceased sibling, as if to compensate for the opportunities that their sibling did not have. Perhaps they strive to perform at a higher level, as if they must positively represent not only themselves, but also their deceased sibling. Some may honor their deceased sibling through certain accomplishments and actions, purposefully bringing good into the world to make up for the positive contributions that their sibling might have delivered. Andrew described an ongoing desire to live up to his brother's promise.

I always felt the need to live up to what my brother's standards would have been. (Andrew)

Edwin believes that his brother's death has prompted him to uphold a strong work ethic.

I am very hardworking. I think of the death of the baby. Sometimes I think it helps me work hard. (Edwin)

Denise, who was born after the death of her sister, spoke of writing a script in her sister's honor.

I think she'll be happy when I actually finish it and put it out. I am doing this script for her. It's like a tribute to her. (Denise)

Sally's volunteer work was inspired by her deceased brother.

For ten years I tutored kids. I saw my [deceased] brother in the little boys. That was my grief process, to give to other boys. (Sally)

Charlotte and Ethan, who are both subsequent children, explain that their brother's death has spurred them to make the most of their opportunities, and that he is an ongoing inspiration.

Because my brother couldn't live, I want to take in any opportunity that I can take in. (Charlotte)

My [deceased brother] is a motivating factor in my life. This totally comes from me, not from my parents. My general premise is to take each day and make the most of it, because my brother didn't get the opportunity to live life and do that. I don't want to waste my time, and I make the most of it. (Ethan)

Like Charlotte and Ethan, many subsequent children have a need or desire to live up to their deceased sibling. Lana spoke with loving admiration for her twenty-year-old sister who died before her birth. She explained that her sister's example provided her with positive encouragement and guidance.

I think it's important [for subsequent children] to look for positive memories of the deceased sibling and to try to carry them forward. So the deceased sibling, if they were a good person, can be an invisible yardstick. My [deceased] sister has been that in some ways. Her beauty and gentleness were an inspiration. (Lana)

Elise believes that she needs to live up to her brother's promise, as his death enabled her to be born.

Marcel was there before me. This may sound weird, but I just always felt like I had to live up to him because he died so I could be here. My parents never said or did anything explicit to make me think that it was my job to replace him, but I have always felt like I was in the womb when he couldn't be. I realized that it was my fate, informing who I think I am and some of my purpose and meaning in life. (Elise)

Andrew feels as if he carries some added familial responsibilities because of his brother's death.

I think that [my brother's death] manifested itself in more responsibility for me. Now I have the responsibility of carrying on the family name. (Andrew)

Finding the Grave

Subsequent children often seek out the final resting place of their deceased sibling as a part of their meaning making process. Many of our interviewed subsequent children, like Jenna, Tanya, and Angelo, reported uncertainty about the location of the grave of their sibling or voiced an ensuing quest or desire to locate the grave. In other families, subsequent siblings felt unable to ask about their deceased sibling's final resting place or were unable to access information, and it remained a mystery.

I don't think that [my deceased brother] was buried. I don't know what they did with him. (Jenna)

[My deceased sister] was born in Florida. Honestly, I don't know where she is buried. I have absolutely no idea. (Tanya)

*The grave got lost. Someone buried [my deceased brother],
and then no one knew where the grave was.* (Angelo)

If they lacked information, some subsequent siblings tried
to piece together where their deceased sibling might be and to
fill in the blanks. Brigit, who was born after the death of an
infant sister, only knew that the doctor reportedly assisted with
her deceased sister's remains.

*The doctor paid for the burial. I think the doctor said he
would bury her, so he may have placed her with his family in
their burial lot.* (Brigit)

Several subsequent children described a process of seeking
their sibling's grave or a desire to do so in the future. Michael,
who reported concern that his sibling's grave was unmarked and
that his parents did not know its location, asked his father to
help him find the grave.

*It just so happened that my father and I were in the ceme-
tery [where my deceased brother was buried] for my father's
co-worker's funeral. After the funeral I told my dad that I
really wanted to see my brother's grave. He was very supportive. We went and asked the cemetery caretaker, found
it on a map, and went out there to find it. It was kind of a
challenge because they are not easily marked.* (Michael)

With research and effort, Sophie located her sister's grave in
the baby area of a cemetery. The babies did not have headstones
but were placed around a tree with stones that bore their initials.
She was able to find the stone with her sister's initials.

*I just wanted to see it; to touch the stone. I put a stone on her
grave that I got in Israel.* (Sophie)

Alan hopes to find his sister's grave in the future.

*My parents were poor and had no money, so [my deceased
sister] was buried in a cousin's family plot. Her name is not*

on the tombstone. We never went to that grave. I don't know where her grave is. I actually want to find out. (Alan)

Other subsequent siblings described finding a lost grave later in life to make meaning not only for themselves, but also for a parent.

> *My brother was buried in a common grave for babies. My mom had no control over the burial as she was unconscious for several days after my brother's birth and death. She did not know where the grave was. When my mom was on her deathbed, my brother and I researched and found the grave. There was no name, only a number. It was a shared grave with other babies. We put some dirt from my sibling's grave into my mom's casket.* (Paulina)

Cathy was able to research and locate her sister's grave. Cathy's mother, who had missed the funeral because she was still hospitalized at the time, shared a desire and need to see the grave for the first time. They made an emotional visit to the cemetery, along with Cathy's other surviving sisters, and finally placed a marker on the grave.

> *The funeral home was able to look up the records. She was buried in the cemetery in town, with one of my mother's aunts who died young. Rather than buying a new grave, they buried my sister in the family plot. With my urging and my mother's eagerness we ordered a plaque with Colleen's name, birth date, and day of death. My sisters, mother, and I traveled together to the little town in Iowa. We brought a little flower arrangement and went to the cemetery. The four of us stood around the grave and mourned Colleen's death. We stood there and cried.* (Cathy)

Many subsequent children benefited from the search and visitation of their sibling's final resting place, as it created an opportunity for meaningful ritual and an honoring of the deceased. Some placed flowers or a special stone on the grave.

Their widespread stories of searching for the deceased sibling's grave illuminate their common need to address unfinished business. The loss of an important but unmet person presents its own unique challenges. Subsequent children often struggle to grasp who their sibling was, as there are no memories of the deceased to cherish and no lived relationship to refer to. The subsequent child will never see themselves reflected in the eyes of their lost sibling. Janet sums up the ambivalence experienced by many subsequent children, who often seek more connection to the deceased but do not want to live in the shadow of loss.

> *On Danny's fortieth birthday I wrote him a little eulogy. To end, I said "Brother, if you can't stay, will you please just go." Because he had been a shadow in my life. All my life, I've been seeking him, seeking someone that was older than me and who could give me direction. Danny was always present in my life, but always absent.* (Janet)

Conclusion

Like all bereaved individuals, subsequent siblings often need to confront unfinished business and make meaning of their family's loss. They face unique challenges, however, because it is challenging to make meaning of an ambiguous loss. Most subsequent children are deeply impacted by their sibling's death, but they have no memories of their own to further a continuing bond and are frequently left with unanswered questions and fragmented knowledge. They may have an intense experience of the loss, but not of the deceased. In their wonderings and explorations of topics such as reincarnation, lost graves, and guardian angels, subsequent children try to make sense of their sibling's death and of their life as the child born after loss. As they try to piece together who their sibling was, they also attempt to define and position themselves and work to assemble a complex puzzle of familial relationships and messages. Their work of meaning making is often an ongoing process that can be revisited throughout their lifespan.

8

Altered Parenting

It is safe to expect that the parenting practices of bereaved parents will be altered and affected by their loss, as the death of a child commonly impacts one's identity, sense of safety, belief system, and worldview. Some parents are less able to attach to a subsequent child because they fear another loss. Others are emotionally unavailable as they are consumed with grief. Many grieving parents, like Annette, describe ongoing anxiety about their subsequent and surviving children. Their worry is rooted in their experience of loss.

> *If the doctor was doing a physical exam on my children and spent too much time palpating the liver, I'd worry that they had liver cancer. If my children had bruises on their legs, I'd wonder if they had leukemia. If they had headaches, I'd think that they might have brain cancer. I remember being terrified that my daughter might get hit by a car if she were in the cul-de-sac. I was afraid whenever she was away from me.* (Annette)

Overprotective Parenting

Bereaved parents are frequently overprotective of their subsequent children because they are acutely aware that a child can die. Some parents, like Betty, Dawn, and Susan, remember being hypervigilant and fearful, and anxiously monitoring all signs pertaining to their subsequent child's health both in pregnancy and after birth.

> I remember watching [my daughter born after loss] at night quite intently, to make sure she was breathing. I had the crib right by the bed. (Betty)

> We took turns staying awake for the first two weeks of his life. We were so afraid that [our son born after loss] would die too. (Dawn)

> I was very fearful, and I hadn't been fearful before the loss. I know that I was overly protective [of my subsequent child]. I would watch her constantly, like a hawk. (Susan)

As they reflect on their childhood and family experiences, many subsequent children describe parents who were overly cautious and protective. Edwin, Kennedy, Susan, and Andrew revealed that their parents went to great lengths to supervise and protect them. In some cases, their parents did not allow them to partake in activities that were common for other children.

> My parents were very overprotective. I was so much taken care of, in a way that I didn't want. With swimming, I couldn't swim because I might go into the water and drown. I also couldn't ride a bicycle because I might hurt myself. (Edwin)

> My parents always had to know where I was. Neither of my parents liked sleepovers. They didn't like it when my sister [who is also a subsequent child] and I were not at home. (Kennedy)

My mum worried about me all the time. I was never allowed to go swimming with other children. One time I snuck off and went swimming without permission. My mum stormed in hysterically. She pulled me out of the shallow end and smacked my legs. She was terrified that I could have drowned. (Susan)

My mom was ultra-protective of me. I don't think she ever accepted the fact that [my brother's drowning] was an accident. She blamed herself, so she became very protective of me and my sisters. She is still very cautious. (Andrew)

Overprotective parenting can hinder a child's ability to grow, develop independence, and explore. Those who were parented with excessive protection often describe unhealthy and controlling dynamics. Linda recollected growing up in a household that was imbued with negativity and fear.

I didn't learn about my body or how to fall, because my mother would always catch me before I fell down. I wasn't allowed to ride my bicycle outside of my neighborhood, because my mother said that I wasn't coordinated, and that she was afraid I would get killed. I felt as if I was always contained. (Linda)

While subsequent children generally recognize the underlying reasons for their parents' worry and overprotectiveness, some, like Edwin, react with understandable anger, while others, like Ryan, feel frustrated or embarrassed.

If I went home now [as an adult] I am sure that my mom would ask me where I was going every day. That would piss me off. They were taking too much extra care of me. It got to the point that I got annoyed, so I left home. I wanted to be myself. (Edwin)

My mom was an overprotective mom. She would freak out if one of us kids walked away for a second when we were out in public as a family. Her immediate hysteria was embarrass-ing. She'd call out for us in panic mode, ask people if they'd seen us. She would absolutely lose it. It must have been a reaction connected to losing my brother. (Ryan)

Many subsequent children also develop empathy about their parents' anxiety. Two subsequent children, TJ and his sister, Sydney, began taking ongoing steps to reassure their parents about their safety after they finished high school and moved away from home.

TJ and I are sensitive and protective of our parents' feelings. As we've gotten older, we have become more understanding, because we know what our parents went through. My mom is riddled with anxiety, so having a set time to speak to me gives her peace of mind. Because she doesn't have control, Mom wants to know I'm safe and at home, and she wants to be able to reach me if I'm out somewhere. I think that she and my dad lost a sense of control because they don't see me everyday anymore, so checking in daily is a big thing for them. (Sydney)

When I was in high school, if my mom was emotional about something I didn't necessarily call her back right away. She'd get so upset if she didn't hear back from me. Now I know to text her saying "Hey, I'm okay. I'll call you back at 5." Most people don't think it's a big deal to not call your parents back right away, but it is a big deal in my family. (TJ)

Experiences vary for subsequent children, and each family is unique. Some subsequent siblings, like Katelyn and Noah, describe parents who were not overly anxious.

My parents were not overprotective. They were good parents who gave me freedom to explore and figure out the world for myself in a good way, with natural consequences. (Katelyn)

I had a supportive and happy childhood. I think that my parents were on the same page as everybody else's parents and were not overprotective. (Noah)

Some bereaved parents shared their conscious and active efforts to avoid overprotecting their subsequent children. Their efforts were rooted in a desire to lessen the unhealthy impacts of loss upon their parenting approaches. Marci, who is Noah's mom, worked hard to ensure that her anxiety did not negatively impact Noah's development.

Sometimes I check myself as a mom. There is something to be learned from friends who have never experienced loss, who are doing a good job raising their kids and are sort of skipping through the tulips, as I used to say. Seeing their parenting has helped me to tone down some of my overprotectiveness. (Marci)

Ann expressed an awareness that she tended to be overprotective as a mom, and an understanding that her concerns stemmed from her experience of loss. She was thoughtful in her attempts to augment her sense of trust and safety.

We went through a process with our [subsequent] daughter's early childhood program that helped us build our capacity to separate from her. We eased into it, having a mother's helper come while we were home a couple times so that we felt more comfortable leaving her. Eventually she went to the program without us, but we were still able to come observe her from an observation room if we wanted to. So every year was a little bit of a growing experience for her, and an opportunity for me to let go. (Ann)

Emotionally Unavailable Parents

Instead of being overprotective in response to their history of loss, some bereaved parents become numb, distant, and unresponsive to their subsequent child's needs and experiences. They may be preoccupied with their own grief, or their lack of connectedness might also be an unconscious protective measure to avoid further pain or potential loss. CR questioned why his mother wasn't more protective of him in the face of his father's alcoholism and unsafe behaviors.

When I was a kid, I started taking care of my dad, because he was always under the influence. My dad was drinking, and my mom was just oblivious or not wanting to see it. I have memories of my dad driving intoxicated with me in the car, several times almost getting in head-on collisions. I wondered why my mom let him drive with me. (CR)

Margie had an ongoing sense of being dismissed by her mother. She recalled walking home from school during a severe winter storm. Her mother called the school frantically to find out where she was, but when she got home her mother did not embrace her or show relief that she was safe.

When I got home my mother just told me to put my feet on the radiator. She never hugged me or said that she was glad to see me. As an adult, I learned that she went into her bedroom and sobbed. She thought I was dead. It must have been terrifying for her. She could barely be in the room with me because it was so terrifying. I was very important to her, but she could never show it, because it would be an admission that she was afraid that I could die. (Margie)

Enmeshed Attachments

Conversely, rather than being emotionally absent or unavailable, some bereaved parents develop enmeshed attachments with their subsequent children that stem from their experience of loss. Fears of another loss and needs for comfort may prompt some parents to be overly present or even intrusive in the lives of their subsequent children. Parents with enmeshed attachment styles are often experienced as smothering, because their children lack space and opportunities to build separate, strong, and authentic identities. Linda, who was born after a stillborn sister, shared memories of a mother who was profusely present and involved.

> *When I went to first grade my mom was there, in the class-room, all the time. I didn't need to tell her what happened at school because she was there, and she already knew. I remember once standing in front of a mirror, and all of a sudden realizing that I was a separate human being from my mother. It was a surprise that I wasn't at one with her, a part of her. At times I still don't feel separate from her.* (Linda)

Eric, who was born after the death of his brother, revealed that his relationship with his mother was overly binding and fused.

> *When I was eight, I had to stop playing with my best friend, because my mother was jealous. She was a possessive mom. I don't think that she wanted me to grow up and leave her. I have photographs of myself as a teenager wearing her watch and her glasses. I experienced myself as if I were her. As a college freshman I was the only one who always talked about his mother. I adapted her worldview toward my generation's culture. I was really seeing the world through her eyes at that time. She had a real problem separating from me.* (Eric)

A Shifted Family Plan

The grief experienced by bereaved parents may lead them to change their plan about their family's composition. Some, like Ryan's mom, choose to expand their families as a protective measure.

> *My brother's death was extremely traumatic for both of my parents, and something that my mom never fully recovered from. My mom had this fear that she was going to lose*

another child, and it drove her to want more kids. There are six of us. My mom told me that she wanted extra kids, just in case she lost another child. (Ryan)

Parenting Through a Lens of Grief

Some subsequent children remember parents who were overwhelmed by grief and who were therefore unable to fully assume certain aspects of their parenting role. Sally, who was born after her five-year-old brother died, lamented the state of her family and her mother's unavailability.

> *There was no chance of a stable home environment after my brother's death. It made my mom unstable. In her head she was homeless and had no roots [after the loss]. She didn't keep the house clean, and didn't keep the family together, which is the role of a mom.* (Sally)

Andrew concluded that his mother struggled with depression during the early years of his life.

> *I think that my mom was depressed for quite a while [after my brother died]. She was probably depressed when she was pregnant with me, and probably went through a lot of grief when I was a baby too.* (Andrew)

Parents who are fearful or ambivalent about attaching to a subsequent baby might also be less physically affectionate. Many subsequent children described parents who avoided physical affection or who seemed reluctant to display love, and they recalled some unmet needs to be held or comforted. Janet remembers seeking out her father's affection as best she could.

> *You couldn't climb on my dad's lap, and you couldn't sit next to him. I remember sitting between his old rocking chair and the footstool. He'd play with my hair, and I'd*

tie his shoestrings in knots. I never had the holding that I wanted. (Janet)

Subsequent children sometimes recognize that they were offered a limited or damaged attachment by their parents. Dana, who was born after the death of an infant brother, spoke of an uneasy attachment with her mother.

I had an anxious attachment with my mom. When I was babysat, I got anxious. I was anxious wondering where my mom was when I wasn't with her. (Dana)

As an adult, Kenneth became more aware of his family's dysfunction and his mother's limitations.

I see mothering now, good parenting, and I realize what I missed. (Kenneth)

Many subsequent children, like Janet and Angelo, carry a deep awareness of their parents' sorrow.

I knew growing up it was just a part of my story, the sadness. (Janet)

My mom never recovered from my brother's death. She says that there is always something empty inside her body. That the pain can never be described. (Angelo)

Conclusion

The parenting that subsequent children receive is informed by their family's grief and its aftermath. Bereaved parents are forever changed by their loss, and they have varied capacities for healing and resiliency. They may be emotionally unavailable or absorbed in mourning. Some struggle to form a secure attachment to a subsequent child as they are fearful or grief-stricken.

Others might form an enmeshed bond with their subsequent child due to their anxiety and needs for comfort. In many cases, bereaved parents are overprotective of their subsequent children. The parenting struggles and practices of bereaved parents are meaningful factors in the origin stories of subsequent children. Family of origin experiences are known to be formative. Parenting is deeply influential upon a person's identity, sense of self, attachment style, relationships, and worldview. Most subsequent children receive parenting that carries the imprint of loss, with repercussions that are significant and woven into their life stories and identities.

9

Surviving Siblings

All family members are impacted when a loss occurs within their family unit, and the death of a child is distinctively heartbreaking. Siblings who were alive when a brother or sister died, who are commonly referred to as surviving siblings, usually face a deep and painful bereavement experience. Their grief and reactions are an important piece of the bereaved family's story.[1] Most surviving siblings mourn for not only their lost brother or sister, but also for the changes in their grieving parents. They may face a complex mourning process because the sibling relationship is significant and multilayered. Siblings can be both playmates and rivals, and they frequently compete, perhaps bitterly, for parental attention and love. They can also be the strongest of allies, sharing family experiences and bonding over the injustices or idiosyncrasies of their parents. Siblings play an important role in identity development. As many parents are prone to comparing their children, siblings often hold each other up as models and rivals through whom they can measure their successes, failures, and value. The loss of a brother or sister is oftentimes life altering, causing immense grief and changed relationships and roles in the family.[2]

Surviving siblings generally experience many emotions in response to their loss, such as fear, shock, guilt, sorrow, and numbness. They may also develop psychosomatic symptoms. Some regress to an earlier developmental level after the loss, reverting to bedwetting for a time, for example, or demonstrating a heightened need for parental comfort and attention. Their parents may be mired in grief and emotionally unavailable, and the experiences of mourning children are often misunderstood. Supportive resources are often lacking for surviving siblings. Bereaved parents are commonly viewed as the primary mourners after a child dies, and the needs of surviving siblings are frequently unseen and unmet. Bereaved children are at higher risk for depression, anxiety, substance use, and declines in their academic performance and social connections, so it is critical to ensure that they receive support. While the loss of a sibling is always devastating and unwelcome, bereaved siblings sometimes experience psychological growth that emerges because of their grief and loss experience.[3]

Surviving Siblings and Their Parents

Surviving siblings suffer not only from the death of a sibling, but also from the loss of their pre-loss parents. Substantial and perhaps permanent changes in a family's equilibrium occur after the death of a child, and parents are forever changed. As they are overwhelmed by grief, bereaved parents often lack the emotional capacity or recognition to meet the bereavement and other needs of their surviving children. Even when well intentioned, parents are often unaware of the sensitivity and pain of their surviving children. Speaking at a conference for bereaved parents, an adult sibling who was eighteen months old when her brother died asked the audience to ponder what she must have felt to be carried in the arms of a grieving parent. Surviving siblings of all ages are acutely attuned to the changes in their family and to their parents' emotional state. Many, like Christine, describe a family environment that was permanently altered by loss.

When I was sixteen, my mom had a stillbirth. I lost my mom when that baby died. She became a different person. (Christine)

Meghan reported that her needs were often dismissed during her childhood because of the overwhelming grief of her parents. They endured several miscarriages, and Meghan witnessed their devastation as the losses occurred. They never explained what was happening, which was confusing, frightening, and caused her to wonder if she had done something wrong.

When I was small, my family lost babies. I remember my mom being in the bathroom. I remember my dad shushing me and telling me to be quiet. I remember seeing my mom sad and my dad worried about her. (Meghan)

Meghan also remembered her mother's ongoing sorrow and emotional unavailability.

My mom was sad and unavailable when I was small. (Meghan)

Patty believes that her brother's death caused a tremendous shift in her relationship and attachment to her mother. She was one year old when her mother miscarried a baby boy.

I know that my mother's behavior toward me changed after my brother died. From what I understand, she was terribly distressed, and she wouldn't pick me up. I was a young infant in the crib, but she wouldn't hold me. (Patty)

Margie, a subsequent child, reflected on the experiences of her older sister, who was two years old when their sibling died. Her sister continues to claim that she has no need to talk about their family's loss and its impact. This is baffling to Margie because she remembers her mother's behavior and acute grief. She wonders if the topic is too painful for her sister to face.

> *What if all of a sudden, a mother isn't interested, is depressed, doesn't play, withdraws, and you don't get held? That was my [surviving] sister's experience. My mother's pattern was to run away from emotions. My sister must have wondered what happened to the baby that didn't come home, and why Dad was crying. It was a significant trauma. As a little girl she had to take care of herself, and she also felt like she had to take care of her grieving parents.* (Margie)

Many bereaved parents do not receive guidance about how to support surviving siblings. In a well-intentioned but misguided attempt to protect their surviving children from pain, parents may avoid discussion of the death, send children away after the loss, or exclude them from the funeral or other mourning rituals. Robin, a bereaved mother, shared her regrets as she considered, in retrospect, her surviving child's difficult experience of the loss.

> *My son was 3½ when our baby died. I don't think we talked about what was going on, except to say that the baby died. We didn't help him process it because my husband isn't really capable of that, and I was in shock. I think I hugged him. I don't remember. We hosted the memorial at our house, and I spent a lot of time planning it. We had a full-time housekeeper who was probably looking after my son. I was around, but I wasn't focused on him.* (Robin)

Susan, whose seven-year-old sister died, reported that her older brother's grief was unrecognized by their parents. She was aware of her brother's suffering and neglected needs.

> *My brother Lesley was very close to our [deceased sister]. She died four days before his tenth birthday. His grief was very much overlooked. He was sent to our grandparents' house and spent a great deal of time living there after our sister's death. I think he ended up being more bonded with our grandmother than with our mom.* (Susan)

Bereaved parents often face a range of strong emotions that impact their parenting after loss. Annette, a grieving mom, described the guilt, anger, and ambivalence that she felt in her mothering role with her surviving child.

I poured my [surviving] daughter a glass of milk. And she hit across the table and said, "I don't want that glass. I want the Mickey Mouse glass." I remember feeling this rage and thinking "My perfect child is dead, and here you are." And also having a horrible feeling of guilt, thinking, "How can I think that?" But it's what I felt. Sometimes I needed to ask friends to take my [surviving] daughter because I didn't have the energy. Other times I needed her to be so close to me because I was terrified that something would happen to her. (Annette)

Meghan stated that her parents were frequently impatient and unavailable. She believes that their frustration was rooted in their grief.

I don't think my parents had space for my developmental needs. They found it disrespectful that I was a normal pre-schooler at such a tough time for us as a family. (Meghan)

Some parents are able to be attuned to the needs of surviving siblings, however, and despite their grief, are purposeful in addressing their surviving children's needs. After Martha lost a twin during pregnancy, she gently shared the news with her three-year-old daughter, and she was thoughtful in her approach.

We decided we had three good reasons for telling her [about the loss]. First, she needed to understand why her mommy was crying or emotional, so she would know it was not her fault and not something she had done. Second, grief could not be pushed under the rug and forgotten. It will find a way out somehow, maybe in some other harmful form. Third, and most important, she needed to be able to claim Laura [the deceased twin] as her sister. (Martha Wegner)[4]

Sheila, a bereaved mom who lost a stillborn daughter, was aware that her toddler son could feel her grief. She was insightful as she considered the possible meanings and felt experiences of her surviving son. She described holding her son more than usual after her loss and observed that it seemed to fit both of their needs. She wondered if her son, sensing her needs for comfort, was taking on a caretaking role, or if he needed reassurance due to her grief.

I needed a child in my arms, and he was a thirty-five-pound toddler. It wasn't just an issue for me. He would ask me to rock him, ask me to sing to him. I don't know if it was some kind of intuition, that he could sense that I needed it, or if he needed it because he could tell that I was sad, but it helped me feel as if my arms were less empty for a little bit. (Sheila)

Like subsequent children, surviving children are sometimes placed in caretaking roles for their grieving parents and become carriers of worry and grief. Mallory, who was six years old when her adolescent brother was killed in a car accident, described a dramatic shift in her familial role.

My role was to make my mom feel better. She would tell me that I was the only reason that she got up in the morning. I felt like I got a message from my father that mom was not doing well, and that I needed to be careful around her and to take care of her. (Mallory)

Lara, a bereaved mom, expressed her awareness of the formative and difficult impacts of her grief upon her surviving daughter.

My [surviving] daughter was only two when her sibling died, and every day I was in tears. There's probably some-thing instilled in her or maybe deep down inside her that remembers how awful that time was for us. She grew up to be a worrier, and I think that might have been caused by all of our grief and distress. (Lara)

Surviving siblings may attempt to be perfect and avoid misbehavior as they fear upsetting their grieving parents. Replacement dynamics may be enacted. Like Christine, surviving siblings might unconsciously feel pressured to please their parents and fill the void of loss.

After my brother died, I was the perfect child and the perfect student. I never did drugs and was a virgin until I was twenty-nine and married. I don't know if my reasons for being that way were ever conscious. I learned in a workshop later that some [surviving] children take on that role. (Christine)

Dynamics with parents, set into place by the loss, are often enduring. Mallory described a lifetime of caring for her mother's grief and anxiety, and the toll of heavy expectations.

I felt like I was constantly on a tether. If I tried to go anywhere or to do anything, my mom was so anxious. I wanted to horseback ride, but my mom responded that horses throw people on the ground and step on them, and that I might die. In high school, when I went out I had to call my mom a lot, at designated times. I lived this limited scope of existence, always worried, always needing to check in. Once I forgot to call and my mom was crying hysterically, asking how I could do that to her. There was so much guilt and responsibility. (Mallory)

Surviving siblings who grew up with poor attachments may remain distant from their parents as adults. Susan, whose brother Lesley is a surviving sibling, described his resentment and avoidance of their mother in their adult years.

His relationship with my mum is strained. He sees her a few times a year and blatantly refuses to help her in the home.

Despite having his own landscape gardening business, he would not even call at my mother's home and mow her lawn. (Susan)

A Disenfranchised Loss

The grief of surviving siblings is sometimes overlooked and disenfranchised. Some mistakenly believe that children cannot truly mourn due to their age and developmental level. This misconception may be exacerbated by the presentation of a child's grief, which usually looks quite different than an adult's. After the death of a child, most attention and care are frequently channeled toward the mourning parents, and the community and extended family may not recognize the significance of the surviving siblings' loss. Their grief is further disenfranchised when their parents are too distraught to understand or address their needs.[5]

> *I didn't feel like I had a right to my grief after my brother died. It was my parents' grief, not mine. There was no attention given to my grief. If I talked about it at school or somewhere, it felt disingenuous, and like I was doing something that I did not have a right to do.* (Mallory)

In some cases, surviving children take on the role of being a memory keeper, holding the loss for the family, ensuring that the deceased sibling is not forgotten, and carving out room for grief and remembrance. In advocating for the recognition of their sibling's death, they push to avoid a disenfranchised loss. Allison, whose mother lost one of her twins during pregnancy, spoke up to ensure that the loss was recognized when a friend came over to meet the living twin.

> *My best friend, Mary, stopped by to visit me and David soon after his birth. No one mentioned Laura [the deceased twin]. As she was leaving Allison said, "You know we had a baby that died. She was David's twin sister. Her name was Laura, and we feel very sad about that."* (Martha Wegner)[6]

Lexi, a surviving sibling, educates others about the immense impact of sibling loss. As she builds awareness, she works to lessen the disenfranchised status of grieving siblings.

> *I go to conferences for grieving families with my father. I give presentations about the sibling perspective about the death of a child in a family.* (Lexi)

Guilt and Self-Blame

It is not uncommon for surviving siblings to believe that they are at fault for their sibling's death. This can sometimes be explained developmentally, as young children naturally have an egocentric sense of the world. They have not yet acquired the capacity to understand or account for the vantage points of others. As they view themselves as central, they often fear that they are at fault for negative events, such as a death in the family. Their worries and guilt are exacerbated when the death is not openly discussed or they are not supported in their grieving process. Diane's younger brother died in his crib. She and her sister thought that his death was their fault because their parents did not explain the cause of death or provide reassurance.

> *My sister and I woke up and found out he had died. We thought that it was our fault. The night before, when our mom was supposed to go feed him, we asked her to read us one more story. We thought that if we hadn't begged her to read one more story, she could have saved him. Years later, as an adult, I told my mom that we felt responsible. She said that we shouldn't have felt that way. Well, no, we shouldn't have felt that way. But that is how little kids interpret it.* (Diane)

Like Diane, Linda was given no explanation about the deaths of her twin sisters, and she believed that she might be to blame. She only knew that they both died within a short time span. One lived for two days while the other was stillborn.

I remember being informed about the [deaths of my twin sisters]. Everybody shut down and quit talking. It wasn't discussed. In those days, even within the confines of your own house things just weren't discussed. My mother never really talked about it, but I have a vivid memory of one thing she said. My brother and I were having a sibling fight, and she said "Well, it's no wonder that God took the babies, because look at you guys!" I felt like it was my fault that they died. It has been a hard thing to carry. (Linda)

Likewise, Meghan worried that she was responsible for her mother's miscarriages.

My mom had lots of miscarriages when I was a toddler and preschooler. I was frightened and overwhelmed. I still need to hear that what happened was not my fault, and that I couldn't fix it or make my mom feel better. I felt invisible and, in some ways, responsible for what had happened. (Meghan)

Eric, a surviving sibling, shared about the guilt and angst of his older brother Hal, who believed that he was responsible for their younger brother's death.

Hal was assigned to watch our baby brother on a three-hour road trip. He was sitting next to him in the back seat of the car. Our baby brother had a cold, and our mom kept asking Hal how the baby was doing. Hal reported back that the baby was sleeping. The baby was dead when they arrived. Our mom did not realize that he had developed pneumonia. Hal believed that the death was his fault until he was an adult and realized that he had been too young to be responsible. He was only five years old when our brother died. (Eric)

A Daunting and Painful Loss

For most surviving siblings, the loss of their brother or sister is their first experience of death, and it is difficult to process such a monumental and tragic event in their family. Christine, a surviving sibling, remembers her sense of the disconnect between the crisis in her home and the ongoing routines of the outside world.

The loss of my brother was so little to the world and so big to my family. I was surprised that the rest of the world went on and didn't stop. I was surprised that when we got home I was so hungry, because you think you're never going to eat again, but you're hungry. And I was surprised at how much it hurt. We didn't have to go to school because my mom said that we're grieving. (Christine)

Most surviving siblings, like Mallory, describe a range of intense emotions about the death.

The shock was so big. It was so unexpected. I remember my trauma, shock, and fear, absolute fear. I was afraid to go into my [deceased] brother's room because I thought his eyes were in there watching me. I had to walk through his room to get to other parts of the house, and I would see his eyes when the lights were out. I was scared and I would run through his room. I also had lots of psychosomatic symptoms, stomachaches, sore throats, and bronchitis. And I remember a desperate feeling of sadness, knowing that things would never be the same. (Mallory)

Some surviving siblings, like Doug, have traumatic memories of their sibling's death and its cause.

My brother had a form of epilepsy. He and I were playing, he hit his head, and he went to bed crying. I still remember my dad running down the hall screaming and seeing the paramedics working on my brother. It took me thirty years to realize that it wasn't my fault. I started seeing a therapist as an adult because my parents didn't want to talk about it. (Doug)

Janet, a subsequent sibling, shared about her brother's terrifying experience as a surviving sibling. He ran to the neighbor to seek help for his mother and saw an ambulance take her away. When she returned from the hospital there was no discussion of the baby's death, but the crib was taken away.

> *My brother saw our mom on the floor hemorrhaging, and he remembers the screaming when our sibling died. He told me that he still hears the echoes of his five-year-old self running through the house to our mom's side and said that there isn't a minute of every hour of every day that he isn't worried about our mother.* (Janet)

Mallory's brother died on Christmas day. She learned of his death with her parents when the police arrived at their home.

> *I remember that it was night, and the police showed up at our front door to tell us that my brother had died in an accident. After that, there is a three-year gap in which I can't remember much at all. I know it is because of the trauma.* (Mallory)

Witnessing their parents' reactions to the death and the ensuing tension in the home may cause additional anxiety and trauma for surviving siblings. Mallory described a mother who was frighteningly distraught, as well as conflict between her parents.

> *After my brother's funeral, my mom basically shut herself in a room for three days, in the dark, in a chair facing the wall. My dad went in and shamed her. He told her that she had two other children and that she had to get out and live her life.* (Mallory)

Some surviving siblings, like Katie, reported that the intensity of their parents' grief reaction gave them a new understanding of the depth of their parents' love, for them and for their deceased sibling.

I saw that my mom's grief was so difficult. It was a strongly emotional time. If anything, it reinforced my parents' love for me and [my surviving brother], because we saw just how deeply my brother's death affected my parents. (Katie)

An Ongoing and Evolving Grief

The grief of most surviving children is ongoing, with a processing and understanding of the loss that evolves as they reach new developmental stages. Over time they may sometimes feel as if they are grieving anew because the loss takes on fresh meaning. Milestones, death anniversaries, and birthdays can cause surges of grief, and various fears and feelings about the loss are often held. Mallory and Lexi both described a painful grief process that continued to unfold.

I struggled to process my brother's death with no guidance. His death was talked about, but grief was not. I had a lot of fear as a child and as a teenager about losing my parents, my other sibling, or of dying myself. (Mallory)

Certain days are a lot harder than others. My sister's tenth birthday was not a good day in our house. We were all sad and moped. I was feeling upset so I decided to try writing to see if it would help me feel better. It kind of made me more sad, but it also made me feel a little bit better because I got my feelings out. (Lexi)

Surviving siblings often make active attempts to process and make sense of their loss. Lexi's father recollected her early drawings of her deceased sister that demonstrated her desire to comprehend how the family fit together post-loss. The confused and ambivalent responses of Lexi's teachers provide an example of the feedback that grieving children frequently receive. Adults are often uncomfortable with the topic of death and may overtly or inadvertently encourage surviving siblings to keep their grief under wraps, creating an additional barrier for their grieving process. Lexi's dad shared his perspective.

> When Lexi was little, she would always include her [deceased] sister when she drew family pictures. She'd draw her sister in the sky as an angel. She caught the teachers off guard when she drew that picture. They called us to ask if it was okay before it was displayed for other people to see. They were uncomfortable, and it was kind of weird. I thought if she was comfortable sharing with other people, why should they care? (Darrell)

Depending on their age and developmental level, some surviving siblings may engage in magical thinking, believing that they can influence events in the world with certain actions, rituals, or behaviors. Magical thinking is often attractive to bereaved children as it can provide a sense of control, which is commonly wished for as they feel no control over the death and upheaval in their families. Mallory, who was six when her brother died, shared about her thinking process.

> I engaged in a lot of magical thinking, tons of it, connecting things that were not real. I believed that I could stop the rest of my family from dying if I was good. So I felt like I had to be good all the time, following the rules, not causing any kind of disruption, not making anyone upset. (Mallory)

As they process their sibling's death, surviving siblings might have a range of thoughts and feelings that may or may not be voiced. Eryn, who was born after a stillborn brother, had numerous questions about what might have transpired if her brother were alive.

> My brother David's death wasn't often discussed in the family, but on his birthday, we would acknowledge it and go to

the cemetery and bring balloons. When I was little, I always wondered what it would be like to have him as an older brother. Now I wonder if my younger sibling would be here if David hadn't died. (Eryn)

Like their bereaved parents, surviving siblings sometimes avoid reminders of the deceased due to their pain. Christine described her experience.

I had two friends with baby siblings who were born around the same time as my [deceased] brother. I couldn't stand to be at their houses with their babies. (Christine)

Surviving Siblings and a Subsequent Child

Some surviving siblings, like their parents, may fear another loss, and be reluctant to attach to a subsequent sibling.[7] Janet, a subsequent child, revealed that her older brother eventually told her about his traumatic experience when their brother died. As an adult he was able to acknowledge his fear and explain the emotionally distant stance that he maintained toward Janet throughout their childhood.

I felt like I was a booby prize for my brother, and that our deceased brother was the sibling that he really wanted. He would see me in the halls in high school and ignore me. As an adult he tried to heal his relationship with me and our sister. He even wrote a letter to his sixteen-year-old self, saying that my sister and I are amazing human beings and that he should get to know us. He witnessed a lot when our brother died and was traumatized, and grew up worrying about our mom. He realizes now that he was afraid to let himself get close to me and my sister after all that he went through with our brother's death. (Janet)

Susan described a similar experience with her brother.

My older brother is very distant. He sees me a couple of times a year now. I think that he keeps a distant relationship with me because of what he experienced when our sister died, and that he does not want to get attached to another sister who might die. (Susan)

Surviving siblings may be envious or resentful if their subsequent sibling is viewed as a gift child who can heal the family. Meghan was aware that her younger sister, born after numerous miscarriages, was cherished and idealized by their parents, whereas she was not.

My sister Molly, who was born after my mom had many miscarriages, is the golden child in our family. She was the one who did everything right. I always had the sense that I was the one who was not quite as loved as she was, or not quite as good as she was. Her needs were always put first and were more important than anyone else's. (Meghan)

In some families, parents are able to be emotionally present for a subsequent child while the needs of the surviving sibling remain unmet. Surviving siblings may inherit difficult roles or feel invisible, much like inadequate replacement children. A bereaved mom, Robin, had a subsequent baby when her surviving child, Zack, was eight years old. Her overprotectiveness of the subsequent baby created additional strain and distance in her relationship with Zack.

When my [subsequent] baby was born I was numb and still had all the sadness feelings inside me. Zack was an "in your face" kind of a kid and I couldn't handle his intensity around the baby. I was really afraid. Parents can be annoyed by their kids when they have a new baby and the kid is poking on them. That's just normal, but I had a hard time, and on top of it I was in shock and I couldn't help my son with his behavior. My husband and I were aware of not being able to support Zack in his relationship with the baby because we

*were so overprotective, and that we made Zack bad some-
how. We were aware of it but couldn't get a handle on what
we were doing.* (Robin)

Grief-Related Growth

The loss of a sibling is often formative upon a surviving sibling's
identity, causing suffering and difficulty but also grief-related
growth. Like subsequent children, some surviving siblings take
on caregiving roles and report heightened sensitivity and empathy for others. It is burdensome to take on significant helper
roles in childhood, but some surviving siblings, like Mallory, also
recognize their skills to help others as a valuable silver lining of
their loss experience.

*I know that my brother's death made me who I am and
drew me to my work as a therapist who helps people in
need. There were many downsides to my experiences with
my mother, who created a world for me in which I had to be
hyperattuned to her needs. But the upside is that I learned to
be hyperattuned and empathetic. I am sensitive and good at
attending to others.* (Mallory)

Conclusion

Most surviving siblings experience deep and enduring grief. The
sibling relationship is expected to last a lifetime, and many surviving siblings maintain an ongoing attachment to the deceased.
They may struggle to cope with their loss and endure a range of
emotions and psychosomatic symptoms. Some carry traumatic
memories of their sibling's death and its aftermath in their home.
They are also prone to believing that the death is their fault and
to harboring feelings of guilt and self-blame.

Bereaved parents are frequently unaware of how to support
surviving siblings and receive little guidance about best practices
or supportive approaches for their surviving children. After the
death of a child, most support is usually focused upon grieving

parents, and surviving siblings might be overlooked, causing a disenfranchised loss. Surviving siblings may feel as if they lost their parents in addition to losing their sibling, because their parents are forever changed and may be emotionally unavailable due to their grief. Some surviving siblings take on worry and caretaking roles for their parents.

Examining the entire family's lived experience of a loss, and the upheaval that a loss creates in the family system, is crucial for the healing and well-being of grieving families. All family members are acutely impacted by the death of a child and by the responses, availability, and functioning of their remaining family members. Like subsequent siblings, surviving siblings need thoughtful support and recognition of the significance of their loss.

10

Born After a Sibling with Special Needs

The seeds for this chapter were sown when a young man, who was responsible for filming one of Joann's presentations about pregnancy after loss, approached her at its conclusion with a request to speak. He shared that he was born after a brother with severe disabilities. Although his brother did not die, he was amazed to realize that his parents' grief and behavior mirrored Joann's descriptions of pregnancy and parenting after loss. He was equally surprised to note that his childhood experiences and family roles resembled those of a subsequent child. He was not alone; many individuals born after a sibling with special needs share similar perspectives and experiences, as described in this chapter.

Having a child with acute special needs is obviously different from having a death in one's family, and it is unthinkable to equate the two experiences. It may create another type of loss, however, as parents mourn for their child's disabilities, and experience shock and grief over the loss of the healthy baby that was expected. Children who are born after any significant loss may have parallel experiences to subsequent children, including altered roles, expectations, and parenting. A family's grief over a child's special needs does not negate their full and unconditional embrace of that child or lessen their love and dedication. On the contrary, their grief is rooted in love. Parents of a child with special needs feel sorrow about any pain that their child may experience or about any limitations that the disabilities create, such as the inability to ever live independently or a shortened lifespan. While we usually think of grief as the mourning that takes place after the death of a loved one, it is important to note that we also experience grief for non-death losses, such as divorce, the diagnosis of a chronic illness, or any type of unexpected impairment for ourselves or someone we love. Children who are born after a sibling with restrictive special needs are, to varying degrees, born into families that are touched by grief.

Like subsequent children, those born after a sibling with special needs may experience replacement dynamics,[1] because hopes may be placed on them to fill a void in the family, to soften their family's grief, or to carry parental hopes and dreams. Replacement dynamics can be enacted after various types of losses in a family. Children born to parents who previously relinquished a child for adoption may be viewed as replacement children if their parents seek to appease their loss through the birth of another child. Those born after a genocide to parent survivors may be seen as the hope for the next generation and as replacements for the many loved ones who were lost. Likewise, parental hopes and expectations for healing are sometimes placed upon children born after a sibling with special needs.

This chapter does not generally pertain to families with mildly or moderately disabled children. Replacement dynamics are more likely to occur when a sibling's special needs are acute or life threatening. Families who have a child with severe disabilities or who know that the child may die young are obviously most prone to a sense of grief and loss. Most of the special needs siblings presented in this chapter have died from their disabilities; only two are still alive, and they currently live in adult group homes.

Parents are often unaware of their child's disabilities during pregnancy, and their child's special needs may be a shock. Some eventually chose to have another baby because of their desire to have a healthy baby or to ensure that their disabled child will have someone to take care of them throughout their lifespan. They might have dreams and cherished wishes as parents that their special needs child will not be able to embody or experience. Like children born after loss, those who are born after a child with special needs may have been conceived in the hopes of fulfilling certain dreams, to heal the family, and to assuage some of their parents' grief. Replacement dynamics might be enacted, as the healthy child is often viewed as the one who can fulfill certain dreams and who can lessen their parents' sense of loss. Scott, who was born after a disabled brother, revealed an experience of taking on some of the hopes that were initially placed upon his sibling.

> *All of the expectations that my parents had for my brother are on me. My dad was an athlete, but Robby could not follow in his footsteps, so I have carried a bit of my dad's hopes. I know that it's just me that is able to carry on for the family. It makes sense.* (Scott)

Amanda was born after her brother was hit by a car, causing him to be severely disabled. He lived for five years, with many hospitalizations and a need for constant home nursing care. She remembers poignant messages that were repeated throughout her childhood about her birth and function in the family.

> *My father told me that they decided to have another child because they wanted some joy in their house. My mom said that I was my parents' hope for a better future.* (Amanda)

Jan and Tom had a firstborn with severe disabilities. Like Amanda's parents, their decision to have a subsequent child was rooted in their hopes for a shift in their lived experiences.

In our support group for families with special needs children, we talked about the risk of having another child. Several of the parents who gave birth to healthy children before having a child with a disability commented on the joy and balance that the healthy child brings into their lives. Tom and I did not have that joy and balance. Our lives were very intense. We needed to find joy in our life, so we decided to have another baby. (Jan)

Children usually feel glad and gratified to bring joy and relief to their families, but they become burdened when they are consistently expected to do so. They may feel unable to express their own needs and identities when they are viewed as the hopes or healers in their families. Unspoken needs and hopes in a family can be powerful and influential. Children naturally seek the approval and love of their parents, and they are very attuned to parental hopes. If their parents look to them to ease their sorrow or to fulfill wishes that have been transferred to them from their disabled sibling, they will want to satisfy their parents and live up to their wishes. Children may feel unable to truly be themselves if they are striving to fill a void or to embody dreams that their disabled sibling cannot reach.

Altered Families and Altered Parenting

Several participants described the ways that their childhood and family life were profoundly altered by their sibling's disability. Amanda shared her experience of growing up in a home that was centered upon her brother's medical needs.

We were raised differently from a normal childhood because we had a nurse coming to the house every day. Both of my parents had a sleep disorder because Dean needed medicine every four hours, and someone had to wake up for that. (Amanda)

Katie, who was born after a medically and developmentally disabled brother named Christopher, remembers a heavy presence of caregivers in her childhood home. Her parents worked full time, and her brother's caretakers played a significant role in her early childhood.

> *I remember having a lot of caretakers around, and the relationships built with them. The caregivers are the biggest thing that sticks out in my memory. A lot of the people that were caring for Christopher were watching me too.* (Katie)

Katie developed a strong, intuitive connection to Christopher, which may have been grounded in her sensitivity as a child born after loss. When she was three years old, she told her mother that Christopher was going to join their deceased brother, Blake, when he was five years old. Her prediction came true.

Children who are born after a sibling with special needs might recognize the stress and worry of their parents. Some reveal that their parents were less present or available for them because of the needs of their disabled sibling. Amanda spent the majority of her early years with her grandparents.

> *I know that when I was very little I was often at my grandmother's house. I had a strong attachment to my grandmother, and I would cry when I had to leave her. My parents really had no time to take care of me because they had to take care of Dean, and his surgeries and hospitalizations. My parents were also often tired from getting up every night to give Dean his medicine.* (Amanda)

Several participants, like Scott, described memories of their parents' grief.

> *I remember [my brother] Robby's eighth birthday. I was six. My mom was sitting in the den, alone and with the lights out, watching videos of Robby crawling around when he was younger. She was crying. It was a very bad scene. I remember saying, "Hey mom, I love you and Robby is the way that he is. And that's never going to change, that's what the doctors have said but we can still love him and that's okay. So please*

don't cry anymore." I gave her a hug and a kiss. Eventually she turned off the television. We went upstairs and played with Robby. I don't think my mom ever got over her expectations or hopes for Robby to flourish. That memory is really strong. (Scott)

Katherine, whose brother was born with Down syndrome, shared memories of her mother's heartbreak.

My mother said that when she went out in public with my brother as a baby, nobody would make eyes at him. Nobody asked her how old he was or what his name was, like people normally do with babies. No one was enchanted by him. It broke her heart that nobody fussed over her brand-new baby. It was also so painful when she would see another child of the same age who was crawling or sitting up, because her child could not even roll over. She said it was like a new wound, every time it happened, like a knife in her stomach every time. (Katherine)

Parents often mourn upon learning of their child's disability. They may also grieve at each developmental milestone that their disabled child cannot pass, as each one represents another loss. Some parents compare their children and feel pain when their healthy, younger child surpasses the capacities of their child with disabilities. When the achievements of a child born after a sibling with disabilities are less celebrated and tinged with sorrow, it can impact the healthy child's identity formation and self-confidence, causing survivor guilt. Katherine revealed that her development and achievements sometimes created conflict for her mother.

My mom was [reportedly] thrilled when I started to crawl, but my brother still couldn't crawl. I think that it was a knife in her gut every time I achieved something, even though she was also proud. She had a lot of conflicting emotions and grief that might have been exacerbated by my just being regular. (Katherine)

Despite the worry that was common in their families, many participants, like Ben, stated that their parents worked hard to be present for them and to maintain a good balance in the home.

> *My brother Tom has been in the hospital system since he was a baby. My parents did a really good job of focusing on him, but also of remembering that they had other kids to care for too.* (Ben)

Family Secrets

Some participants reported secrecy in their family about a disabled sibling. Marianne, who was born after a disabled brother, did not learn about her brother until he died. Before Marianne's birth, her parents followed their doctor's advice, placing her brother in an institution and cutting off contact. Marianne remembers her shock, at the age of nine, of learning about her brother and his death, and spoke of the impact of the unveiled secret.

> *It was a total shock, learning about him, and that he had been in an institution. I also remember thinking that I had to be good enough, or that my parents might give me away too. He had been dead to our family all of those years, and I thought that I might end up that way too if I misbehaved.* (Marianne)

Marianne's experience highlights some of the outcomes of replacement dynamics. As a child she was frightened to learn that her brother had been sent away, causing her to think that she had to be a "good enough replacement" to ensure that she did not face the same fate. The harboring of secrets, which is fairly common in families with replacement dynamics, also impacts family cohesion and a child's sense of safety. Children can usually sense parental distress, and it is more anxiety producing if it is unspoken and with an unclear cause.

Meaning Making

Some of the participants, like Peter, were able to recollect their process, as children, of trying to understand, adapt, and make meaning of their sibling's disability or death.

> *My earliest memories are of playing house with my sister. I knew that she was bigger and older, but in my early years I already understood that we were playing at the same level. Sibling rivalry stopped when I realized that I was bigger than her, and I knew that winning every fight with her wasn't right. I was about four when this happened. I felt like I was being the older brother for the rest of our childhood until I got a more subtle understanding. I felt like I had a three-year-old sister.* (Peter)

Amanda was two years old when her brother died of his injuries. She remembers trying to understand his death through play, which is a common vehicle for children to try to make sense of difficult experiences and work through them.

> *I have a faint memory of being brought over to the casket to see [my brother] Dean. After that I would sometimes play a game called "Dean in the Blue Box." That was how I coped at the time. I think I was remembering him and trying to understand where he was and what happened.* (Amanda)

Others shared a process of meaning making that they undertook as adults. Marianne explained a quest for information about her institutionalized brother to better understand her childhood, family relationships, and experiences. Like many siblings born after a loss, she also felt a desire to establish a bond with her unmet brother.

> *I knew nothing about my brother's life, except that they did not have a funeral and donated his body to science.*

My parents would never talk about what happened. I kept wondering who he was and what happened to him. I finally reached out to the institution and got his medical records. I haven't told my parents about this. I just needed information. (Marianne)

Marianne believes that her relationship with her mother was impaired because of her mother's grief about her brother. Her sense of a damaged bond mirrors the experiences of many children born after a deceased sibling.

My brother's life really impacted my life. My mom did not want to connect to me. She was so hurt by her experience of having a disabled child that she didn't want to bond to me. (Marianne)

Shifted Birth Order Roles

The roles that siblings commonly adopt, based upon their birth order, may shift if one child has special needs. Like Ben and Katie, children who are born after a sibling with special needs may be treated as if they are older than their sibling, especially when they surpass their sibling developmentally.

My brother Tom was born first, then Pete, and then me, but it definitely felt like Pete was treated as the oldest and I was treated like the middle child. Tom seemed like the youngest because he was the baby that needed a lot of medical attention. I felt like I had the middle child syndrome, even though I wasn't actually the middle child. (Ben)

I've always seen myself in the firstborn role because of Christopher's disabilities. I sometimes felt a little jealousy over being expected to be high functioning and taking care of my own stuff while Christopher received more attention. Obviously, that just goes along with the territory of growing up with a sibling with special needs, but as a child you don't quite understand fairness. (Katie)

Shifted birth order roles may be experienced as a loss. It might feel burdensome, as the second-born, to take on the traditional responsibilities of the oldest child, or upsetting, as the youngest, to be unable to be the baby in the family. Altered birth roles are generally caused by the heightened needs of siblings with disabilities. Many children feel sadness and resentment about the time and care needed by their sibling with disabilities, and guilt about their resentment. Elements of rivalry are customary in sibling relationships, but it is often complicated and conflictual to compete with a disabled sibling.

The Gifts

Many individuals who were born after a sibling with special needs described strengths and gifts that they developed because of their experience. Several participants specified that they acquired a heightened sense of empathy for others. Scott, whose older brother had special needs, shared about his childhood efforts to be caring toward all disabled children at his school.

Thanks to my brother, Robby, I had more awareness of the community. In school I looked out for people who seemed not to have friends or who were sitting alone, because I knew that they needed a friend. I remember going over to different kids' houses and playing with them, kids who had Down syndrome or were on the autism spectrum. I knew that they needed friends too. I must be honest, it wasn't the exact type of play that I might have ideally hoped for, but I remember having fun. I knew that they were like my brother and that they might not have many friends, so I was happy to do it. (Scott)

Some, like Katie, Ken, and Katherine, described a stronger sense of compassion and connection to all people with disabilities, and a drive to advocate for them.

Having my brother [with disabilities], Christopher, in my life allowed me to have more empathy and compassion toward other people with special needs. They have their own personal value. (Katie)

I think I was more sensitive to people with disabilities. In high school, there was a group of kids with developmental delays, and when other kids would make fun of them, I would say, it is not their fault for the way they are. (Ken)

When they passed legislation for my brother to go to school and people joked about the short bus [the bus for people with disabilities], I told them that they were disrespecting the dearest part of my life, and not to make it a joke. I wouldn't let it go. It was not OK to see him as deficient when he was the best thing in our lives. I always look for the secret gift in each person. People should be celebrated in all their complexity. (Katherine)

Ken was surprised to learn, later in life, that he and his family had become role models for some of the community who observed them.

A former neighbor recently told me that his family learned so much from ours. He reflected on how we took my brother to church and other events, as if he was "normal." We didn't know at the time that we were teaching anybody anything. But my neighbor said that it had a big effect on his family and other kids too, because during those times we didn't have many people with disabilities around us. (Ken)

Many participants shared that their siblings with disabilities positively shaped their life choices and personalities. Katherine's father encouraged her to protect her brother, and that role became an important part of her identity. She described a sense of pride about helping her brother, even when she was just a toddler herself. She taught him to sit up and walk so that he would be mobile, like her.

Instead of feeling like it was a burden to look out for my brother, I felt like I had a job to do. I had a mission. My siblings and I were proud to take care of him and to make sure that he was never bullied. (Katherine)

Ben remembers being protective of Tom and of feeling good about his role as Tom's ally. He and his other brother were vigilant, watching out for Tom in public spaces.

My brother and I had a game in public. When we'd see people staring at Tom, we'd stare back at them intently. It's not OK to stare at people with disabilities. (Ben)

Helping to care for a disabled sibling promoted a sense of self-worth, purpose, and resilience for some participants, while also deepening their connection to their sibling. Ken describes helping others to understand his brother's speech throughout his childhood.

For some reason, I always knew what my brother was saying when no one else could understand him. I helped others understand him. (Ken)

Ben's values and friendship choices are anchored in his experience as Tom's brother. Tom continues to be an important part of Ben's life in adulthood, and he is beloved by Ben's closest friends. Ben reflected about Tom's critical influence upon his life and identity.

I honestly can't imagine what my life would be like without Tom. I work at a children's hospital, and I really only work there because of Tom. His existence has shaped who I am in my life and what I do. Tom has changed my outlook on life and how to treat people. I have more empathy for others, because I grew up with someone close who needed empathy. It's very sobering to think that someone who can't speak, walk, or do so many things has shaped another life in that way. He has such an emotional effect on the direction of my life. I wouldn't trade my life with Tom for anything. (Ben)

The gift of witnessing, giving, and receiving immense love was another common experience. Katie described the influence of her mom's outlook and actions.

I definitely learned about love. My mom lost my brother Blake, who died at birth, before having Christopher, who was disabled due to severe birth trauma. The depth of her love for both of them was foundational for me. It built my understanding of love and of how unconditional it can be. (Katie)

Katherine spoke with deep admiration for her brother. She considered him to be a role model of love and compassion.

When my brother died, they did an autopsy. We discovered that his heart was three times the normal size of an adult male. They thought they were telling me a medical fact, but I believe they were affirming something that I already knew, which was that my brother simply had the biggest, best heart. (Katherine)

Peter described his family's expanded worldview about disabilities and what matters.

My mother instilled in me a sense that it's okay if a child isn't born healthy. We need a world that doesn't automatically discount a birth that isn't normal, or someone that is unhealthy. There are so many ways of being human. Disabled people can live an equally great life with proper support. (Peter)

Conclusion

Having an older sibling with acute special needs can be a life-altering experience that brings sorrow and strain, but also growth and cherished family bonds. While the experience is different from being born after loss, there are some possible commonalities in family dynamics and repercussions. Children born after a sibling with severe special needs may have been conceived to ease their parents' sense of loss and to fulfill dreams that were unattainable for their disabled sibling. Replacement dynamics will occur if they are viewed as the child who can embody parental wishes and fill a void in the family. Their parents may be grieving, which can negatively impact attachment, bonding, and family functioning.

Families must often live and plan differently when one member has acute special needs. Some parents may be stressed or preoccupied with the care of their special needs child and less physically and emotionally present for their healthy children. Nursing staff might have a significant presence in the home. Healthy children can have a range of reactions, including resentment of their disabled sibling, guilt about their resentment, and guilt about their own wellness and health. They may also feel the need to take care of their parents and disabled sibling. Many develop a deep sense of empathy for others and express immense love and gratitude for their disabled sibling. Families with a special needs child often demonstrate resilience and can recognize both the gifts and the challenges of their experiences.

Eulogy for Tom

Tom, one of the special needs siblings represented in this chapter, died while this book was being written.

My sweet son could not speak, but it never ceased to amaze me how he could communicate with so many. Tom taught so much. We learned patience, kindness, and the knowledge that the simplest of gestures can impact another person. He never walked, but led so many down his path, in education, faith, healthcare, and life. His brother Ben said "I will miss the way you told us what you wanted without saying a word." Tom gave us an opportunity to slow down, to listen with our ears and eyes, to read his body language. To be patient, and meet him in the middle.

Tom lived what he learned. He wasn't cruel and didn't lie or hurt anyone. He was seen by some as a burden, less than desirable, and yet he was the best little person. I admit, I am biased. But Tom taught so many lessons. We will remember his spirit, his fun, his giggles, his sense of humor, and his delight in all that was new.

Tom enriched our lives with focus, determination, patience, adventure, strength, kindness, laughter, inspiration, and so much love. Through him we know empathy, compassion, and the meaning of service. His dad and I only wanted the best for him. We nourished all of his needs and so he stayed for thirty-eight years but he is more than that. He is a lifetime of love that will heal our wounds, dry our tears, and soften our physical loss. Tom was as whole as God intended him to be. It was my joy and honor to be his champion, guardian, advocate, chauffeur, cook, caregiver, cheerleader, his source of everything, and mostly his mother.

(Eulogy by Cindy, bereaved mom)

11

~~~~~

Survivor Guilt
and Idealization

Many subsequent children wonder why they were fated to live while their sibling was fated to die. Some struggle to make sense of those outcomes because they feel arbitrary or unfair. They commonly experience survivor guilt, which involves feeling stress or guilt about being alive when another person has died, guilt for not saving or helping the deceased, and a sense that one's survival is unfair. Subsequent siblings frequently sense a connection between their birth and the death of their sibling, which may be distressing and cause them to feel blameworthy and uneasy.

In their varied attempts to make sense of their loss, subsequent children might join their parents in idealizing the lost sibling, imagining the deceased as a perfect family member, protector, confidante, and friend. For subsequent children, survivor guilt and idealization are often linked, because it can be reassuring to envision their deceased sibling as a loving person who does not begrudge them for being alive or for having positive experiences. However, an unfortunate hierarchy is created when a deceased sibling is idealized, because subsequent children will feel unable to measure up to their perfect, lost sibling and their self-esteem will suffer.

Survivor Guilt

For many subsequent children, connecting their opportunity to live with the death of their brother or sister fosters survivor guilt, angst, and sorrow. CR, who was born after the death of a sister, expressed unease with the correlation of his birth and her death.

It's really hard, knowing about my sister, and knowing that her death is why I'm here. It really dawned on me that the only reason that I'm alive is because my sister died. My parents were not going to have another child. They only wanted one child. (CR)

Doris, who was born after a stillborn sister, shared feelings of guilt, as she knew that her birth would not have occurred if her sibling were alive.

One problem I've faced over the years is feeling guilty. My parents really only wanted two kids, so if my sibling had lived, I would not exist. And that's not fun to think about. I recognize the pain that my parents must have gone through, but I like living. (Doris)

Elise was aware that she could not have been born if her brother survived.

My deceased brother was born in August, the year before I was born. If he was carried to term, it would have overlapped with the start of my mother's pregnancy with me. Basically, I couldn't have been conceived if she was still pregnant with him. (Elise)

As they contend with survivor guilt, subsequent children sometimes ask their parents if they would have been born if their deceased sibling were alive. Parents may respond in various ways, as illustrated in the responses of two mothers, Lynnda and Annette. Lynnda was direct and factual as she addressed the questions of her subsequent daughter.

We only wanted two kids. If her sister had lived, she wouldn't be alive. I was very forthcoming with her about that. She didn't like it, but why lie? (Lynnda)

Annette was careful to address the feelings of her subsequent son, Nick, and to provide reassurance.

When Nick was twelve, we went out to the cemetery. He looked at Courtney's stone, and I could see him go ashen. I said, "Nick, what's wrong?" He said, "Mom, if she hadn't died I wouldn't be here." I put my arm around him and said, "Nick, I don't know how all of this works but I really believe that you were meant to be a part of our family. I don't know if you would have been born a year later or if you would have been born at another time, but I truly believe you were meant to be with us." (Annette)

Varied family members may be aware of the ongoing survivor guilt that subsequent children experience. Brynne, an older sister, commented upon the struggles of her sister, who was the subsequent child.

She would have temper tantrums. I think they would happen because she knew that she might not be around if Morgan had not died. It affected her a lot. She always said that if Morgan had lived that she wouldn't be alive. It's been really hard for her. Our mom always responded that we love her, that we're glad that she is here, and we're glad that she is alive. (Brynne)

McGee, an older sister, shared similar stories about her sister Jill, who was the subsequent child. She reflected upon the anguish and difficulties that Jill faced in the subsequent sibling role.

My sister Jill [the subsequent child] told me that from a young age she always thought that she existed only because Heather died. When she got in trouble as a child, she felt like mom and dad were thinking that Heather would never have misbehaved like she did. (McGee)

Caroline, whose son Ethan is a subsequent child, described Ethan's need for comforting, which was a developmentally appropriate part of his grieving process.

When we went to Disneyland, I had to give Ethan permission to be happy about the trip. He was sorry that his [deceased] brother could not come. I told him that his brother would want him to be happy. (Caroline)

Subsequent children may also feel as if they are to blame in some way for their sibling's death, which exacerbates their survivor guilt. Natalie felt guilty and implicated when she learned the story of her sister's death.

When my sister died, my mother was asleep. She was taking a nap in the middle of the day. No one heard my sister go into the pool [where she drowned]. Then it clicked in my head. . . . That my mother was napping because she was pregnant with me. It hadn't connected for me before, that she was taking a nap because of the pregnancy with me. I felt pretty, pretty bad for about two years, and guilty about it. (Natalie)

Idealization

As a part of their mourning, longing, and remembrance, bereaved parents often idealize their deceased children and believe that they were perfect. Parents may refer to their deceased child, in spoken or unspoken ways, as the ideal model of what a child should be. Subsequent children consequently feel self-conscious and chagrined about their own imperfections and unable to compete with their perfect and absent sibling. However, some subsequent children follow their parents in idealizing the deceased, which may be an attempt to lessen their survivor guilt and distress, and to align with their parents.[1] Many subsequent children harbor fantasies about their lost siblings and envision them as the protectors, friends, and confidantes that they always wished for. Janet imagined her deceased brother as the ally and loving sibling that she lacked.

> *I lived with an imaginary sibling in my mind. He would have been my best friend, and he wouldn't have teased me. Whenever something negative was happening with one of my other siblings, I imagined that Daniel would never have done that.* (Janet)

Like Janet, Dorotha experienced some sorrow and strain in her family, and she visualized her deceased brother as a helper and friend.

> *Growing up there were times that things were tough. I remember crying and wishing that I had my older brother. I imagined that he would have done the things that I needed or hoped for.* (Dorotha)

Lana, who was born after her twenty-year-old sister died of pneumonia, admired her sister's photographs. She envisioned her sister's beauty and kindness, and she imagined the positive relationship that they might have built.

> *There is a fantasy element in my mind about who my sister might have been. She was very elegant in her pictures. She looks delicate, glamorous, and very tender in a certain way. [If she were alive,] I might have someone who I could*

confide in as a sister. There is a rift between me and my other sister. (Lana)

Some subsequent siblings, like Andrew and Janet, seek relationships in their lives that resemble the connection that they wish for with their lost sibling.

I often think about the fact that it would be really nice to have a big brother. And I've gravitated toward a roommate who is like my brother. He and I get along so well, we've been friends for so long, and he's older than me. In every sense of the word, I think of him as a big brother. Maybe I have friends that kind of fill in the blanks in some ways. (Andrew)

I've always had a close male friend who is just a couple of years older than me. I'm very aware that I was seeking the best friend and the older brother that I imagined Danny would be. (Janet)

Conclusion

Subsequent siblings are born into complex family dynamics and environments. Most have a need to process their sibling's death and their role as the child born afterwards, but they may not find outlets or support systems to make sense of their experiences. They frequently engage in their own explorations and struggles as they try to understand their sibling's death. Many subsequent children grapple with their identities as the child born after loss and wonder why they lived while their sibling did not. As their process their sibling's death and its significance, they often need to give the loss a fitting space in their minds, hearts, and life story.

Survivor guilt is commonly experienced by subsequent children, as most question why they are alive although their sibling died and also wonder if their birth depended upon their sibling's death. They might experience guilt and torment about taking their sibling's place and wrestle with the injustice and strangeness of living while another child did not. When subsequent children idealize their lost sibling, several purposes may be served. The admiration and recognition that they bestow upon their sibling may lessen their survivor guilt. Imagining the deceased as a loving ally who would not resent them for being alive might assuage their guilt and provide comfort. The act of aligning with their parents' idealization might also assist in abating familial conflict and in repressing uncomfortable feelings of anger or competition.

Idealization can promote coping, but it also has costs. Subsequent children who envision their deceased sibling as a perfect child are likely to feel inadequate in comparison. Repressed negative emotions, like resentment or rivalry, may remain unprocessed and feel forbidden and unthinkable. Nevertheless, imagining their lost sibling as a benign and protective figure may promote a positive continuing bond and foster a life narrative that feels manageable and healing.

12

Gender Considerations

Many bereaved parents place strong hopes and meaning upon the gender of their subsequent child. Their pronounced reactions highlight the struggles and replacement dynamics that may play out when parenting after loss. Subsequent children sometimes inherit family hopes and plans that were originally held for their deceased sibling. Those who are a different gender than the deceased might feel as if they are a disappointment to their parents and siblings, and sense that their families would have preferred a subsequent child of the same gender as the deceased. To satisfy their family's longings and become a more acceptable replacement, they may take on traits or participate in activities that are stereotypically associated with the opposite gender. More rarely, some families have ardent hopes that the subsequent child will be the opposite gender from the deceased, as they seek to avoid comparisons or reminders of their loss. Dynamics and pressures about gender are often unspoken, and families may or may not be conscious of their bias.

Current Gender Perspectives

Gender identity is now understood to be fluid and much more expansive than a male or female dichotomy or a gender assigned at birth. However, the stories, terminology, and observations of our participants primarily align with a two-gender perspective. Our society's comprehension and discussions about gender have shifted relatively recently, so it makes sense from a historical standpoint that the narratives of our adult participants, who were asked to share about their childhoods and their parents' perspectives, are grounded in another time and do not always reflect our current beliefs and understandings. Our book's aim is to be inclusive of all people and genders, and we hope that readers will bear in mind that most participant stories are from a previous time frame. One transgender individual shared his perspective in our interviews, and it will be important to seek and hear additional, diverse voices in future research about families, subsequent children, and gender.

Gender and Replacement Dynamics

It is common for bereaved parents to want a subsequent child who is the same gender as the deceased due to their underlying wish for a replacement. Sally described her parents' disappointment about her gender, as she was born after the death of a brother.

> I was a planned but unwanted child. Once I was born, they ignored me. My dad did not want a girl. My dad wanted a boy, and my mom did too, because of losing [my brother]. (Sally)

Agnes, a subsequent child, was her father's favorite for a short time, but she was rejected by her father once a brother was born. It was clear to her that her newborn brother was the boy that her father longed for, and she felt immediately displaced.

> When my brother was born, it was like my dad divorced me. And that's when I got sick. I felt terribly lonely. My mother

has apologized to me about the way I was treated after my brother was born. (Agnes)

Surviving siblings may also hope that the subsequent child will be the same gender as the deceased. Janet, who was born after a deceased brother, was aware that her older brother was disappointed about her gender.

I remember thinking that I was a replacement child, and that I certainly was not what my brother wanted. He wanted another brother. (Janet)

As they look back on their childhoods, some subsequent children observe that they took on roles that probably would have been held by their deceased sibling, perhaps participating in activities that are traditionally attributed to the opposite gender. Tanya, born after the death of a brother, felt that her choice to play so many sports may have been an attempt to fulfill her dad's desire for a son, and that it provided a way to connect with him.

If I had had an older brother maybe things would have been a little different, because I was a tomboy growing up. My dad always coached my little league games, and he coached various other sports that I played. If there had been a boy maybe I would have been more girly. (Tanya)

Like Tanya, Dierdre was born after a deceased brother. She believes that she became a tomboy to satisfy some of her father's needs and hopes, and to lessen his sorrow about the son that he lost.

My dad always treated me like a boy. I ended up being a tomboy, because he never had a boy after my brother died. So I did all the boy stuff. I guess I did it to be there for him in that way. (Diedre)

Some subsequent children, who felt like their gender was a disappointment, described their parents' joyful reaction to another child who was the same gender as the deceased. This painfully reinforced their sense of being inadequate replacements. Tret, who had a difficult relationship with her mother, shared that her mother's response to the birth of her younger brother bolstered her sense of inadequacy.

My mother didn't want any more children after me, but she couldn't get over losing my brother and decided to get pregnant again. My father told me that my mother wanted a boy to replace the boy she lost. She wasn't happy until she had my brother Scott, five years later. I have a vivid memory after his birth, of my mom holding him up in the window of the hospital to show us, with this beaming smile on her face. I'd never seen her that happy in my memories of my early childhood. I just have this impression of seeing joy in her face that I had never seen or felt in years prior. (Tret)

Mia, who also had a turbulent relationship with her mother, had a similar experience when she observed her mother embrace a male grandchild.

I think the crowning recognition came when my oldest brother and his girlfriend had a baby. When the baby came over for the first time my mother took the child to the living room, got down on the floor, and held the baby. Everybody else was waiting to be greeted but she was just going through this thing, and in love with this grandson. I instantly thought that this never happened with me, and knew that she never had that enthusiasm or that connection to me at all. (Mia)

Several parents also shared feelings and experiences pertaining to their subsequent child's gender, including replacement enactments and concerns. A bereaved and pregnant mother, Gabrielle, voiced her mixed feelings as she wondered about her subsequent baby's gender. Her response to having a baby boy, after losing a son, illustrates the identity linkage that parents may construe when the genders of their deceased and subsequent children align.

I was very torn when I was pregnant and wondering about the gender of my [subsequent] baby. Hoping for another boy would feel like I was trying to replace [my deceased son,] Sam. But hoping for a girl would feel like Sam wasn't good enough. When Brian [my subsequent baby boy] was born, less than a year after Sam died, I hugged my mom and told her "I have Sam back. I just know it's him." (Gabrielle)

Gender, Culture, and Identity

Cultural beliefs pertaining to gender are often passed down through the generations, becoming embedded in the values and worldview of parents and causing specific ideas and hopes about the identities, roles, and traditions that their children will embody. After losing a child, parents may choose to have a subsequent child to fulfill some of their hopes that are rooted in culture and gender. Their cultural and gender-based expectations can be influential upon the identities of their subsequent children and the rapport that is formed with them. Dierdre revealed that her dad's Italian background was an additional influence upon his desire for a son, and that her ability to be a tomboy, without a brother to compete with, allowed her to form a closer bond with her father.

Being a tomboy allowed me to connect with my dad. He is Italian. He might not have made as much of an effort with a girl if a son had been around. In Italian culture, girls are not as important as boys. His father criticized him for having no sons. (Diedre)

At times, the identities of bereaved parents may be tied to parenting a child of the same gender as the deceased, and they may also unconsciously wish for a replacement. Sheila, a bereaved mom who lost a daughter, had hopes and a vision of parenting a girl and always imagined herself as the mother of a daughter. She also yearned for her deceased child. She was initially upset to learn, during pregnancy, that her subsequent child was a boy. Her response is not uncommon; many parents ache for their deceased child to return, while also knowing that their subsequent child will be a different baby. Parents are starkly reminded that the deceased will not return when the subsequent child is a different gender than the deceased. Like Sheila, some will need time and guidance to process feelings of sorrow and disappointment about the gender of their subsequent baby.

The news that my [subsequent] baby was a boy hit me pretty hard. I didn't tell people immediately, because I needed time to deal with it and process it myself. It was not a disappointment in my baby, but I did feel disappointment about not being able to raise a daughter. (Sheila)

Wishing for the Opposite

Less frequently, bereaved parents may adamantly wish for a child of the opposite gender of the deceased, perhaps in the hopes of avoiding reminders or heightened grief for their loss. Eric, who was born after the death of a brother, was aware that his mother wanted a daughter. He believes that his mother's strong wishes impacted his ability to be comfortable with his gender identity.

My mother wanted a girl. I ended up feeling like I wasn't really a male, that I was not a good example of a male, and that I couldn't do it. I absolutely believe that her wanting me to be the girl that she wished for created several issues in my life about gender identity. (Eric)

Margie, who was born after a deceased sister, learned that her parents only picked out potential boy names before her birth.

It's clear that my parents felt as if I wasn't the right baby. I was supposed to be a male. (Margie)

Cathy, who was born after a deceased sister, had parents who desperately wanted a boy. Her mother's sorrow and disappointment were an integral piece of her birth story.

For my birth story, my mom told me over and over again how badly she wanted a boy. It wasn't until I was born that they found out I was a girl. She would laugh as she told me that she kept me in the hall at the hospital after I was born, and that everyone thought that her baby had died because she was crying so hard. (Cathy)

The Weight of Parental Wishes

Children are very attuned to the feelings, wishes, and disappointments of their parents, even if they remain unspoken. One participant shared that throughout her childhood, she repeatedly asked her father if he was disappointed that she wasn't a boy. He would always reply that it was a silly question. After he died, she and her older sister found a death certificate for a baby boy, a deceased brother whom they had never been told about. She had clearly sensed her father's unspoken loss and yearning for his son.

CR's mother wanted another daughter after their loss of his sister and hoped for a female subsequent child. CR was born female but soon realized that he was transgender, identifying as male. He struggled to be himself and to transition because he was aware of his mother's intense desire for another girl.

After my sister died, my mom and dad worked very hard to have me, with some intervention. They really wanted a daughter. I was born and assigned female at birth. My parents talked openly about my sister, my mother especially. It was an important piece of my mom's identity to have another daughter. So I pretended to be what she wanted. I struggled as a young adult, reconciling frustration, anger, and feeling pressure to be the daughter that she wanted. From very young I was uncomfortable as a girl. I felt like a boy on the inside but didn't have the vocabulary to express it. In college, I finally transitioned. We've been through a lot but now my parents embrace me for who I am. I told them that I'm their child and it doesn't matter what gender I am. (CR)

Like CR, some subsequent siblings shared that their parents eventually accepted their genders and identities, despite their initial disappointment. Cathy felt loved by her mom.

Even though she cried and cried when I was born, she would always smile as she told the story, and she would playfully say that they decided to keep me anyway because I have brown eyes like my father. (Cathy)

Conclusion

Gender is usually viewed and experienced as a core piece of a person's identity. Fervent hopes and emotions about gender often surface when bereaved parents and surviving siblings anticipate and welcome a subsequent child. A family's focus upon the subsequent child's gender, and its alignment or lack of alignment with the gender of the deceased, points to powerful replacement dynamics that are sometimes enacted. It also illustrates the common connections that are made in families between the identity of the subsequent child and the identity of the deceased.

If bereaved parents are carrying a wish to replace their deceased child, they may automatically hope for a subsequent child whose gender matches the deceased. Conversely, some parents might adamantly want a subsequent child who is the opposite gender of the deceased because they fear painful memories and feelings of loss. Family relationships and the subsequent child's identity might be molded by gender and replacement expectations. Replacement dynamics are problematic and at play when subsequent children feel like they disappoint because of their gender or when they strive to compensate for their family's dissatisfaction. Subsequent children fare best when their families embrace and welcome them as they are and when they are supported to be their authentic genders and true selves.

13

Rebellious and Disruptive Behavior

Many subsequent children harbor anger and distress about their family's grief and its impact. They may resort to acting out behaviors that are fueled by the pressures and hardships of their role, such as replacement dynamics, poor attachments with caregivers, expectations to heal the family, and feelings of invisibility. While turbulence and defiance are usually unwelcome in families, they can sometimes be a sign of health and resilience. Subsequent siblings are often pressured to meet heavy demands that impinge upon their ability to develop their unique identities. Their rebellion may be prompted by a need to truly be themselves and to reject the replacement dynamics or loss-related demands that they are experiencing in their families. Rebellions sometimes escalate into unsafe behaviors that warrant urgent intervention and concern. Disruptive and rebellious behaviors may serve a range of purposes for subsequent children and may be a cry for help, an expression of rage, and a testimony of their family's struggle and dysfunction.

Acting Out

When children act out, it demonstrates that they feel unable to put their feelings and needs into words. They are resorting to expressing their needs through their actions. They may feel unheard and unseen by their caregivers, and their rebellious behaviors may be a heightened or desperate attempt to express their needs and discomfort. Some subsequent children who experienced impaired bonds with their parents describe deliberate acting out and attention seeking. In Kenneth's case, there was clearly a hope that his mom would become more attentive to him and his needs. Kenneth was born after his brother died, and he grew up with a mom who struggled with severe alcoholism.

> *I did stuff that I knew would upset my parents. I'd run away from school. I cut school constantly, even when I was very young. I got sent to the principal's office a lot and in school I'd be disruptive so I had to spend lots of time in detention. I knew that would upset my father. By that point my mom didn't care very much.* (Kenneth)

Like Kenneth, Susan acted out both at school and at home and demonstrated an underlying need for attention and validation. Susan was born after the death of her seven-year-old sister.

> *I was no angel. My memories of myself as a child are of being quite difficult. I would complete work in class very quickly and then make it my business to disrupt the class, probably not intentionally, but there was just a sense of needing to be the center of attention. Invariably, this brought me very negative attention. I was probably labeled as the naughty kid.* (Susan)

Tret, who was born after the death of a baby brother, described rebelling to get attention from her entire family. Her acting out allowed her to feel seen and to avoid feeling invisible.

I rebelled and got in trouble a lot through my young years and high school years. A lot of it was to get attention, not just from my mother but in my family. (Tret)

The defiance described by some subsequent siblings points to their underlying anger in their childhood and adolescent years, and its need for an outlet. Scott, who was born after his brother died of spinal meningitis, shared about his anger and rageful behaviors.

I was the ornery one. I was a hot-tempered little kid. I remember misbehaving in a way where I didn't get to go out for recess. I don't remember the behavior, but it was serious. So while everyone was out for recess I went around and broke all the other kids' pencils. (Scott)

Elise, who was born after her brother died, enacted a long-standing and defiant rebellion.

I was described as being a rebel without a cause. I was the one rebelling and causing all sorts of problems. I was dating another older guy, going out with friends my parents didn't want me to go out with, and pushing limits in ways my siblings hadn't. (Elise)

Some subsequent children act out in alarmingly unsafe ways, frightening those around them and putting themselves at risk. Susan ran in front of a bus on a busy street and would sometimes hide for hours, even when she knew that her mother had called the police. Her choice to wait for someone to find her points to a deep need to be seen and to underlying anger about feeling invisible.

I locked my mum and stepfather out. I had to be coaxed through the letter box to let them in. Then I hid again. I remember when my mum finally found me. She was really angry. (Susan)

Susan's dangerous behaviors were numerous, including taking an overdose of medication as a child. Unconsciously, she seemed to understand that dead or ill children were loved and seen in her family.

> *I remember standing on all these things to get to the medicine in the medicine chest. There was this red medicine that was quite putrid. Then my mum came up and said, "What have you done? How many spoons have you had?" I had no idea. Of course, I was rushed immediately to the hospital.* (Susan)

Kenneth often hid as well. We can speculate that a pattern of hiding can connect to the subsequent child predicament of feeling unseen and their desire to be found and recognized. Like Susan, he also engaged in some dangerous behaviors, going to unsafe neighborhoods alone.

> *The first thing I'd do, in every house we'd move into, was to find little hiding places. The other kids in the neighborhood were building their forts, a communal effort, but I would just do my own little thing. I would put these boards over me and wouldn't tell anybody. I'd also go to places that were away from everybody else. I'd hide at the railroad tracks. I'd go to industrial parts of town where there's no kids, no playground, away from everything. I knew once I was away, they'd be worried about me.* (Kenneth)

In retrospect, some subsequent children are able to connect their childhood acting out behaviors to emotional or mental health struggles. Alice, who was born after a deceased brother, recognizes that she suffered from depression as a child.

> *According to my mother, I was a difficult toddler, and I remember that I was explosive as a child. I think it was depression. I bottled stuff up until some little thing upset me, like I would lose it if there was no more milk, or somebody*

ate all of the cereal I liked. I would slam and break stuff and run into my room in a rage and in tears. I did a lot of self-injury during those times. My mother would put me in a room alone. I was completely disorganized and dysregulated. I would hurt myself when I was in there. (Alice)

Rebellion with a Cause

Much of the anger and pushback from subsequent children may be adaptive, to demand needed attention, express authentic feelings, and reject replacement dynamics. Anger, resentment, and rebellion are understandable responses from subsequent children who experience replacement pressures in their family. Pierre was born after his eight-year-old sister died of leukemia. His mother made ongoing, negative comparisons between him and his deceased sister, who was reportedly very intelligent, until he angrily rebuffed her.

My mom kept calling me a moron. Then I lashed out, and she never used that word again. (Pierre)

Candace, born after an infant sister died of sudden infant death syndrome, was viewed as a gift child by her parents. She described an ardent rebellion during her adolescent years. We can speculate that she may have needed to rebel to truly be herself, and that her rebellion might have allowed her to dismantle an unwanted identity as an idealized replacement child.

I was a terror as a teenager, a hellion. I was rebellious, always yelling. (Candace)

Rebellion Guilt

While the rebellion of subsequent children might serve a range of valuable purposes, including setting healthy boundaries and fostering a more authentic sense of self, many subsequent siblings harbor intense guilt about rebelling because it is difficult to upset or oppose grieving parents. Rebellious behavior defies the attunement and care for bereaved parents that is often ingrained in subsequent children. Kenneth felt guilty for rebelling and upsetting his parents, despite the neglectful and tumultuous parenting that he received.

As an adult I feel kind of guilty that I caused my parents all that stress that they don't need. (Kenneth)

Likewise, Candace was remorseful about her disobedient and acting out behaviors, and she felt guilt over upsetting her parents.

Throughout my life I felt horrible about being a very difficult teen. (Candace)

Conclusion

When children act out, they might be pointing out familial dysfunction and seeking help for their family system. Rebellion stories are sometimes testimonies of childhood distress, and the rebel may be the healthiest family member who is pushing for needed help and change. Therapy may assist families to stabilize and to make sense of rebellious and disruptive behaviors. While acting out behavior causes stress, strain, and disharmony in a family, it may serve a greater purpose, allowing family members to step into new roles and ways of connecting, promoting an individual's growth and separateness, and breaking up familial patterns that are problematic or burdensome. Some disruptive behavior may ultimately allow families to regroup in a more positive formation and to discover a new balance. Listening carefully and empathetically to the significance of rebellious behavior can often allow for deeper understanding and create inroads for positive change. Obviously, help must be accessed immediately if unsafe behaviors occur.

Rebellious behaviors sometimes surface in a school setting. Early childhood educators, teachers, and school counselors can play a positive role when they attempt to understand the underlying sources of disruptive behaviors in the classroom and guide families toward appropriate supports and resources. It is important for educators to be aware that family grief and loss may be an impetus for acting out behaviors and childhood distress.

Subsequent children may rebel to free themselves from pressures and constraints of their role and to address unmet needs. Like all children, they need to be recognized and embraced as unique individuals. Subsequent siblings often struggle to be themselves as they are born into a role to replace someone else. Rebellion may be an expression of their frustration and of their need for independence and recognition. It might also be a critical means for them to access, establish, and give voice to their true and authentic selves.

14

Fears, Phobias, and Morbid Preoccupations

Many of us are drawn to stories that mirror our own issues and backgrounds, because they provide a means to make sense, comprehend, or work through our experiences. Our attraction to a specific topic might be based on a need to master a challenge in our own lives. Research has shown that subsequent children may become preoccupied with death, dying, and morbid topics, because they were born into an environment of grief.[1] The stories of our participants demonstrate that some write about death and loss, are drawn to narratives of tragedy and crisis, or work and volunteer with bereaved people. A focus upon death-related material may consciously or unconsciously allow them to process and integrate their experience of loss. Subsequent children may also be prone to developing fears and phobias that stem from their sibling's death, or from their parents' grief reactions.

A Preoccupation with Death

Several participants described a preoccupation with death and grief, and reflected that it was caused by the loss of their sibling. Denise, who was born after her two-year-old sister died of leukemia, is an actor and writer. She divulged that loss and bereavement are a central focus of her work.

Everything I write about is extremely emotional and extremely sad, and extremely depressing. Everything I write about is about death. I have this weird connection with stuff like that. I don't think I am very normal when it comes to thinking about death. I'm very connected to death. It's very familiar. (Denise)

Paulina, who was born after an infant brother died, shared a similar preoccupation with death.

There was lots of talk of death in my family. I continue to be fascinated by death, to think about it a lot. I continue to have a "death wish." I am not suicidal ever, but I believe that death is like a person who visits us often, and lives amongst us. I have conversations with death. I say "not yet." I play games with death. (Paulina)

In some cases, subsequent children choose work environments in which they ongoingly confront death and dying. CR, who was born after his infant sister died of heart disease, worked in a hospital for animals. He identified with the pain of the losses that he witnessed.

There were a lot of deaths around me every day. I literally felt all of the pain that people and animals experienced. I related to it so much. It's hard for me not to just feel it and take it all in. (CR)

Andy was born after the death of a baby sister. He expressed an awareness that his writing about death-related topics was a vehicle for him to better understand his own loss narrative.

A good deal of the stories that I write deal with missing people or miscarriages, things like that. So it's something that I feel like I still don't fully understand. Through my writing I'll continue to poke into that, and maybe get glimpses into it in some way. (Andy)

An Interest in Tragic Stories

Some subsequent children describe gravitating toward the morbid or tragic stories of others, perhaps in current events, books, and films. Their own grief histories might elicit a need to understand how others cope with crisis and tragedy. The grief-related stories of other individuals may unconsciously allow them to feel and unleash repressed emotions about their own experiences. The loss narratives of others can also provide a sense of universality, as loss is a common human experience. They additionally confirm that death, and its threat, are always close at hand. Liz, who was born after her sister died of sudden infant death syndrome, shared about an enduring interest and concern for catastrophic news stories.

I think a lot about the suffering in our world, from starvation to tsunamis and refugees. I'm very drawn to those stories in the newspaper and to listening to them on the news. (Liz)

Janet, who was born after her brother's death, described a passion for loss-related topics.

Grief and loss is my passion. It always has been. As a little child I read Little Women, Where the Red Fern Grows, Eight Cousins, *and all the books that had death in them. Over and over again, I was drawn to stories where someone had a death, a loss, became blind, or became disabled. I read them somehow to figure out how you could live through this and go on.* (Janet)

Mired in Grief

While a focus upon death may sometimes assist subsequent children in processing and integrating their experiences of loss, intense preoccupations can become problematic and harmful if they negatively impact a subsequent child's daily life or functioning. Liz and Katie both shared that their focus and attunement to the suffering of others had detrimental consequences upon their lives.

Issues of suffering occupy my thoughts. I get sick to my stomach, and not able to sleep. (Liz)

I definitely have a very strong sense for other people's emotions and grief, and they affect me more than other people might be affected. (Katie)

Fears

Many subsequent children are fearful of dying or of experiencing another significant loss. Some, like Mia, felt unsafe in their families of origin, because they were aware of their parents' inability to prevent their sibling's death. Mia was born after her two-year-old sister died.

It's a lingering fear. You have these ghosts, and you have these fears as a result of your sibling's death. Your parents failed! They let a child die. What does that mean for you? You're vulnerable and you're dependent. (Mia)

Mia's sense of being unsafe created a fear that she would not be adequately cared for, especially by her mother. Her fears were exacerbated when her father was sent away for a psychiatric hospitalization, leaving her alone with her mom. The upheaval in her family made the world seem like an unpredictable and unsafe place.

I just had the notion that at some level I wouldn't be taken care of. I don't think it was formulated in a formal thought. I think it was more of an inchoate fear and feeling. My dad got sent away [due to mental illness], my brother had a horrible surgery, and my sister was dead. So my mother ran the show and controlled things. She had a lot of power, and that power frightened me because I didn't sense it was tempered with much love or affection. (Mia)

The world often feels frightening and unpredictable to subsequent children, as they are acutely aware that loved ones can die at any time. Susan, who was born after the death of a seven-year-old sister, described her childhood fear of death and separation.

I can't remember a time when I didn't know about death. I used to be very frightened as a child that my mom would die and leave me alone. I always knew that everybody dies. I always knew that age doesn't determine who dies. There are no rules in death. (Susan)

Subsequent children may harbor specific death-related fears and phobias that echo the death event from their own histories. Gregory, who was born after his infant brother died, was afraid of anything that could impair his breathing, because he was aware of his brother's cause of death.

Since my brother died of [sudden infant death syndrome], my mother was always protective about us playing underneath the covers. Anything that could smother you or cut your breath off, any horseplay, was a big thing to my mom. There was always lots of emphasis on [the risks of] being smothered. I was afraid about that growing up. (Gregory)

Subsequent siblings sometimes inherit a range of fears from their parents. Jenna, who was born after a stillborn brother, grew up in an anxious household. She and her surviving sibling naturally adopted some of their parents' fears.

My parents are scared to death of everything, like dogs, and driving at night, and lightning. It's horrible. And they gave it to us. (Jenna)

Some subsequent children, like Andy, describe themselves as being more fearful and cautious than many around them. Their early exposure to loss may make them more risk averse.

I feel like I have more fears that I carry with me than my wife, for example. My wife jumps out of airplanes and bungee jumps. I don't even want to get on a roller coaster. I don't want to jump out of an airplane. I feel like I need my feet on solid ground. (Andy)

Conclusion

As they attempt to make sense of the loss in their families, subsequent children may gravitate toward death-related topics, immersing themselves in a world of loss to better understand their own experiences. Their explorations are common and usually a healthy response to the subsequent role. They stem from a desire for mastery and understanding. Less frequently, some subsequent children may be mired in grief or have ongoing and intrusive fears about loss. A preoccupation with death and loss may churn the inner pain of subsequent children who are stuck in trauma and grief. Those who are impacted by ongoing fear and distress would benefit from therapeutic help to mourn, process their histories, and take steps toward healing. Grief-informed therapy in individual or support group settings can provide relief and opportunities for growth. It is important to also note that while a focus upon death-related topics does not signify that someone is at risk for self-harm, immediate assessment and action are vital if there are ever any concerns about safety.

Subsequent siblings who are frequently exploring death and loss through writing or other modalities demonstrate a need to work through their own grief experiences, and their creative explorations and reworkings are often adaptive and healing. Explorations of loss-related phobias may be beneficial for subsequent children as well. Fears often soften when their source is identified and when they are understood and acknowledged. Subsequent children were not present when their siblings died and missed funerals or primary mourning rituals, so their fears and morbid preoccupations may be grounded in a need to make sense of their sibling's death, to feel included, and to discover models of survival, mastery, and healing.

15

⤳⤳

Caregiving Roles
and Sensitivity

Sensitivity and helpfulness are common expectations for a subsequent child because bereaved parents anticipate that their child born after loss will provide comfort. In response to spoken and unspoken parental expectations, many subsequent children become caregivers in their families and beyond, and are highly sensitive to the needs of others. They are attuned to their parents' grief and try to assuage it, out of care, a desire for love, and the hope that their parents will be functional and present for them. As adults, they frequently recognize that emotional attunement and capacities for caretaking are some of their central personality traits, influencing their histories, family roles, and career choices.

While sensitivity and caretaking are valuable traits, they are also burdensome and unhealthy if children become caregivers for their parents. Roles are flipped when parental needs are prioritized and children regularly support their parents, emotionally or otherwise. In the mental health field, this role reversal is referred to as parentification, because children assume a parenting role. Negative repercussions are common for parentified children because their needs are unmet and their caregiving dis-rupts their development, forcing them to grow up too quickly. Several subsequent siblings described distinct caretaker roles in their families of origin that exceeded typical expectations and responsibilities for children. Sheree, who was born after her mother had several miscarriages and a stillborn daughter, shared childhood memories of acting like a parent for her mother.

> *I had to treat my mom like she was the kid, and calm her down, or bring her things because she worked too hard. She wasn't necessarily responsible about money, so I had to look at what she was spending to make sure that we were going to be okay. I was more responsible than she was. I really had to raise myself in some ways. It was normal to me. I never thought too much about it, or about myself.* (Sheree)

Andrew, who was born after the death of his three-year-old brother, described a high level of ongoing attunement to his parents' emotional state and a sense of responsibility for their well-being.

> *I was very responsible [as a child]. I was always trying to make sure that my parents were happy and pleased.* (Andrew)

Margie, who was born after a stillborn sister, recollects being a caretaker in her family, despite being a child.

> *I was the person who took care of everybody in the family. I was expected to know what to do to take care of things, to clean the house. I was also the one they called when there was a tough emotional circumstance. My mom had a nervous breakdown when I was ten years old. Instead of asking my older sister to help, my parents gave me the role of taking care of the other kids.* (Margie)

Like Margie, Dorotha recounted taking on an adult-like role as she assisted with parenting of her younger siblings. She was born after a brother died.

I was always the third parent. If any of the other kids in the family had problems, my parents always turned to me to handle them. My grandmother used to say that I never had a childhood. (Dorotha)

Marianne, who was born after a disabled brother who was institutionalized, commented upon her caretaker status as a child and its negative impact upon her development.

Developmentally, I think I had to leap ahead quickly to become an adult. I was the third parent in the family. I was also the go between my parents. I was old really young. Part of my healing has been to let the young part catch up. (Marianne)

As a part of their helping roles, many subsequent children described keeping the peace in their families. Like Margie, they soothed family members and untangled conflicts while avoiding discord and the expression of their own needs. They were also often seen as confidantes.

I was the peacekeeper. I didn't ruffle any feathers, did what I needed to do, and tried to keep the peace. (Margie)

Denise, who was born after her sister died of leukemia, had a strong sense of her role as the family's helper.

I'd describe my role in the family as the peacemaker, the one who is always trying to make everything OK, the one who is like a therapist, the one that if someone needs advice they are going to call me, the one that's going to fix stuff, the one that's going to hold it together, the glue, the staple, definitely the band-aid of the family. (Denise)

The helpfulness of subsequent children frequently extends beyond their family and becomes a pronounced behavioral trait. Ryan, who was born after a deceased brother, shared his identification as a caretaker for others.

I am sensitive to people's feelings, and I think people would say that I'm pretty giving. In high school, kids used to make fun of me for being too helpful. (Ryan)

A Never-Ending Sense of Responsibility

Like Andrew, many subsequent children hold on to their caretaking roles into adulthood and feel a lifelong need to protect their parents and mitigate their family's grief.

I am still fiercely protective of my mom. She and my father came into the city for dinner recently. It was ten o'clock at night, and they were going to take the subway. I told them to take a cab. I'm very physically protective of her and emotionally protective of her. I feel very responsible for both of my parents. Now it is funneling itself into making sure that they have enough money for retirement. When they get older, I have been thinking about how I am going to help support them. (Andrew)

Some subsequent siblings, as adults, are hesitant to move far away from their parents due to an ongoing sense of responsibility and worry. Many express an ongoing struggle to balance their parents' needs with their own. Jane, who was born after her nine-year-old sister died of an autoimmune disease, was conflicted and emotional as an adult about her pending relocation.

I have lived in New York all my life, as have my parents, and now I am moving to another state. I'm excited because I think it's going to be great, but I also feel very choked up about it. It's hard for me to leave my parents, partially because they are older, but it occurs to me that maybe I have some feelings that they already lost one child and it might be more difficult for them to have another daughter move away. They have always had me living close by. (Jane)

Eric, who was born after the death of a baby brother, grew up with a rather fused relationship with his mother. As an adult, he was ambivalent about moving away from her.

I've had opportunities in other parts of the country that I have turned down so that I can stay close to my mother. It's a little bit of a challenge. Eventually I may have to tell my mom that I'm moving. I know I'll need to go if that's where my life is taking me. (Eric)

While it is not unusual for adult children to live with aging parents or to care for them, subsequent children sometimes feel a heightened drive to caretake for their aging parents, which seemingly connects to entrenched patterns of trying to heal and help their family. In some cases, subsequent children become caretakers for elderly parents despite difficult dynamics. Lori, who was born after a deceased sister, described a strong sense of responsibility for her mother that influenced her choice to live with her.

When my mom came to live with me, I felt overprotective of her and overly responsible for her, as if it would be my fault if something happened to her. There was a lot of screwy psychological stuff going on and I resented it. (Lori)

Candace, who was born after her infant sister died of sudden infant death syndrome, chose not to marry and became the primary caregiver for her elderly parents.

My parents sold their house and moved in with me [when they were elderly]. I was their caretaker for seventeen years. It was tough, very tough, but I have no regrets. I would have done anything to keep my mother out of a nursing home. I was very devoted to them. They became my babies. It was a total role reversal. (Candace)

Helping Roles in Careers and Adulthood

Subsequent children often choose helping professions, and they may also utilize their aptitude for caregiving in volunteer work or other endeavors. We interviewed subsequent siblings who were employed in an array of helping roles, including nurses, clergy members, doctors, and social workers. A helping profession or life mission may feel like a natural fit for them, and many seem to do their jobs with an attunement that is based upon their own experiences. Some subsequent children, like Andrew and Liz, describe a dedication to volunteer work that is embedded in their awareness of the pain of others and a drive to help.

> *I try to volunteer as much as possible. I bring food to people who are housebound with AIDS. I try to do it at least once a week, and I have my regular people that I visit. There is so much pain there.* (Andrew)

> *I'm very aware of the suffering of the world. I spent a year doing volunteer work in Mexico at an orphanage. I worked in this conservation organization that dealt with impoverished people, helping them get homes.* (Liz)

An array of helping fields were represented in the sample of subsequent children who were interviewed. Some gravitated toward a focus upon grief and loss. Dorotha became a nurse who specializes in working with bereaved parents.

> *I have a passion for working with loss. I find a great deal of reward and satisfaction in it, and I've never tired of it.* (Dorotha)

Mia works in the court system with children who have difficult histories, including backgrounds of trauma. She was drawn to this population because she understands the impact of family stress and its significance for a child.

> *I decided to become a mental health professional because I came from a nutty family. I had my own experience of being nuts with it, and of working my way through it. I became more aware of who I was, and I went off in the direction to help others.* (Mia)

Sophie has dedicated her life to advocating for the well-being of children and to promoting heightened understanding about their needs.

I'm a professor of early childhood development, and I specialize in infant mental health. I guess I feel for vulnerable children. I try to teach teachers how best to work with those families. (Sophie)

Some linked their professional choices to their lived experiences in their families and spoke of an effort to ensure that others did not suffer as they did. Natalie, who was negatively compared to her deceased sister as a child, became a teacher who carefully embraces each of her students as a unique individual.

I'm an adult teacher right now, and I have taught children in the past. I am always extremely, extremely careful not to compare my students in any way. (Natalie)

Janet has devoted most of her career to helping children. Her childhood experiences of feeling invisible led her to prioritize the validation and care of children.

Part of the reason I'd become an early childhood educator was to give those children that which I didn't have, which was individual attention. (Janet)

Mary became a foster mother, and she provided loving care to babies that exceeded her own childhood experiences. Her work with children brought up many emotions for her.

I would tell the babies how beautiful they were. I remember going to bed one night, just sobbing, because I don't think anybody ever said that to me. And I thought, you know, I was a baby too. (Mary)

In some cases, subsequent children are initially unaware of the link between their professional work as a helper and their identity as a subsequent sibling. Christine described her experience.

I thought that I became a nurse because I loved children. During a work workshop about bereaved children, I realized that my background as a bereaved sibling drew me here. I was so choked up that I couldn't talk. (Christine)

Likewise, when Mary attended a workshop on pregnancy after loss, she suddenly understood the significance of her role as a subsequent child.

When I learned about grief in families and the implications of pregnancy after loss, all of the sudden I realized, oh my God, that was me. (Mary)

One subsequent sibling poignantly wondered when she would be cared for as she considered her lifelong history of assisting others.

Who cares for the caretaker? I've been a teacher, a pastor, a counselor, and a chaplain. All of those things had me caring for someone else. (Janet)

Heightened Sensitivity

Sensitivity is a common trait for subsequent children because their family roles foster keen attunement to the feelings and needs of others. While it is a gift and asset to be attuned to others, the sensitivity of most subsequent children has difficult origins and costly repercussions. It is unhealthy for children to be overly identified as helpers for their parents, as it is a role reversal. Children need parenting, care, and help for their own development. Andrew and Natalie, both subsequent siblings, shared their identification as highly sensitive people. They acknowledged that their childhood experiences of family grief and struggle were primary sources for their attunement.

I think I am a very sensitive person. I am more attuned to heartache in people. I understood depression at a very early age because I got to see it, and I understood that you can't necessarily work through stuff and that sometimes life may run you down. (Andrew)

I can always tell when somebody has something on their mind that they are not talking about. Like if somebody is tense, and if they are just making small talk, I can always tell if there is something in the background. Because there was always something in the background when I was a kid. (Natalie)

Many subsequent children, like Margie and Katie, describe care and sensitivity that extended beyond their families and informed their interactions with the world.

I was always the one that would go to the underdog. I was a very sensitive little kid, and if anyone was in trouble, I would go to them. (Margie)

I'm very connected to my emotional state and other peoples' emotional states. It has its pros and cons. Being too sensitive can be a problem sometimes, but other times it does allow you to be a blessing to other people. (Katie)

Some subsequent children are highly empathetic and perceptive of others who are experiencing a loss, which clearly connects to their own histories of being born into grieving families. Renie, born after a stillborn brother, became a designer, and she creates personalized cards for others who are grieving.

Empathy is a huge part of who I am. My design work is to think about how it is for somebody else and design something for them. I had a friend who lost her father, and I made a card that had a lantern that would light up and send a wish message to heaven. My grandfather was all about trees, so for his funeral I designed a family tree. (Renie)

Subsequent children may attempt to assist others who are grieving because they are aware of the isolation that can occur for the bereaved, and they hope to relieve it. Ethan, who was born after a deceased brother, shared about supporting a colleague who lost a child.

Grief is never something I've avoided. A lot of people don't know what to say when they see someone who is grieving. They fear exacerbating it by talking about it directly. But you have to stare into the soul of what's going on. (Ethan)

Liz and Katie shared similar stories and a strong desire to help others who are grieving.

My neighbor lost her baby to sudden infant death syndrome, and then lost a lot of friends too, because they didn't know what to say. They avoided her at the grocery store. I made sure to reach out to her because a lot of other people were just too scared or thought it was too painful to address. (Liz)

I think there is part of me that values being able to soothe other people. When I was a freshman in college, I petitioned my psychology department to begin a grief group. My father died two years earlier, and I wanted to help other freshmen and sophomores who were grieving as well. (Katie)

In some cases, subsequent children describe a troubling level of sensitivity, as they feel deeply and take on the suffering of others. Some subsequent siblings, like Liz, Johanna, and Charlotte, struggle to care for themselves or to separate from the pain of others, which connects to their early experiences in their families.

I've always been very sensitive to other peoples' pain. I feel their pain physically and worry about that. That's always been a challenge to figure out how much to engage with people that are going through painful times. I have to work to move away from it. Living with pain, it's something I bear a lot. (Liz)

If I take on the energy of someone who is going through a hard time, and attempt to put myself in their shoes, it hurts, physically and emotionally. It almost becomes physically debilitating. My muscles get tight, and my joints get sore and shaky. It's hard. I have to remember that no one goes through life without pain and sorrow, and try to separate out my own emotions. As an adult, it is getting clearer for me that I can care for someone and be empathetic but still be able to go on and live my life. (Johanna)

I take on my friends' sadness, and that can be overwhelming. (Charlotte)

Mary's empathy for her foster children was rooted in her own feelings of neglect as a child. She grieved for their losses and struggles.

Even now, I can probably not talk about my experience as a foster mom without crying. There are five or six babies that I cannot talk about without crying today. (Mary)

Subsequent children are not alone in describing themselves as highly sensitive individuals. Their sensitivity is frequently noted by their family members as a pronounced and remarkable trait. Annette described the strong emotional attunement of her son who was born after loss.

He can sense emotions. He's got a good radar, always knowing if I am sad. I think he can pick up feelings a lot better than a lot of men can. He knows when others are sad. (Annette)

Annie described the remarkable sensitivity of her daughter born after loss and connected it to her daughter's experience of having a grieving mother.

From the beginning, my daughter seemed to have this extra level of empathy that I just didn't expect from a very tiny person. Even at a couple months old she seemed to understand even if I was just thinking about [her deceased sibling]. She knows when people are sad; she goes over and comforts them, much more than I ever expected a two-year-old to be able to do. I think a lot of that comes from her experience during my pregnancy with her, when I was experiencing so much grief. (Annie)

Bereaved parents may be drawn to seeing their subsequent child as a helpful and sensitive being because they are placing conscious or unconscious hopes upon that child to be helpful and to lessen their grief. One mom shared her belief that her subsequent child, while still in utero, was already working to reassure her.

Whenever I felt nervous that she wasn't doing okay, she would kick. I could probably count twenty or thirty times when I was nervous, especially later in pregnancy, about her not being okay, or not having felt her kick for a while, and she would kick. I think that her compassion is a wonderful thing. (Ann)

Many parents, like Ann and Laura, described subsequent siblings who, as children, were very aware and helpful of peers in need.

I have seen my daughter, Madeline, try to help others in our family, and now I'm seeing it happen outside of the family too. She noticed a little girl who was feeling sad, like an outsider. She tried to include her and to find some common ground. (Ann)

My son is thoughtful and goes out of his way to help other kids. He made friends with a boy who had autism, just naturally helped him out. It wasn't like I needed to encourage him to do that. (Laura)

Wanda and Lydia explained that their subsequent children were exceptional among their peers, demonstrating unusual capacities for empathy and care.

All of the teachers have said that Alana is very empathetic. A child was sad, and Alana went right over to her and took her under her wing. Alana is always the first one to introduce herself to a new kid in class and to try to make them feel welcome. (Wanda)

My daughter is very willing to help people who are in need. She loves kids. She's very compassionate. She also has a very keen sense of fair play, of what's right and what's wrong. She has a lot of compassion for the underdog and for people who are different, people with alternate lifestyles, and homeless people. She is much more sensitive and caring than some of her friends. (Lydia)

Some parents, like Caroline and Ann, also shared stories of subsequent children who tended to take on too much responsibility for the worries and issues of others, to the detriment of their own needs.

My daughter Charlotte is very empathetic. However, she has a propensity for allowing herself to be taken advantage of by people. She is often the personal therapist for friends who do not give much in return. (Caroline)

Her care for others is a wonderful thing, but she can do it to the detriment of herself. She is a worrier, and she takes a lot on. I am just trying to remind her that she needs to be concerned about her behavior and not those around her. (Ann)

In second grade, my son Ethan repeatedly tried to help a sad child. The social worker had to intervene. She explained to him that it was great he was looking out for that kid, but that he did not need to be responsible for him, and there were adults to do that. (Caroline)

The sensitivity of subsequent children may make them prone to high levels of worry, which can be carried into adulthood. Some may harbor ongoing concerns about their parents' well-being. Growing up with grief and loss might also create fears of another death in the family, as described by Susan.

I phoned home this morning, and my mum wasn't there. I had this moment of feeling quite anxious. Did she have a heart attack and die? Feeling anxious like that, it almost takes me back to being a child when I used to worry about her dying. I always worried about my mum dying. (Susan)

Conclusion

The caregiving and sensitivity traits embodied by subsequent children can be understood as gifts that are rooted in difficult origins. Some subsequent children may discover meaning, purpose, and heightened self-esteem through their service and care for others. Their helpfulness and attunement benefit those around them, with a range of positive repercussions. In our interviews, we met with subsequent children who became nurses, psychotherapists, clergy, teachers, and volunteers for an array of charities. Princess Diana, who was a subsequent child, devoted herself to assisting children in need and to causes such as eliminating land mines. We can speculate that her role as a subsequent sibling may have led her toward this work, which was a gift to the world. As adults, many subsequent children embrace and take pride in their sensitivity and strengths as caretakers. Their capacities to empathize, understand, and help others can be viewed as a valuable silver lining of their subsequent child role.

There are also costs, burdens, and pressures that prompt the caregiving roles and acute sensitivity of subsequent children. It is not accidental that those who were born after loss are prone to caregiving and emotional attunement, because they are conditioned to care for others as a part of their role. Patterns of caregiving often follow subsequent children into adulthood. When children become caretakers, their own needs are usually unmet, and their development may be negatively impacted. Seeking balance and care for themselves is critical for their well-being and for the realization of their full identity and potential.

16

The Pain of Bereaved Parents

The pain of bereaved parents is an influential presence in a family. Some parents mourn visibly and actively, and might be immersed or overwhelmed with grief. Others may rarely or never discuss their loss, but it might be acutely felt, with unspoken enactments in the family's dynamics. Grief is not static or linear, and parental mourning evolves over time. Regardless of their family's grieving style, most subsequent children describe growing up with an ongoing consciousness of their parents' pain. Roles are reversed when children worry for their parents, and those born after loss often attempt to protect their parents from additional heartache and upset. Parental suffering after the loss can shape family behaviors, rules, and relationships.

An Awareness of Their Parents' Suffering

Children who grow up with grieving parents are usually acutely aware of their parents' sorrow and fragility. Tyler, a seven-year-old who was born after a deceased brother, noted that his parents and family were different than others.

My parents were sadder than my friends' parents. (Tyler)

Janet and Tret, who were both born after brothers who died, described the consistent sadness of their parents.

My mother is a very deep woman, and she carries a lot of sadness in her life. I know that she never got over the loss of my brother. I'd find her crying. (Tret)

I think there was definitely a sense of shadow. In my early years, I was raised in a fog of grief. (Janet)

Subsequent children, like TJ and Ryan, are frequently witnesses of their parents' grief.

They relive the tragedy of my brother's death every year. It's hard to explain unless you're there and you experience it. (TJ)

It's brutal, heartbreaking, and very painful. There's a picture of both of them holding my brother David [after he died]. You can see the emotion on both of their faces, of just being crushed. It's obvious to me how hard this is, truly the worst nightmare. (Ryan)

In some cases, subsequent children may be hesitant to seek answers that they need due to their sensitivity to their parents' grief. Martin, who was born after a four-year-old sister died of leukemia, rarely had the opportunity to discuss his sister's death. As an adult, he had many unanswered questions.

My sister's death wasn't a topic of conversation. I think, subconsciously, I got the understanding that it wasn't a comfortable thing to bring up. If there was a reminder you would see little things in my mother's face, bringing back pain for her.

There were times that I wondered things, but they were less important than not upsetting my mom, just leaving it alone. (Martin)

Grief for Their Parents' Suffering

Subsequent children sometimes feel anguish about their parents' suffering. Pierre and Brynne describe grieving for their parents' grief.

I remember being taken to the cemetery by my parents. On high holidays, they would cry and take care of my sister's grave. I'd be upset because they would cry. It has been sad to live with this. (Pierre)

In my psychology class in college, we were shown a video of mothers sharing about miscarriage, stillbirth, and baby loss. It was so upsetting that I couldn't watch it. I was just thinking about how my mom's experience with the baby was exactly the same. I realized how much of an impact it had on me. (Brynne)

Subsequent children may feel the need to protect themselves from their parents' suffering because it is too difficult to bear. Allison was proud when her mother published an autobiographical book about losing a child, but she declined to read it as it was too distressing to face.

I don't like to think about how it must have been for them to lose my sister. I know it was a painful time. Maybe when I have my own children, I will read my mom's book about my sister, but right now I just don't want to know. (Allison)

Protecting Parents from Additional Sorrow

Subsequent children often make conscious, ongoing efforts to protect their parents from additional distress or grief. Andrew,

Anna, and Liz were watchful of their mothers' grief and well-being, and careful to avoid causing upset.

You never wanted to make my mother cry because there was always so much pain there. (Andrew)

I had to be very careful not to be a burden for my mother. I was always the one who was very calm, and I always did what mother said. I was easy for her. (Anna)

I always wanted to be a very easy child. I never wanted to upset my mother. I didn't always agree with her, but I would avoid telling her anything that she didn't want to hear. Whether it was conscious or not, there was always the thought that my mother went through the loss of a child, so I should not burden her. (Liz)

Subsequent children sometimes describe an unspoken pressure to be fine and well, and to avoid causing any worry. Like Mia and Janet, they may feel unable to express problems or needs.

I always had to be fine. The notion wasn't formulated as a formal thought. It was just more of a fear and a feeling that you don't show any need. There was no room for me to need anything. (Mia)

I always had to be a little adult, who did not make a problem. I always had to be okay. I could not let my parents see me cry or be sad and gloomy. (Janet)

Johanna, who was born after the loss of an infant brother, described hiding her issues to avoid worrying her parents or causing sadness.

I knew that I couldn't protect my parents from the pain of losing my brother, something I had zero control over and wasn't even present for, but I thought that maybe I could protect them from any pain that I might cause. That caused me to not be open with them when I was struggling, because I didn't want to give them more grief. (Johanna)

As they know that their parents cannot manage the threat of another loss, concerns pertaining to health or well-being often feel unspeakable and forbidden for subsequent children. Susan and Katie shared that they also avoided risk for their parents' sake.

I knew as a child that I had to do everything I could not to die, so as not to hurt my mum. I always felt like I had to stay alive and be well, because two of my mum's children were dead. (Susan)

I don't put myself in risky situations. I don't want my mom to go through anything else. I would never want her to face the situation of losing me. I protect myself for her sake in some circumstances. (Katie)

Subsequent children who become sick sometimes describe parents who avoid or discount their illness. Like Margie, they may hypothesize that their bereaved parents were too frightened to confront their illness and another potential loss.

I developed chicken pox and a heart murmur. My mom was dismissive and downplayed my illnesses because I think that she was unable to acknowledge that I might be really ill. When I was three years old, I had a heart catheterization, and I spent the night at the hospital. My dad instructed me not to cry when they left me there, but I did. When I went home, my grandmother was the one who cared for me. (Margie)

When left alone and hospitalized as a six-year-old, Janet believed that she was dying, and her biggest fear was about upsetting her mother with the news of her impending death. She clearly internalized a message that she was not allowed to die or cause further upset in her family.

I had bladder surgery when I was six. I was terrified, and there was no one there to comfort me. I thought that the blood in my catheter meant that I was going to die. I was scared to death that my mom was going to come in the morning, see the blood in the catheter, and that she'd know that I was dying. (Janet)

Of course, subsequent children have differing experiences, and some do not feel a need to protect their parents from sorrow. Sophie had surgery on her eyes when she was four years old. In stark contrast to Janet's hospital experience, she described her parents' presence and loving care. Her mother stayed with her in the hospital, and her father gave her a music box to comfort her.

After my surgery I had bandages on both of my eyes, so I couldn't see. My mother described the trees and sounds outside to me, and she was so kind. (Sophie)

Even in adulthood, subsequent siblings are often reminded of their parents' worry about any possible threat to their well-being or survival. They feel an ongoing need to protect their parents from sadness and anxiety. For Charlotte and Johanna, the fears and anxieties of their parents loomed large after they left home and went to college.

When I was in college, I got the same text from my mom every Friday night. She would remind me not to Uber alone, not to take drinks from strangers, and not to walk near water if I was drinking. Then she'd text me every Saturday and Sunday morning, even if I didn't go out that weekend, to ask if I was alive. She said that she had to check because she did have one kid who died. (Charlotte)

My lifelong need to protect my parents' feelings has been a very twisted mindset to live with. As an adult, when I dropped out of school I didn't tell my parents right away because I wanted to protect them. I didn't want them to be upset. (Johanna)

As an adult, Janet continued to receive unmistakable signals from her parents that she must not cause them worry or distress.

After a dear friend died, my dad gave me a card that I'll never forget. The front of the card had a picture of a man sitting alone in the rubble, and it said, "Take good care of yourself." On the inside it said, "We have more than enough to worry about without adding you to our troubles." It sums up the role I played in my family, and the person I became. (Janet)

A Caregiving Role

Like Susan, many subsequent children adopt caregiving roles for their parents. Despite a desire to be helpful, they often experience the caretaking as difficult and burdensome.

I felt responsible for my mom's happiness. It still feels a very tedious responsibility. I'm the only person that can take care of her, and what I do will make her happy or not. I became obsessed with her happiness, buying her gifts or doing things to make her happy, but her sadness is chronic. She can be happy, but not happy from the heart, like most other people can be. Hers is a deep, deep sorrow. She was my parent, but I have always been hers as well. (Susan)

Negative Outcomes of Parental Grief

The devastating loss of a child can have many destructive impacts upon a family, including harmful repercussions upon a marriage or parental relationship. Parents might grieve differently from one another, causing resentment, distance, and a sense of unmet needs. They may feel unable to support one another due to their own intense grief. They might also feel transformed by their significant loss, and sense that they have grown apart. Some bereaved parents divorce, struggle to stay together, or, like Sydney's parents, work through their marital issues with counseling support.

> *My parents went to couples therapy after my brother died. They struggled with their marriage after losing him, but they are still married, and now they are doing well.* (Sydney)

Andrew learned that his parents endured a difficult time in their marriage as well.

> *My grandfather mentioned that my parents had a really rough time when I was three years old. I was the same age as my brother was when he died, so maybe that was one of the reasons. I think it was a significant time for my mother. I don't know if they split for a while or not. I know that they were talking about separating, but they stayed together.* (Andrew)

Diane's parents were unable to stay together. She believes that the loss of her brother and its aftermath were the primary cause of their split.

> *My dad never talked about Freddie's death, but somehow, he blamed my mom for it. And my mom blamed him for not being there. She felt stranded. I think it was the start of the end of their marriage.* (Diane)

Sometimes one parent must delay their grief to take care of the family, because the other parent is bereft and unable to be present. This generally places a heavy strain on the caretaking parent and the marriage. Natalie shared about her parents and the upheaval caused by her sister's death.

I think that my father didn't deal with my sister's death for a long time, because he was the one who did everything after I was born. He took a leave from work and took care of me. When I was in high school, my parents separated for three years, but now they are back together. (Natalie)

Melba and her husband divorced after the death of their child, but they were able to have a heartfelt conversation later in life about their experiences.

My husband never talked to me about our deceased baby. When I was sixty-seven years old, I finally had a long talk with him about it. I asked him how it affected him, if he cared, and if he had any grief about it. He told me that he cried about it a lot. I replied that we should have cried together. Now he realizes that he wasn't there for me, and that he should have been. He told me that he is sorry. (Melba)

The loss of a child may also cause or exacerbate a parent's mental health issues. Margie's mother developed severe agoraphobia and postpartum depression. She would not leave the house and wanted someone to stay with her at all times. Margie missed school on a regular basis to stay with her mother or to care for her younger siblings. Her mother became an alcoholic and did not become sober for decades. Margie remembers her mother's return from a psychiatric hospitalization.

She came back so altered from the hospital. I remember the little yellow pills. She would take a half a pill and drink beer out of a juice glass. (Margie)

Likewise, Sally's parents suffered from mental health issues post-loss.

My mom was hospitalized for a nervous breakdown after my brother's death. My father needed treatment too, but he never got it. (Sally)

Some parents experience an array of trauma responses due to the loss of their child, including terrible nightmares or intrusive thoughts. Melba, a bereaved mother who lost a baby, described ongoing struggles.

The death of my child was totally unresolved for me. One night, years after she died, I woke myself grasping in the air to catch her, my baby. I was dreaming and hallucinating that she was walking across the dresser, and I was having violent headaches. I went to meet with a psychologist, who asked me when I was finally going to bury my baby. That was my first realization that I had suppressed my grief. (Melba)

Bereaved parents may feel the need to move to another home after losing a child, because their former home holds painful memories and associations. Tret shared her mother's experience.

My parents ended up moving after my sibling died because my mother kept hearing a baby cry in that house, even though there was no baby. (Tret)

Lara, who was born after the death of a brother, learned that her parents moved repeatedly after her brother died. She believes that their frequent moves were caused by their trauma and troubled state of mind. They were able to settle permanently after she was born.

I was told that my parents moved seven times in the year after my brother died. They finally moved into the house that I was born into, and they have lived in that house for thirty-three years. They never moved again. (Lara)

The pain and trauma of losing a child may put a parent at greater risk of substance use. Substances are frequently abused when people are in pain, struggling to cope, and feel a need to self-medicate. Parents who were abusing substances before losing a child are likely to increase their usage after their loss. Others may begin using substances to dull their pain. A grieving parent's substance abuse is usually impactful upon the whole family and carries perilous consequences. Kate's father began using substances heavily after her brother's death, and he was diagnosed with depression. He eventually left her mother, severing contact with the whole family and engaging in behaviors that were hurtful and difficult.

> *My dad never showed his feelings. He is on drugs. After he left, we also found out that he was having an affair with the babysitter. He took his name off the gravestone at the family plot, and it looks terrible now. My [deceased] brother is at the head, where my mother will be buried.* (Kate)

Kenneth, born after a deceased brother, believes that his sibling's death incited his mother's substance use.

> *My mother was clearly abusing alcohol while she was pregnant with me. I was born with fetal alcohol syndrome. Her grief about losing my brother probably caused her drinking patterns. The alcohol caused me to be in special classes at school, and I couldn't really read until maybe I was a sophomore in high school.* (Kenneth)

Likewise, Liz believes that her father's alcoholism is connected to the death of her sibling. His alcoholism is an ongoing issue.

> *My father has an alcoholic history which has not been fully addressed. He went through treatment and then has never given up drinking but that's kind of his secret.* (Liz)

Disenfranchised Losses

Losses that are not fully understood or recognized by others are, by definition, disenfranchised losses. Certain types of losses, such as stillbirths and miscarriages, are commonly disenfranchised, because friends and family members may inadvertently minimize their importance. Bereaved parents are more likely to experience a prolonged and complicated grieving process when their losses are unrecognized or unspoken. Katelyn's mom, who had a miscarriage before Katelyn's birth, struggled with a loss that was often discounted.

> *My mom did not feel entitled to her grief because she had a miscarriage. Her sister told her, "Well, at least you never had to meet your baby." That hurt my mom a lot. I think there was a lot of underlying trauma for my mom.* (Katelyn)

Brad's mom, who had a stillborn baby before Brad's birth, experienced heightened pain because her loss was misunderstood.

> *The only time that I ever heard my mom talking about her [two] stillbirths, I could sense the absolute pain of those losses. We were discussing someone who had lost a child on a television show, and she just blurted out "People say they are sorry, but they have no idea what they are talking about." She felt like people did not understand, and I know she carried a lot of grief.* (Brad)

An Overshadowing of Grief

Many subsequent children, like Charlotte, describe the ongoing presence and impact of parental grief in their families.

> *I think that there was a shadow over my family. I always had [my sibling's death] in the back of my mind, even from a young age. We knew that our parents were going through something so terrible and difficult. Losing a child is so dark.* (Charlotte)

Some subsequent children, like Ethan, were also careful to point out that they had happy childhoods, despite their family's history of loss.

I don't know what my life would have been like if my brother had lived, but I had a happy childhood. My brother's death was very tough for my parents and will always be a source of sadness. There was a shadow of grief, but I never felt under a shadow. My brother is a part of my existence and part of my life. (Ethan)

Healing Over Time

Layers of healing occur for some bereaved parents as they take on new roles, make meaning, help others, and expand or shift their faith and sense of self. Several subsequent siblings shared observations of their mothers and expressed gladness that their moms uncovered sources of purpose and solace over time.

My mom is an artist, and now she makes angels for a non-profit memorial garden for deceased infants. I think it must be really healing for her, after her own loss of my two siblings, to be contributing in this way to the Garden of Sleeping Angels. I think it is great. (Marie)

My mom was a dancer, and she thought that my deceased sister was going to be a dancer as well. I think she had to mourn for her dancing career, and for that connection to my sister. She's a decorator now. She is more secure in herself now that she has something else. (Natalie)

My mother, even to this day, goes to church every week and sings in the choir. She used to work in the church as well. I am sure that her faith became a big part of what allowed her to get through. (Martin)

Conclusion

Parents who lose a child often experience a devastating grief that evolves and endures over time. The repercussions of their loss are frequently impactful upon all aspects of their lives, including their physical and mental health, their identities and belief systems, their marriages and familial relationships, and their family dynamics. Their parenting approaches are likely to be influenced by their loss, and their grief may have lasting effects upon their children and home environment. Most subsequent children have a deep awareness of their parents' suffering that shapes their attachment and relationship to their parents and is a formative force upon their identities. Families have varied strengths and capacities for resiliency which do not erase their grief but may assist them as they navigate its shadow.

Parenting a Dead Child

We heard his borning cry.
We named him
Matthew.
We loved him.
Swaddled in his birthing blanket
we cradled him in our arms,
though the blanket
was to shield us
from his cold, cold body.
We baptized him.
His picture hangs
on our bedroom wall.
He is in our family tree.
On his birthday
we gift him
with tears of love.
At Christmas

we gift him
with a donation
to a foundation
in his name.
He is in our
Last Will and Testament.
We dressed him
for his journey
to the Kingdom
beyond where the
rivers and the streams flow
beyond where the
pines and wildflowers grow.
We laid him to rest,
though, it was in
The Field of Stones.
Still, and still, he is here
with us
in the shadow of our smiles.
(poem by Lloyd, bereaved father)

17

Loss in the Family and Continuing Bonds

All subsequent children are born into a family that has experienced grief, but each family's culture, coping style, and grieving process is unique. A vast range of dynamics and reactions occur within families after loss. Some subsequent children describe growing up in an atmosphere of mourning. Their sibling's loss may have been very present in their family's daily life, and perhaps their family was moored in grief. In other families, the deceased sibling may have been a secret or perhaps the loss was rarely spoken about. Bereaved family members frequently struggle with the question of how to hold the loss, individually and collectively as a family. Members of the family often have differing needs, desires, and grieving styles, which complicates their dynamics and mourning practices.

Many of us yearn to hold on to our deceased loved ones. We may choose to maintain an ongoing connection to them after they die, which is known as a continuing bond. Our relationship to the deceased does not necessarily end, but can continue and evolve, in an altered form, as we carry the deceased with us.

Some of us nurture a continuing bond to our lost loved one, using thoughts, rituals, or activities to uphold the relationship and connection. We might speak to our deceased loved one, write them letters, engage in a favorite shared tradition, seek out a sense of their presence, or wear a piece of their jewelry or clothing. Perhaps we imagine the advice that they would give if they were present, internalizing them and leaning upon their wisdom for support. Living with loss is often a balancing act. A healthy outcome often includes maintaining a lasting bond to the deceased, if we choose to do so, while also staying invested and involved in the present. A continuing bond will not erase our grief, but we may find it helpful and comforting as we strive to live with our loss, and it might foster a sense of resilience and strength.[1]

The concept of a healthy continuing bond represents a dramatic shift in grief theory perspective. Early grief theorists believed that the bereaved need to relinquish their attachment to the deceased as a part of a healthy mourning process. They encouraged severing ties to the deceased in order to reinvest energy and love into new relationships.[2] In more recent years, however, grief researchers have understood that many bereaved people need to maintain an attachment to their deceased loved one and that the creation of a continuing bond is often an adaptive response to loss.

A Continuing Bond for Parents and Families

Many bereaved parents, like Marci and Annette, maintain a continuing bond to their deceased children and find it to be comforting and helpful.

> *I still have my box of the pictures of Sarah, who died at eighteen weeks gestation, and that's a private place that I go to because it's part of the landscape of my life. I feel like I can walk beside Sarah in a personal space and that she doesn't overtake me. In spite of losing her, my life is so rich, so full, and so joyful, and my ongoing relationship with Sarah enhances it. No matter how painful it was to lose her, my*

experience of loss and my connection to her are part of what makes me a good mother and a good grandmother. (Marci)

I connect with [my deceased daughter] on a totally different level that isn't physical. I guess it's spiritual. Probably the closest place I feel to her is in my parents' church. When I really want to be close to her in spirit, that's where I go. (Annette)

Bereaved parents often hold on to a continuing bond to their deceased child throughout their lives and also as they face their own mortality. Like Ryan's mom, their planned final resting place may include a desire for proximity to their deceased child, symbolizing their everlasting connection.

Before my mom died, she made it clear that it was important to have my brother reburied with her. They laid his casket on top of hers. I think that it shows their spiritual connection. She wanted him to be moved and to be with her. It also shows the lasting impact that his loss had on her and how important he was to her. She didn't talk about him a ton, but she did make it clear that this was one of her desires when she passed away. To her it symbolized having him go into the afterworld with her. (Ryan)

Grieving and the formation of a continuing bond are often organically modeled by bereaved parents for their subsequent and surviving children. Caroline described speaking openly about her deceased son with her other children. She maintained mementos and practices to remember him while also staying focused upon her family's evolving life beyond the loss.

My other children always knew about Sebastian [their deceased brother], and I would speak about him in matter-of-fact terms, explaining that he had gone directly to his next life. We did not do anything ritualistic to incorporate him into our daily lives. We put a couple of decorations for him on the Christmas tree, and I have footprints and a pair of his tiny shoes next to my bed. Other than that, we just got on with things. (Caroline)

As subsequent and surviving children experience their parents' continuing bond to their lost sibling, they may develop or enhance their own connection to the deceased. Andrew explained that his deceased brother was frequently referenced and commemorated in his family.

He was never forgotten about. He was always a part of whatever we did. If we sat down for a meal and my mother said a prayer, she always included him in the prayer for the meal. At the holidays, she would put a stocking up for him, and we had pictures of him around the house. He was never put away; he was always kind of there also, in conversations or in pictures. (Andrew)

Elise's parents used an art piece as one means to include and remember her deceased brother.

My mother sewed birth samplers for me and my siblings. They were stitched with our name, birthdate, and weight, and they were framed and hung in our childhood bedrooms. I remember that she made one for Marcel as well. I think that it was hung in my parents' bedroom. It was much smaller than ours and more simple. It had two baby footprints, and the name Marcel stitched on it. It was a reminder of his presence and his part in our family. (Elise)

In some families, the deceased child is purposefully commemorated during important family milestones. Annette describes the honoring and remembrance of her deceased daughter, Courtney, at her other daughter's wedding.

Courtney [my deceased daughter] continues to be a part of the family conversation periodically. When my other daughter, Allison, was married, we played a song of tribute for

Courtney, and we placed a tiny rose bud in a vase in her memory. It was very meaningful for us. (Annette)

Another family celebrated the deceased child's birthday every year by going to the cemetery and sending off balloons. The surviving and subsequent siblings attached letters to their balloons, building their sense of attachment and connection to their deceased brother.

We wrote notes to [my brother] Connor, put them in balloons, and let them go. (Jack)

The way that the deceased child is commemorated in a family frequently illuminates a family's communication style and their ability to share and process the loss. As Charlotte reflected upon her mother's inclusion of her deceased brother, Sebastian, in her family's life, she also commented on her mother's mourning and coping capacities, which include the use of humor.

My mom keeps a print of my deceased brother's footprints next to her bed. She hangs ornaments for all of her children on the Christmas tree, and he has one too. She says that she never goes a day without thinking about him, but she's not like sitting there with sadness anymore. She will sometimes joke, "You know who's my favorite child? Sebastian, because he never complains." (Charlotte)

Some subsequent children, like Andrew, state that their parents' inclusion of their deceased sibling in their family's life and practices was helpful for them, assisting them to make sense of their family's narrative of loss.

I think it was good for us [myself and my siblings] that my brother was kind of remembered and not put away somewhere. I feel like I understand him because of how much he is a part of our lives. (Andrew)

In the act of keeping their deceased child present, with visible reminders and familial acts of remembrance, bereaved parents share their continuing bonds with the family, and set a pattern for themselves and their family members of keeping the deceased close. They also encourage surviving and subsequent children to participate in remembrance and to form their own continuing bond to their deceased sibling.

Secret or Unrecognized Losses in the Family

Some subsequent siblings grow up in homes in which their deceased sibling is rarely spoken about or is a secret. Their parents may harbor a private continuing bond, or perhaps their parents have chosen to detach from the deceased child, avoiding memories and connectedness in an attempt to cope. Their subsequent children may worry that their deceased sibling was seemingly forgotten and even question the strength of their own relationship with their parents. Michael, who was born after the death of a brother, learned of his brother's existence when he was nine years old. He shared his uneasiness about his family's lack of remembrance of his deceased sibling.

> I remember that my first question and concern was if my brother had a gravestone, because I thought that was the most important thing to remember him by, or at least to honor the fact that he was alive at one point. And my parents were sort of like no, or they weren't sure. They had moved on so much in their lives. It was like they were unconcerned. They were unclear if there was a marker at his grave or not. I wanted to make sure that he was remembered. It worried me, as a kid, that he was kind of forgotten. I would also have liked to know a little bit more about him. (Michael)

Karen, who was born after a brother died of sudden infant death syndrome, wished that her family had mourned more openly and collectively.

I wish that there had been more to commemorate [my deceased brother]. Like we could have said a prayer for him at dinner or gone to the grave. Instead, he was just this memory in my mom and dad's minds. (Karen)

Mia, born after the death of a two-year-old sister, was skeptical of her mother's explanation of the family's commemoration for her deceased sibling. She did not believe that her deceased sister was truly honored or memorialized.

We never visited [my deceased sibling's] gravesite except when my grandmother died and was buried at the same cemetery. In my religious tradition, there's supposed to be an annual acknowledgment of the deceased. You light a candle, and it burns for twenty-four hours. But for my [deceased] sister, there was no celebration of her life or observance of her passing. I questioned my mom at one point as to why we didn't make that observance of my sister. She was very good at thinking on her feet and said that we just lit one candle for everybody. I'm glad she was aware of that, because nobody else in the family had any idea. (Mia)

Several participants learned about their deceased sibling by accident and claimed that it was startling and upsetting news to process. Tret's hauntingly clear memory of discovering a photograph of her secret, deceased brother points to the weight and shock of her experience.

My biggest recollection was of finding a picture of a baby's coffin in my father's desk when I was seven. I asked my mother about it, and she said that was my brother, whose name was Brian. I don't even remember if she told me much about it. I can picture the desk. I know the room. I know the drawer. I can still see the photo of the white casket. (Tret)

Tanya, born after an infant brother died of spina bifida, also discovered a hidden photograph of her secret sibling.

It was a total fluke when I found out. I was eight or nine years old. It was Christmas. I was going through a drawer, getting the placemats and the Christmas runner for the table. Under the placemats, I saw these three pictures of my mom, my dad, and this kid. And it was very clearly not me. (Tanya)

Subsequent children whose parents avoid their grief may internalize a message that it is best to sidestep and negate the impact of a loss. They often yearn for more information if their sibling's death was a secret or unspoken. It is usually more complicated to grieve when a loss is silent or unrecognized because there is no forum to make sense of the loss, mark its importance, or gain support. Katelyn, who was born after the deaths of two siblings, expressed a wish for more communication and openness about her family's losses.

As a child it would have been nice to have my parents acknowledge that I had two siblings that didn't make it. I didn't know that my parents had other pregnancies before me until I was in late elementary school. It was only brought up once and never talked about again. I think that my mom was not ready to talk about it again with her living children. She thought that we didn't understand how it was for her. It's tucked away very privately. (Katelyn)

Alan was born after his two-year-old sister was killed by a drunk driver. He grew up in a home in which his deceased sister's death was unspoken; he learned about her existence from a cousin. His need to make sense of her death and to commemorate her was unwavering. After his mother died, he felt more able to express and explore a continuing bond.

My parents were so traumatized that they did not want to talk about [my sister's death]. This is something that we respected as children. There were no pictures of my deceased sister in the house. Later, one picture was found. Mom would just say that it was a picture of a little girl.

After my mom died, me and my brothers and sisters had the picture restored, and we all have it in our houses now. (Alan)

Continuing Bonds After a Miscarriage

Miscarriages are often secret or disenfranchised losses, and they may be quietly and deeply mourned. Family members may or may not feel the desire to commemorate a miscarried baby. Some might want to find ways to remember or acknowledge the miscarriage, and, just as with other losses, subsequent and surviving children might feel the need for information and recognition of the loss. Several subsequent children in our interviewed families expressed a desire to name the miscarried baby. The naming seemed to provide a means to honor the miscarried baby's identity and place in the family.

> *John [my five-year-old son born after my miscarriage] was quiet for a moment after I told him about the miscarriage, but then he said "Mommy, we need to give that baby a name."* (Clare)

> *When they learned about my first pregnancy and miscarriage, my daughters [who were both born afterwards] asked me if they could name their sibling. I said yes. So they named her Sarah, and when our family sent out cards they signed her name on them for many years.* (Carrie)

Tyler, a seven-year-old subsequent child who was interviewed, also wanted his miscarried sibling to have a name and explained his name selection.

> *There was a boy or girl who died in my mom's stomach when she was pregnant. I named it Happy, because that's not a girl or a boy name. I tried to figure out a name that could go either way. I could think of them as Happy.* (Tyler)

These examples of wanting to name a miscarried baby seem to highlight a common need, on the part of subsequent and surviving children, to make meaning of a loss in the family. When losses are secret, unnamed, or unspoken, it is more difficult to mourn them or to give them the recognition that they need.

Balancing Grief, Remembrance, and the Family's Present Life

Families hold, observe, and share their losses in unique and differing ways. It is challenging for many families to achieve a balance between a focus upon the loss and a focus upon the present. Maintaining a continuing bond to a deceased loved one is helpful for many bereaved people. Living in a home that upholds a perpetual atmosphere of mourning is usually detrimental, however, as it does not allow the family's present to be fully lived or cherished. Keeping a loss as a secret or taboo topic can be harmful to a family's cohesion as well. A family's quest for balance is further complicated by the likelihood that the needs and grieving styles of each family member will not align. In most families, their holding of loss will change and evolve over time.

While some subsequent children express comfort at the way that their deceased sibling was remembered in the family, others share a sense that the loss was overly present in their family's life, with negative consequences for them. Jane, who was born after the death of her nine-year-old sister Sylvie, described growing up in a bedroom that was laden with reminders of her deceased sibling. When Sylvie was ill, a group of artists created and inscribed images to her, and they were hung in her bedroom. Jane inherited the room and its decor, which included approximately a dozen images.

> *I think that it is important for a deceased sibling to be talked about in the family, but not dwelt upon. I think that my mother may have gone a little overboard. I just remember, growing up, I felt like Jesus, I can't get away from this. I think it was fine that they talked about her and said all these*

*great things, but I think that they could have put the paint-
ings away for a while. Or maybe not had so many around.
People would come to the house, [see the paintings inscribed
to Sylvie], and say "Oh, who was Sylvie?" And I'd have to
say that she was my sister who died. It was like, do we have
to keep talking about this all of the time?* (Jane)

Natalie, who was born after the death of her three-year-old
sister, stated that her mom kept the loss very present in their
family's life. Her sister's room was maintained untouched, like
a shrine, and her mother often brought up the loss to strangers
and acquaintances, as if she wanted everyone to know about it.
Natalie shared her wish for more connection, care, and focus
upon living family members.

*I wish that we could have had more rituals to bring us
together and closeness with the family that was still there.*
(Natalie)

As she discussed her experiences as a subsequent child,
Marisol commented more globally about the perils of keeping a
loss front and center.

*Maybe I shouldn't say this because it might be controver-
sial. This thing with the World Trade Center anniversaries
. . . Every time September 11th comes, they have the whole
nation harping on it. What are we supposed to do? Is the
whole nation supposed to mourn all the time? And why are
we doing it? Is it really good for the situation?* (Marisol)

Some parents seem to be unaware of their surviving or subsequent children's sense of being overshadowed by loss. Grieving parents might also be so immersed in their grief that they
are unable to focus upon the family's present members, current
needs, and daily life. In some families, however, bereaved parents
are mindful of the potential burden that subsequent and surviving children may experience. Caroline and Marci, both bereaved

mothers, spoke of their efforts to ensure that their homes and families were not shrouded in mourning.

I made a choice that I did not want Ethan and Charlotte to be burdened [by their sibling's death]. I never told them that Sebastian died on Mother's Day. In the earlier years, when the loss was more intense, I would compartmentalize, allow myself to grieve as fully as I could a few days ahead. That way, I could be happy and present for my living children on Mother's Day. I also employed that attitude for other holidays. That system served me well. It will be twenty-four years since Sebastian died, and not a day has gone by that I have not thought about him. However, we definitely do not live life in the funeral home here. (Caroline)

I made a conscious decision to really focus on the joy that my [living] kids bring me and not to be peppered by my past losses. I committed to myself and my kids and decided that I'm going to enjoy every minute because my living children are truly a miracle and a gift. They should not have to carry the burden of my losses. (Marci)

The Subsequent Child's Continuing Bond: Andy's Story

Some subsequent children need to explore and establish their own connection to their deceased sibling as they seek to make meaning of their loss. Andy's story, which was captured in interviews with Andy and with his mother, highlights the loss, questioning, and longing which may be experienced by a subsequent child, as well as the differing needs and coping mechanisms that can coexist in a grieving family. Andy's sister, who died before he was born, was a family secret. He learned about her as an eleven-year-old when he discovered her name in the family bible. She was born prematurely and lived for eleven hours. Eleven had always been Andy's favorite number. In retrospect, his connection to the number eleven seemed symbolically important to him, as if he had always carried an awareness of his sister and a bond to her.

I've been trying to pay attention to little things, and what significance they might have. I kept seeing the number eleven. It turns out that my sister lived for eleven hours, and that she died at eleven AM. (Andy)

Andy's need for information and commemoration did not align with his parents' coping style or grieving process. His father struggled with the baby's death and did not want to discuss it. Andy's mother, Ruth, explained that she and Andy's father did not speak about their deceased child or feel the need to do so.

By the time that Andy was old enough to discuss his sister, she was no longer front and center in our thoughts. She was never far away from our thoughts, but she was not a part of our family conversation. (Ruth)

Yet the loss was front and center for Andy, and he clearly felt the need to make sense of it and to integrate it into his life story. In college he majored in film studies, and his first film was about a young man who was looking for his sister. In the film, a photographer follows a mysterious woman that no one else can see. He sees her in his viewfinder as he attempts to take her picture, but when he puts the camera away, she disappears. He later learns that she has died.

At the end he crosses over a little bridge, into a park with swings. He puts the camera down and meets up with his sister, and you can see them talking. In the next shot, you see that the swing is broken. The film tells my story. I had a sister, who was born and lived for eleven hours. (Andy)

Andy was proud of his film, and he sent it to his parents. They both liked it, but they continued to avoid any discussion of his sister's death. They seemed unable to broach or understand Andy's experience of loss. His mother eventually began to understand the film's significance.

I discovered his journal after he moved off to college and found that he had been journaling to her [his deceased sister] for an extensive period of time. I was flabbergasted. I hadn't realized what her death meant for him, and that it had been a mistake to keep the loss silent and unspoken. I was amazed at his response, both in the journal and in the film, which was something that I would never have imagined. I was concerned that he felt the weight of carrying the life of two people rather than one. (Ruth)

Andy believes that his writing is channeled through his sister and says that she is his muse. He senses her influence and presence in his work, and through writing he feels an ongoing bond to her.

Whenever I write, the words seem to write themselves. I think it's my sister. It feels automatic. I was thinking back to when I found out about her, and that coincides almost exactly to when people started labeling me as a writer. So I've always kind of attributed that part of me to her and believed that she writes through me in a sense. (Andy)

Parental secrecy and a lack of familial commemoration propelled Andy to explore his family's story of loss and to do so on his own terms. He used the film to explore and make meaning of his sister's death, while also honoring her, forging a continuing bond, and taking control of his own needs for mourning and remembrance. In giving her the role of the muse, his loss became less nebulous, and he discovered a means for commemoration and closeness.

Conclusion

Families have countless ways of grieving and of holding a loss. Their patterns will be informed by many factors, including cultural backgrounds, belief systems, learned behaviors, coping strategies, and the grieving styles of individual family members. While relationships certainly change after someone has died and is no longer physically present, they do not necessarily end. Bereaved parents and siblings often take comfort in maintaining a continuing bond to the deceased, and it may assist them in making meaning of their loss. Subsequent children often want to uphold an ongoing connection to the deceased as well, and many express gladness and relief if their deceased sibling is openly remembered and discussed in the life of their family.

While some families are able to balance the remembrance of a lost loved one with a healthy investment in each other and their present life, other families become mired in grief. Subsequent and surviving children can feel overshadowed by the death of their sibling if the family home remains shrouded in mourning and remembrance. Families may also suffer when the death of a child is kept secret or as an unspoken topic. Secrets can harm a family's bonds as they often create distance and confusion, and it is burdensome for children to harbor questions or worries that they feel unable to discuss.

Family members often have varied needs as they strive to grieve and remember their lost loved one, and their coping styles may conflict. One family member's desire to frequently reference and discuss the deceased may be painful for another. Alternatively, if one family member prefers to keep the loss unspoken there may be detrimental consequences for the family unit. The death of a child is known to be one of the most painful losses that a parent can endure, and families generally cope as best as they are able. As families navigate their grief, they can benefit from consciously considering the needs of surviving and subsequent children, and from seeking balance, even if it is imperfect, between commemoration, a bond to the deceased, and a healthy concentration upon the present.

18

The Mourning of the Subsequent Child

While most subsequent children are painfully aware of the absence and loss of their deceased sibling, it can be challenging and counterintuitive to grieve for an unmet family member. Some feel as if they have deeply mourned for their deceased sibling, while others reveal that they have not grieved. Subsequent children missed the mourning rituals and social support that occurred in the aftermath of their sibling's death. Their loss may be disenfranchised as family members and others often believe that they are untouched by a death that occurred before their birth. In some cases, they have very little information about their sibling or their sibling's death, which further complicates a potential mourning process.

As most subsequent children are profoundly impacted by their sibling's death, they commonly feel a need to make meaning of their loss and to grieve. Many remember feeling grief for their deceased sibling during their childhood coupled with an effort to make sense of their loss, which is a vital part of the mourning process. Natalie, who was born after her three-year-old sister died by drowning, had an imaginary relationship with her deceased sister. It allowed her to play out some of her wishes and fantasies, and also illustrated her confusion and attempts, as a young child, to understand the finality of her sister's absence. In her play, hopes, and evolving understanding of the loss, she also gave shape and expression to some of her grief.

There was a time when I was little when I was using [my deceased sister] as an imaginary friend, and I thought she was coming back. I assumed she would be coming back in time to go to school. I had this whole thing in my head that we were going to wear matching outfits. Even though she was three years older than me, it didn't click in my head that if she had been alive, she wouldn't have been in kindergarten with me. When I found out she wasn't coming back, I was bummed out. (Natalie)

Dana, who was born after the death of an infant brother, remembers feeling sorrow as a child.

When I was little, I remember feeling sad and feeling bad for my mom. I looked at it like I was deprived of a sibling. (Dana)

Like Susan, many subsequent children may yearn for a replacement for their deceased sibling and hope for another brother or sister.

I used to beg mum to have a little baby. I was just desperate. I pretended that my little niece was my sister. I even brought someone home from school and said this is my little sister. (Susan)

Tyler, a seven-year-old subsequent child, described his family's ritual for his deceased brother's birthday. He was glad that his deceased brother was remembered but also expressed feelings of sorrow and confusion.

On the night of [my deceased brother's] birthday we leave a cupcake out for him, and when we wake up there's not much left. He knows that we always leave him something for his birthday. Sometimes I think that he may be somewhere but invisible, so that you can't see him. So sometimes I think that he's there, but sometimes I don't. It's kind of hard and sad because I can't see him. (Tyler)

Some subsequent children, like Edwin and Candace, recollect being grief-stricken when they were told about their deceased sibling for the first time.

I grieved a lot when I found out [about my deceased sibling]. I was about seven or eight years old. I grieved a lot and wished that my brother would come back. (Edwin)

I think that when I was first made aware [of my sibling's death] as a child I felt sad. Then it subsided. I remember wishing for siblings to play with. (Candace)

Parents, like Ethan's mom, sometimes describe their subsequent child's sadness and quest for understanding.

He told me that he was sad and upset not to have seen his brother, not even once. He also said that he feels cheated. Ethan believes the death of an infant is the most unfair death of all. He asked me how God could send me Sebastian and then take him back. He thinks this is cruel. (Caroline)

Ethan's mother also shared that Ethan demonstrated a preoccupation with his lost sibling and an ongoing need throughout childhood to process and make sense of the loss.

Ethan still talks about Sebastian daily. One time I found him holding the framed image of Sebastian's footprints while lying in bed with his sister Charlotte. He explained that he wanted all three of the siblings to be together. He noticed who in the neighborhood had been born in the same year as his brother. He also commented upon how many people were in various families and said that we were the only ones in our extended family who had to celebrate the holidays without all of our family members. (Caroline)

The Reconstruction of a Deceased Sibling

Subsequent children often construct imagined mental images of their deceased siblings, because they did not meet them. They have no memories to bring them solace or to help them with meaning making. As they piece together a narrative of the deceased with the fragmented information that they have, they reconstruct their lost sibling and build imagined representations of them for connection and understanding. The need to reconstruct significant and unknown deceased family members is explained in the literature about children who lost an unremembered parent. Reconstruction is an important process for grieving, as "one cannot deal with a loss without recognizing *what* is lost."[1] Reconstructions of a lost loved one are flexible images that can evolve as one passes different developmental stages and remain present throughout one's lifespan. They can help with the creation of a continuing bond to the deceased because they clarify the deceased's identity, one's relationship to them, and the meaning of their death. Jane, born after the death of a nine-year-old sister who died of a rare autoimmune disease, shared extensive musings about her deceased sister. Her thoughts illustrate her attempts to understand and form more of a tangible impression of her sister, which could assist her in mourning and integrating the loss into her life story.

> *As the years go by, I find myself thinking, if she were alive today, how old would she be, and wouldn't it be cool to have an older sister, and what would she have been like? Would she have gotten married and had children? I think she probably would have. What kind of life would she have had? What would she have done? Career wise? Would she have*

stayed home with the children like my sister and I do? Would she have been a career woman? What would happen to her? She would have been coming of age in the 1960s. Would she have been a hippie? You wonder, what if, what if, what if? What would she have looked like? Would she look like me as an adult or different? Whom would she have married? Where would she have gone to school? What would her life have turned out like? (Jane)

Likewise, Janet described her need to reconstruct and imagine what her deceased brother would have been like, as she has so little information about him.

I have this rich imaginative life about this brother who was fictitious to me. There were no pictures, no handprints. The pictures of mom pregnant with him were removed from the slides. My deceased brother was a ghost in our household. (Janet)

Some subsequent children reconstruct their sibling as an ally. CJ's parents' marriage was turbulent, and their fights caused him stress and worry. He sometimes missed his deceased sister and wished that she were present to help him.

I would miss her even though I didn't know her, because if she was here at least we could be together instead of me being alone and trying to figure out what to do with what I'm hearing and feeling [when my parents are fighting]. I was depressed and I missed her, but that didn't make sense to me because I never knew her. (CJ)

Brigit, who was born after a stillborn sister, imagined her lost sibling as helpful and kind.

I don't know if I mourned for [my deceased sister], but in my younger years I used to think about her more. She would have been the oldest of all these boys, all these brothers. If she were around she would defend me, and my brothers would be teasing her and not just teasing me. (Brigit)

Grieving in Adulthood

Many subsequent siblings, like Jane, Andrew, and Denise, describe grieving as adults and throughout their lifetimes.

I have grieved for my sister. I always thought it would have been so nice if she had lived. I'd have this other sister. I bet she'd be really nice, someone I'd have something in common with. And I've always thought that there's something I've missed, the sense of having her. I once had a dream. There was this image of these two Siamese twins, these girls, and it's like they sort of had two heads. I can't tell if they had two bodies or one body, but they were merged. After I woke up I wondered, do I feel like part of myself is missing because I lost a sister? (Jane)

The grieving I did was feeling the loss and wishing I had this older brother around. And kind of a wishing of what might have been. Never really actively grieving, but more of a longing than anything else, I think. (Andrew)

In my acting, and anything that I write, it is all about loss. I'm very connected to it. I'm not afraid to write about it or experience stuff like that in my acting class. I think I am a person who can channel things that are really emotional and really sad, and I think it's because of [my deceased sister] and my grief about her. (Denise)

As described by Jane and Paulina, milestones can sometimes elicit fresh sorrow and novel insights.

When I had my own children, I was sort of mourning for my sister all over again, thinking about what my parents went through and how hard it was for them. Until you have a child, you don't know how attached you get. And it made me think of how traumatic it must have been. (Jane)

I grieved when I found [my deceased brother's] grave. (Paulina)

Some subsequent siblings, like Lana, believe that they may have unresolved grief. Lana was born after her twenty-year-old sister died of pneumonia.

I have unresolved grief because I never got to know my sister. It is hard to work through. (Lana)

Angelo, who was born after his three-year-old brother was killed by a drunk driver, shared about his lingering sorrow.

I have gone through sadness. I'm the one who wants to talk about it. When I ask my mom questions about it, [my surviving siblings] say that I shouldn't bring it up. But I need answers. Maybe I have some unresolved grief. (Angelo)

Like Angelo, Jane wonders if she has unresolved grief about the death of her sibling.

My sister's death definitely made me feel sad. It still does. I think my grief is unresolved in the sense that I'll always feel sad about it. I don't know if that is unresolved or not. (Jane)

The Transgenerational Transmission of Grief and Trauma

Some of the literature about subsequent children correlates their experience to children who are born after the Holocaust to parents who are Holocaust survivors.[2] Of course, the death of a child in a family is completely different from the Holocaust, and the two experiences cannot be compared. In both circumstances, however, parental grief and trauma can impact future generations, because grief and trauma can be passed down to children in a process known as a transgenerational transmission. Researchers have found that those who are born after the Holocaust or a genocide, who are known as the second generation, seem to frequently absorb psychological burdens from their parents. The children of genocide survivors often deeply identify with the experience of their parents, as if they went through it themselves, and define the Holocaust as the single most critical event that has impacted their lives, despite the fact that it occurred before their birth.[3]

The transgenerational transmission of grief and trauma can occur in numerous ways. In infancy, even before verbal communication begins, babies who are born after a traumatic event will absorb the sorrow, anxiety, and emotional or physical absence of their parents.[4] Psychoanalytically oriented theories suggest that emotions which were too difficult to be consciously experienced by parents are given over to the second generation, so that second-generation Holocaust survivors often unconsciously shoulder the repressed and insufficiently worked-through Holocaust experiences of their survivor parents. It has also been found that the trauma of parents can sometimes be inherited, just as hereditary diseases may be passed from one generation to another. The genetic memory code of a traumatized parent can be transmitted to the child through electrochemical processes in the brain, and memories of fear can be carried across generations through genes and physiological processes.[5] Grief can be inherited as well. When grief is prolonged or complicated, and parents are unable to fully or adequately mourn, a pattern of complicated grief is often passed down to the next generation.[6]

As the transgenerational transmission of grief and trauma is primarily an unconscious, invisible, and unspoken process, it is not simple to recognize. Subsequent children may not be aware that some of their feelings are inherited or that they are holding their parents' grief. Those with more intense grief and trauma responses to their sibling's death might be feeling some inherited emotions that were too difficult for their parents to tolerate. Johanna, Pierre, and Michael were able to describe grief reactions that were closely tied to the feelings of their parents and might be a transgenerational transmission of their parents' grief and trauma.

> *I remember one anniversary of my brother's death that hit my mom and dad really hard. It made me so sad and stricken with grief that I had no idea what I was feeling. I remember seeing my mom cry and dad cry, and going up to my room and bawling my eyes out for no reason for someone I didn't even know but missed so deeply that it physically hurt.* (Johanna)

> *I think I grieved more for my parents' grieving for my sister than for myself.* (Pierre)

> *My [deceased sibling's] death impacts me in the way that it impacts my parents.* (Michael)

The impact of inheriting the trauma and grief of one's parents can be devastating and far reaching for subsequent children. "To grow up with overwhelming inherited memories, to be dominated by narratives that preceded one's birth, is to risk having one's own life stories displaced, even evacuated, by our ancestors. These events happened in the past, but their effects continue into the present."[7] Like replacement dynamics, a transgenerational transmission of grief and trauma can obstruct subsequent children's ability to form their own authentic identity or to invest in their own life experiences, because they are saddled with others' burdensome emotions and grief reactions.

A Lack of Mourning

Subsequent children have varying experiences and reactions to their sibling's death. Some feel no need to mourn, while others feel as if they have been unable to ever grieve. Pierre and Tanya expressed their inability to grieve for an unmet sibling.

I never met her. I can't grieve for someone I never met. It's hard. I would have liked to meet her. (Pierre)

I never grieved because for me, personally, I can't say good-bye unless I say hello. (Tanya)

Michael, who was born after the death of a two-year-old brother, thoughtfully described some of the complexities of his mourning experience. His words illustrate the importance for subsequent children of having open communication about the loss. His grief was impeded by a lack of information.

I think I haven't grieved but I have definitely paid respects. I might have a little unresolved grief because there is so much I don't know. I would have liked to have known more. (Michael)

Some subsequent children, like Ryan, commented on the confusing nature of their loss, which makes it difficult to mourn or understand. Ryan was born after the death of a brother.

I lost somebody, but do you lose somebody before you ever had somebody? It's hard to miss what you've never had in some regard. What sits with me more is I was probably supposed to have a relationship with him, what could have been, and what would he be doing now. (Ryan)

Like Megan, some subsequent children did not feel allowed to grieve.

In my family, it was always about my mom. She suffered so many losses and felt so alone in the world that we worked so hard to make her forget. My mom was allowed to be sad, but we all had to be strong and quiet for her. (Megan)

Many describe a disenfranchised loss and an encumbered grief process. Megan and Lori, both subsequent siblings, did not feel entitled to mourn until they reached adulthood and recognized the significance of their losses.

> *How was I to grieve when I didn't even know I was a sibling? I am thirty-nine years old, and this is the first time that I have thought of myself as a bereaved sibling with the rights to have my own feelings and my own grief for my losses.* (Megan)

> *I had no idea that the loss of the baby who was born before me could have any effect on my life until just in the past year or so.* (Lori)

Subsequent children like Ethan and Brigit use a frame of their spiritual beliefs to make meaning of their loss.

> *I know I had a brother before me. I never got to meet him, but I was raised to believe that I will get to know him in another life, hopefully sometime away.* (Ethan).

> *My deceased sister is at peace. With the world we're living in now, she's at peace. Sometimes she's better off, with the way things are going now. The world is crazy. The creator has a master plan for everybody. It was meant to be.* (Brigit)

Conclusion

Subsequent children have a complex loss to bear. Many feel as if the death of their sibling is a central and formative force in their family, but that their loss and experience is disenfranchised. They might question how to mourn or if mourning is necessary while also holding feelings of sorrow and confusion. Most subsequent siblings carry ongoing feelings of grief and need to make sense of their loss, because their role in the family is intricately linked to the deceased. As they never met their siblings, they might seek to reconstruct them, forming an image in their mind to better understand what and who they have lost.

The mourning of subsequent siblings may be additionally complicated by a transgenerational transmission of grief. Some subsequent children unconsciously inherit feelings of grief and trauma from their parents. Replacement dynamics, survivor guilt, and a lack of information about their sibling can further exacerbate their grieving process and capacity to make meaning. Their grief may also be compounded if the loss was an unspoken or taboo topic in the family. As for all types of losses, each subsequent child will have a unique approach to mourning, and their needs and feelings of grief will vary. A drive to grieve is often connected to a drive to heal, and subsequent siblings may find some relief and growth in their process of mourning.

I Only Knew Him in My Heart

I only knew him in my heart.
I never saw him in life.
I will never see him in my life.
I will only see him in heaven.
My brother, Matthew, died
when he was an hour old.
He was born before me.
He died before me.
I wish he could be with me now.
I only knew him in my heart.
(poem by Ryan, fifth grader and subsequent child)

19

❧

Subsequent Children Consider Parenthood

People who were raised in grieving families may experience intense emotions when they consider having children. Memories of their family's grief and fears of loss can surface. Some subsequent children feel worried or ambivalent about becoming parents or choose not to have children because of their backgrounds. Others feel less impacted by their family's history of loss as they consider parenthood. Subsequent children have a range of possible experiences. Their sibling's death might affect their choices and feelings about parenthood because their family's loss is often influential upon their identities and life choices.

Susan was born after the death of her seven-year-old sister, and she grew up with a strained relationship with her mother. She was informed by her mom that her birth was a mistake and that she would have been aborted if abortion were legal. Her feelings about potentially becoming a mother herself became understandably complex. While she was drawn to parenthood as a young child, she ultimately opted not to have children.

As a little girl I loved my dolls, and I did have some intense times of wanting a child. However, my mum said that being pregnant is hard work, and that birth is excruciating and frightening. Experience also showed me that there are no guarantees that your children won't die before you. There was a period as an adult when I could not walk through a department store and see the clothing for children and babies without an uncontrollable urge to cry and a deep feeling of sorrow. I decided not to have children because birth is quite scary and hideous to me. My identity as childless seemed preordained. (Susan)

Some subsequent siblings describe their choice to be an aunt, uncle, or foster parent rather than having a birth child. Born after the loss of two brothers, Katie made the decision not to have children. She was aware of her mother's fears about pregnancy and claimed that she did not want to burden her. Katie's interest in fostering instead of birthing a child also hints that she might have carried some pregnancy fears of her own after witnessing her mother's anxiety.

My mother still feels very unsafe around pregnancy. When our alpacas on the farm are near to giving birth, she's constantly terrified that she'll find a miscarried baby. I do not want to have kids and have known that since I was thirteen. I do think about fostering children. I would love to impact young people's lives, but not create one of my own. (Katie)

Tanya, who was born after an infant brother died of spina bifida, explained that the risk of loss informed her choice to remain childless.

Because of the loss of a child in my family, there was always some inherent sadness, a certain dark cloud that kind of permeated everything. I'm not a mother and have no plans on being a mother. That was part of the arrangement that my husband and I made when we got married. We are a terrific aunt and uncle duo, but we are not parent kind of people.

Because anytime something happens to your child there's always going to be an inherent kind of darkness. (Tanya)

Likewise, Janet, who was born after the death of a brother, decided not to have children. It became another experience of loss for her, despite being her choice.

I made the decision not to have children. As part of my processing, I wrote a letter to the children I'd never have. Interestingly, as a chaplain I was once called to do a handover of a newborn from the biological mom to the adoptive mom. The biological mom had written a gut-wrenching letter about all the things she would never have with her little boy. It totally echoed what I had done in my letter to the children I never had. (Janet)

Fears of Loss

It is understandable that a subsequent sibling might feel afraid of losing a child. Like their bereaved parents, they are acutely aware that a death can happen. Karen, who was born after her brother died of sudden infant death syndrome, expressed uncertainty about becoming a mother herself because of her fears. Her anxiety was intense when she cared for her infant nephew.

When I babysat for my nephew, I was so paranoid, like my mother, of sudden infant death syndrome. I remember having his playpen in my room. I'd put my hand on his back, waking up and checking on him. It might be genetic. Who knows. I was so afraid. Because of losing my brother, I know it can happen. (Karen)

Katelyn, who was born after the loss of two siblings, expressed her worries about motherhood and pregnancy.

I know that I want to have kids, but I also know that I'll be worried that something might happen when I'm pregnant, because my mom lost two babies. (Katelyn)

Subsequent siblings who decide to have children, like Andy
and Elise, may have more anxiety than most during their pregnancies, especially if their parent's loss was a stillbirth, infant, or
pregnancy loss.

*Other people are so giddy when they are having a baby. They
can't possibly understand what my experience is like, coming from a family that lost a baby. When we were pregnant, I
kept worrying and thinking about the worst-case scenarios.*
(Andy)

*I don't know how much [my brother] Marcel's death influ-
enced my need for self-protection during my pregnancies,
but I always waited to tell anybody that I was pregnant, recognizing that the risk of miscarriage is always high. I was
super anxious. We didn't buy anything until after the twenty-
week ultrasound. I would wake up in the middle of the night
wondering when the baby last moved and drink juice to
make sure he was kicking. When he was born, I immediately
asked if he had ten fingers and toes.* (Elise)

Noah, born after several miscarriages, did not believe that
he would be anxious about pregnancy and parenting, but he
became aware of his underlying fears when he faced his partner's
first ultrasound appointment.

*I had trust in God that he would help us through whatever
happened. I got through it and didn't realize I was holding
my breath until the doctor confirmed everything was OK. I
also know my mother worried during our pregnancy.* (Noah)

Renee, who was born after a stillborn brother, wonders if
her anxiety, absorbed from her in utero experiences with a grieving mother, caused her to have her own repeated miscarriages
and to be unable to have a birth child.

*I wondered if I miscarried because I was anxious. Was it
impossible for me to have a birth child because I carried so*

much of my mother's fear? Was it connected to the shadow of grief in our family? Every time I thought I was pregnant, I had instant anxiety. Knowing that my mother carried me with anxiety during her whole pregnancy, I realized that I was experiencing that same anxiety myself. (Renee)

Some subsequent children, like Marie and Liz, make a marked effort to enjoy their pregnancies despite their family's history of loss and attempt to minimize fear and worry.

We made sure that the doctors reviewed the records of my mom's pregnancies. They treated my pregnancy as high risk, even though I was twenty-five and had no health issues. But I tried really hard not to let my mom's pregnancies interfere with how I felt about my own. I still wanted to enjoy my pregnancy. (Marie)

I was still really excited and happy when I was pregnant, even though there was that thought that something could go wrong. Each milestone in the pregnancy was a great milestone for us, and we celebrated them. I think I was trying not to let the past sadden what we were experiencing. (Liz)

Compensating for Their Own Experiences

Margie consciously chose to nurture her son while he was in the womb, knowing that her pregnancy would impact his development. She believes that her own prenatal and early attachment experiences were negatively impacted by her mother's grief, so she purposefully attempted to provide a more positive beginning and attachment for her child.

When I was pregnant, I just knew that if I was upset, he would be upset. It was a deep knowing. I remember listening to music for [my baby] Adam and knowing that his brain was forming. It was important to me that he was cared for in a way that I wasn't and that he had a sense of self. (Margie)

Mary became a foster mother while she was raising her own five biological children. She was drawn to helping young children in need of mothering and nurturing. Over the years, she fostered fifty-five newborn babies. She recognized that her care for foster infants was linked to the lack of nurturing that she received as a baby and to a desire to compensate for her own childhood deprivations.

> *My reasons for mothering newborns were not lost on me. I believed that some of them were denied during pregnancy, and I recognized that was not a good thing. I used affirmations with them, telling them that they were so beautiful. I told them they were special, worthwhile, and wonderful to have on earth. Even if my foster babies left my care after a few weeks, I believed that my affirmations would somehow stay in their hearts.* (Mary)

Imprints from Their Parents

It is unsurprising that the parenting practices of subsequent siblings might mirror their parents' approaches. Rebecca, whose mother was quite overprotective of her, described enacting a similar pattern with her own children.

> *I have three children. I am overprotective of them, and I think it is because of what happened in my family, because of my sister's death.* (Rebecca)

The self-image that subsequent children construe in their families of origin may influence their approaches and self-confidence as a parent. Both Lori and Pierre seemed to struggle to trust themselves in a parenting role. Throughout his childhood, Pierre's parents negatively compared him to his highly intelligent, deceased sister, and he felt unable to measure up. As Pierre spoke about parenting his young son, he described relying upon the intelligence of his older, surviving sister, pointing to his ongoing sense of being less smart and capable.

*I have a seven-month-old son. My [surviving] sister has been
so helpful. She has been invaluable with my son. My wife
and I don't know what we are doing. My sister has tested
cognitive abilities.* (Pierre)

Lori, who was born after a deceased sister, described her
negative self-image, which fueled her doubts about taking on a
parenting role.

*I never thought I was emotionally stable enough to have
children until I was thirty. As a child, I always felt like I was
screwed up and crazy.* (Lori)

Some subsequent children, like Jane, describe perspectives
about parenting that were altered by their parents' loss and sibling's death.

*My sister's death and that background certainly makes me
more grateful for having healthy children. And I do have a
son who has a severe speech delay. He is in special education.
We don't know what the full prognosis is, but I step back
and tell myself that this is difficult, but that it can't be anywhere near as difficult as having a child who is sick and died.
I try to use that to give myself perspective.* (Jane)

Furnishing a Replacement

In parenthood, subsequent children may unconsciously continue to try to provide the replacement that their parents ached
for, and their family's replacement dynamics might be passed
into the next generation. Subsequent children sometimes contemplate the idea of naming their child after their deceased
sibling, a symbolic and relatively common act of commemoration and replacement. Deirdre's ambivalence about potentially
using her deceased brother's name for a future child points
to the complex issues and meanings that may arise with a
renaming.

I might name my child [the same name as my deceased brother] for my parents, if I ever have a child. But you know, I think that might be jinxing it, so I might need to think of another name. (Dierdre)

Kim, a subsequent child born after her mother relinquished her sister for adoption, chose to become an adoptive parent. While Kim's reasons for adopting included infertility, we can hypothesize that adoption might also have been her unconscious attempt to satisfy her mother and to replace her sibling lost to adoption.

As soon as we adopted our son, he and my mom were thick as thieves, quite a bonded little duet. I'm sure that it had special significance for my mother that we adopted a child into the family. Adoption sent one child away and brought one in. (Kim)

Subsequent children who experience pregnancy or child loss might enact replacement dynamics with their own subsequent children. Renee, who had multiple miscarriages, eventually adopted two children. She designed a tattoo for herself with symbols to represent her adoptive children. Interestingly, the tattoo also included secret symbolizations of her miscarriages, although she has chosen not to tell her adoptive children about those losses. The hidden miscarriage references, interwoven with the images for her children, seem to illustrate an unspoken shadow of loss and potential replacement dynamics. Within her tattoo, the identities of the adoptive children are linked to her prior losses. The adopted children, even in a tattoo that was reportedly created to honor them, share the stage with unspoken miscarried babies.

A Deeper Understanding of Their Parents

Some subsequent siblings, like Jane, shared that their own experiences of parenthood illuminated the significance of their parents' grief and loss.

After having my own children, I became more aware. I have two sons, and it's this deep thing, this deep love. So I thought about how horrible and traumatic it was for my parents to lose a child and what they must have gone through. I gained a new awareness of their experience. (Jane)

The Influence of a Special Needs Sibling

Like subsequent children, those who were born after a special needs sibling may feel anxious about becoming parents. Their feelings and decisions about parenthood might be heavily influenced by their family's experience of having a special needs child. Katherine, whose older brother was born with Down syndrome, reported that her pregnancy brought up complex emotions and choices.

I was sure that my body could not produce a healthy child. I had all the tests, because I felt that it would help me to know and prepare myself if I had a child with a disability. I felt really guilty about having the tests, however, like I was betraying [my brother] Dougie's memory. It was a really painful thing that I stumbled through. I was very surprised when my daughter was born and nothing was wrong. (Katherine)

Johanna was born after a brother with special needs. He died as an infant. Like Katherine, she has some worry about becoming a parent due to possible hereditary issues, but her brother's disability will not stop her from having children.

My mom has always told me that [my brother's disability] was a one-time thing, not that it couldn't happen to me, but that it was just a luck of the draw. If I were to have a special needs child, I know that my future husband would handle it with me. I would just be a different kind of parent. I do worry about it, but it's not a fear so to speak. I think I could handle it as a person and as a mother. (Johanna)

Reactions of Their Parents

In addition to managing their own potential fears, subsequent siblings may contend with an array of reactions and worries from their parents as they move toward parenthood. Their parents may be reminded of their own pregnancies and parenting experiences, and of their terrible loss. A new pregnancy or birth in the family might awaken their parents' grief or trigger anxiety. Due to their histories and trauma, some parents are unable to be excited, present, or supportive when their subsequent child becomes a parent. Marie, who was born after the deaths of two siblings, shared that her parents were anxious and unable to be joyful during her pregnancy.

> *It was really hard, because parenthood is something that I was excited for, but I felt like my mom wasn't excited to be a grandma. She was nervous and scared the whole time I was pregnant and wasn't able to enjoy it with me. After I had the baby, she gave me a huge hug and was teary-eyed. She said "Now I can breathe." She was definitely more nervous than I was, and my dad was as well.* (Marie)

Katelyn, who was born after two losses, noted that her sister-in-law's pregnancy caused a surge of emotion for her mom.

> *My brother's wife is five weeks pregnant. I get the sense that my mother really needs to process her own losses again because of this.* (Katelyn)

The testimonies from bereaved parents confirm that many of them struggled when their subsequent children became pregnant and had a child. Nina, Marci, and Melba, all bereaved mothers, described their fear and grief.

> *When my daughter was pregnant, I was very detached. When you love someone and they're going through something that you've gone through, you hope that the end result isn't terrible*

like yours. That great fear is dangling. It was hard for me and for [my daughter] Marie. Even after her first daughter was born, I was still standoffish. Her daughter had some complications, so I didn't want to get attached. When her second daughter was born healthy, Marie said "Do you think you might get a little closer to this one?" I told her that I will try. (Nina)

The anxiety rose into my throat, but I kept it in check very specifically. My kids and my daughters-in-law knew that I had experienced all of those pregnancy losses, so it was definitely present and under the surface for them. (Marci)

The birth of my first grandchild triggered my grief wide open. I was frightened, and I withdrew out of fear. My daughter and I didn't connect about her pregnancy or share a feeling of excitement over the baby. After the pregnancy, she expressed her disappointment that I wasn't excited for her. I explained that I was afraid to be excited and didn't want to pass my fear on to her. She told me that she thought that I was tangled up in the grief over my first baby. She gave me a great gift, because I began to think about it, and I could see how it was connected. (Melba)

Some subsequent children experience their own tragic pregnancy or child loss. Sheree, who was born after a stillborn sister and several miscarriages, had her own miscarriage. She reported that her mother was very supportive, despite their formerly turbulent relationship.

I was twenty-one when I had my own miscarriage, the same age as my mom when she had her stillbirth, so I definitely think that there was a connection. My mom and I had a little ceremony, and I felt like she could really help me because of what she went through. (Sheree)

Conversely, Lara's parents distanced themselves after Lara and her husband lost their second child, and Lara felt unsupported and misunderstood by them. Perhaps Lara's parents struggled to support her because of their own history of loss.

After the loss I needed help with [my oldest child], but my parents didn't want to come. We planned a memorial service, but everybody was like, "Why are you having one?" My parents came, but nobody talked about our loss. At the memorial, my mom told me about someone who lost a baby who was a toddler and said that would be so much harder than my [newborn] loss. I really didn't want to talk about that. (Lara)

Conclusion

As subsequent children consider and experience parenting, their inherited anxiety and loss is likely to influence their decisions and parenting approach, both consciously and unconsciously. Their new role as parents might also trigger a range of reactions in their families of origin, perhaps igniting grief and fear in the hearts of their own parents. While many subsequent children become capable and loving parents who raise thriving children, it is important to recognize the unique challenges that they might face. When unconscious fears or replacement dynamics are recognized, they can be processed, lessening their potential impact and harm.

Sarah's Story: A Subsequent Sibling Becomes an Adoptive Mom

I did not realize it initially, but my parenting story connects to my identity as a subsequent child. For as long as I can remember, I wanted to adopt a baby. It was my plan since childhood. My husband and I adopted a son from Korea, and our choice to adopt was not based upon infertility, but upon a desire to adopt. He is our beloved and only child.

Our son was ten months old when he arrived, which is common for international adoption. He lived in a loving foster family before coming to us. Unfortunately, the adoption agency did not allow us to go to Korea to get him, despite our desire and request to do so. Their policy was to have all children escorted to the United States by a hired caregiver. We met our son for the first time at a New York City airport.

From the perspective of my ten-month-old son, the experience was surely overwhelming, sad, and traumatic. He was attached to his foster parents and believed them to be his forever family. At ten months of age, he was placed in the arms of a stranger, and he spent twenty-four hours on his journey to us. The caregiver was a very kind man who took excellent care of our son, but the trip was long and confusing, and he surely missed his foster parents. Upon arrival he was greeted by us, two strangers, and brought into our home. Everything in the new home was different, such as our voices, the language, the smells, and the sounds. Even the toys and bedding offered to him were new and unfamiliar. He did not know us, and he longed for his foster mother and father.

In the early months he showed signs of his grief and confusion. He was impossible to soothe, reaching for me but then pushing me away when I picked him up in my arms. He was restless and in constant motion. It was almost impossible to get him to sleep at night. We would sit by his crib for hours to get him to sleep, refusing to let our traumatized baby "cry it out" as recommended by the pediatrician. We saw our son's determination and distress and knew instinctively that he would have screamed for hours if left alone. He ended up sleeping in our bed for several years as it was the only way to get him to sleep.

The adoption agency provided firm advice and instructions to assist with the attachment process. As we had missed the early months of our son's life, in which important bonding takes place, it was imperative we do everything possible to form a strong attachment. We were told that no one else should watch our son or even hold him, as he needed to understand that we were his parents. While this advice was understandable and well-intended, it also made it impossible for us to feel as if we could ever ask for help with our baby or have a break to rest. Our baby continued to be hyperactive and hard to soothe. Our hearts broke for all that he was going through, and we were overwhelmed as new parents.

During my maternity leave, I remember getting together with a mom who had a baby of the same age. Our sons sat side by side in their strollers, and the differences in our rapports with our babies were painfully pronounced. I watched her playful interactions with her happy son, who smilingly reached for her and laughed. My son was stony faced, and I felt a crushing sense of inadequacy. At the beach I heard a little boy calling "mama!" as he insisted on holding his mother's hand; I wondered if my son would ever feel that way. When he woke up from his naps screaming and screaming inconsolably, a regular occurrence, I grieved for his grief and trauma, and vowed to continue to shower him with love, over and over. I'd whisper my love to him as he fell asleep in my arms at night. He always turned to face away from me, and I wondered if he was wishing for the comfort of his other mother.

We learned that he had sensory integration issues, and, later, attention deficit hyperactivity disorder. He was frighteningly fearless, and his body was in constant motion. He crashed into walls and furniture as he was a sensory seeker, and he was often covered in bruises despite our best efforts to keep him safe. His bruised little face reinforced my sense of failure as a mom. I often thought about his foster mom. I could tell that she had loved him and that he had been bathed in love. I felt it as soon as he was placed in my arms at the airport for the first time. His skin was pink and perfect like a rose, and he squirmed in his little pajamas. He was plump and perfect, doted upon and cared for. I had an ongoing, sinking sense that she was surely a much better mother than I was. I often wished for her guidance and longed to pick up the phone to call her. I imagined her as the mother that he missed and wanted, and felt unable to measure up.

Years later, the realization hit me. As an adoptive mom, I became a subsequent mother. History was, in a sense, repeating itself. I was a replacement, for both a birth mother and a foster mother. My son was grieving, and I felt unable to compete with the mother who was longed for. I had a desperate desire to assuage my son's grief and felt as if I was never good enough. I wondered if my desire to adopt was connected in some ways to an unconscious need to repeat and master my replacement role. A therapist friend made an additional observation, pointing out that I may have unconsciously chosen to adopt because I could empathize with the grief of an adopted child. I was born into grief myself.

I share my story to highlight the complexities of parenting that subsequent children may face. Perhaps we are drawn to grief and prone to reenacting replacement dynamics in our relationships and families of procreation. In my case, I also firmly believe that my son was meant to be with us. There is an old Asian proverb about an invisible red thread connecting those who are destined to meet. I am grateful for all the forces and factors that led me to be his mom.

20

≈≈≈≈≈

Silver Linings and Supportive Bonds

Challenges and difficulties may provide opportunities for growth. No one would ever wish to be born into a grieving family or to lose a sibling, but the capacity to find silver linings within a painful experience is often an indicator of health, healing, and meaning making. Sometimes, in facing adverse circumstances and surviving them, we build our confidence to confront additional struggles in the future and feel stronger and more capable. Subsequent children frequently face hardships, but some are also able to recognize strengths that they gained because of their role and their family's loss. Sensitivity, attunement, and a capacity for care and service are frequently identified as positive attributes that were developed because of the subsequent child role. Resilience, defined as a means to withstand difficulties and a positive capacity for recovery, may also be prompted by their life experiences. Many subsequent siblings recognize a range of gifts that they gained in their role, which points to their capacities as survivors and their resilient spirits.

Silver Linings

Some subsequent children believe that their role caused them to grow stronger, because it provided a unique perspective, and they witnessed their parents' survival. Martin, who was born after his four-year-old sister died of leukemia, was inspired by his parents' resiliency.

> *Now that I'm older, I look at my parents and what they went through. I gained some strength by understanding that they survived, and they went on. When I consider that, it's inspiring.* (Martin)

Sally, who was born after the death of a brother, grew up in a strained and neglectful home. The lack of nurturance that she received fueled her determination to survive and care for herself.

> *I was my mom's nurse. When I left on my own, I was strong. I took care of myself better than they ever took care of me.* (Sally)

Pressures of the subsequent child role, to be helpful and to avoid causing distress, are generally a negative and burdensome experience for subsequent siblings. However, some subsequent children, like Michael, concluded that parental pressure to be a good replacement also steered them away from negative behaviors and poor choices.

> *I felt strong as a kid, and I think I had to be strong because I was born into that role, born after my brother who died. My older brother and sister ended up making some bad choices. Maybe I stayed on a good track because I was in that role with my parents, and I felt like I had to be the good kid.* (Michael)

The experience of being a gift child, despite its significant difficulties, sometimes has a silver lining for subsequent children.

Some, like Liz and Rebecca, felt treasured and believe that they helped their parents to cope with their loss. They were both glad to provide some comfort to their parents, and they valued their close rapport with their mothers.

> *My mother was just so happy that I was in this world. I really felt like a special child.* (Liz)

> *I feel like I was able to maybe not fill [my deceased sister's] shoes obviously, because she was a different identity, but that I was able to give my mother the gift that she wanted. I felt good that through me, God granted her wish.* (Rebecca)

Some subsequent children, like Karen and Andrew, expressed gladness that the loss of their sibling promoted their spiritual growth and sense of meaning. They both believe that their deceased brothers are watching over them from heaven in protective and helpful roles, and they describe their sibling's death as a formative factor in their spiritual development.

> *I feel like [my brother's death] gave me a spiritual piece. I felt like wow, I have this older brother in heaven looking out for me. So every time I don't pay attention and almost get hit by a bus, I never do, maybe that has something to do with it. I believe that he is looking over me. He's more like an angel.* (Karen)

> *I learned early on about what happens to you, how people die. I was forced to think about something more than just what is in front of us, and I am glad to know that there is something larger out there. I believe that there's another spiritual world, a place where your soul may go, because I was always made to believe that my brother was in that place and that he was watching us.* (Andrew)

Susan shared a similar sense of enhanced spirituality and perspective that is rooted in her experience of loss.

I have great motivation and resilience, and although I carry a deep sorrow, I feel being a subsequent child enabled me to understand quite quickly what some people spend a lifetime trying to grasp. There is no certainty, only uncertainty. The human spirit is remarkable to carry on in the face of this, knowing that the unknown can bring unfathomable pain, and yet we risk still connecting, loving what we most might lose. (Susan)

Jane and Lana, who were both born after the death of a sister, claim that their subsequent child status and the memory of their sibling gave them positive perspectives and aspirations.

One positive has been a certain perspective. An appreciation of life. (Jane)

Seeing a picture of [my deceased sister], someone so beautiful and elegant, it created something to look forward to and live up to. It was very positive. (Lana)

Healing

In addition to identifying silver linings, some subsequent children shared developments in their adult lives that were healing for them. Nurturance provided later in life cannot replace the care that was needed in childhood, but it might foster relief and positive change. Margie felt invisible during her childhood, but as an adult she gradually developed a deep connection with her mother. Their bond was amplified when her mom was dying. She was grateful for the warmth and connection that were integral in their last moments together.

When my mom was dying, I got up in the bed behind her, just cradled her in my arms and on my lap. I could see she was struggling to go. God told me to just sing to her, [the song] "Turn your eyes on Jesus, look towards his wonderful face and the things of earth will grow strangely dim." I sang that through, and the second time through I actually felt her leave her body, like she went through mine. She gave me a last big hug all the way out. It was such a blessing. (Margie)

Janet was very moved, as an adult, when her parents engaged in a small but important step to repair their relationship with her.

My parents made baby books for all of my siblings when they were infants, but not for me. My sister-in-law decided that I needed one too. She approached my parents for needed information and involved them in its creation. So my parents were in their sixties as they were writing about their memories of me as a baby. They made no mention of my deceased brother. It was just a dedication to me, and that was healing. (Janet)

Janet later had a dream that vividly illustrated her evolving family narrative. It symbolized her heightened sense of belonging, without discounting the challenges of her childhood.

I had a dream about my family table. Captain chairs were at each end for my parents, and there were two chairs on each side for the four children. I walked around the table and realized that our family was complete. There was not a chair for [my deceased brother] Daniel, but it was OK. It was a short dream, but it was healing for me. It did not negate Daniel, but it changed the way that I look at my family. I always thought that Daniel was the missing piece. We never removed him from the family story, but in that dream, I realized that my family was still whole. I have an imperfect, perfect family. (Janet)

Supportive Bonds

For all children, the development of resilience and a positive sense of self relies upon connections to at least one supportive adult who sees and embraces them for who they are.

As children grow, they need to be recognized as unique, lovable human beings. Subsequent children, who may not always feel accepted for who they are, benefit tremendously if they are able to experience a positive bond; it is critical for their development, well-being, and mental health. Supportive adults can come into a subsequent child's life in various ways, and they might be a parent, grandparent, older sibling, close family friend, or teacher. Some subsequent children report growing up with one parent who enacted replacement dynamics while the other parent did not. The parent who is emotionally available, and who embraces the subsequent child as an individual, generally plays a vital role in promoting the child's positive identity formation, resilience, and overall well-being.

Several subsequent children revealed that their fathers were the ones to understand, support, and lovingly recognize them. Anna felt like she was a burden to her mother but described a nurturing relationship with her dad.

When you needed warmth and comfort, my father was there. Not my mother. She was kind of cold and hard. I didn't sense the feeling of embracing from her. (Anna)

Margie, Michelle, and Tret shared similar stories. Their mothers were often distant or emotionally unavailable, but their fathers were attuned to their needs.

Dad interacted with me much more than Mom did. I always felt like I was more Dad's baby than Mom's baby. (Margie)

My dad and I were close, much more than my mom and me. He was my rock. He was the one who recognized me, loved me and saw me, loved me and appreciated me. (Michelle)

I have memories of trying to get my mother's attention and not being able to. But I had enough attention because I had my dad. When I look at the pictures from when I was little, I can see the adoration that my father felt for me. There are pictures of my mother holding me too, but her expression is not the same as my father's when he was holding me. It's just very different. (Tret)

Natalie described a mom who saw her as an inadequate replacement, but also a dad who understood and validated her. He became Natalie's ally and advocate, challenging her mom's idealization of her deceased sister and replacement enactments.

My mom always shared little anecdotes, about things that [my deceased sister] had said. My sister didn't say much, she was only three, but I felt like my mother started embellishing the anecdotes, making her say things that a three-year-old would not say. Things about her clothes or about how neat she kept her room, whereas I was the total opposite. Then one day my dad called my mom on it. He said that he didn't remember that, and that my sister just screamed all the time. So then my mom stopped [the anecdotes and comparisons]. My father was always my ally. (Natalie)

Natalie experienced her dad as a nurturing parent from her childhood into adulthood. Like other subsequent siblings who experienced one caregiver as a loving advocate, it is probable that Natalie's positive bond with her dad fostered her resilience and her spirited determination. She insisted upon forming her own identity despite the pressures to replace her sister, and her resistance was advantageous for her well-being. Her bonded relationship with her dad and his ongoing support played a vital role in fostering her growth and her healthy capacity to push back against her mom's replacement enactments.

Supportive and special bonds were described with mothers as well. Some subsequent children had close rapports with their moms while their fathers were more distant. Sophie, who was born after the death of an infant sister, was fortunate to have close bonds with both of her parents, and she described a mother who was warm, supportive, and attuned in her mothering.

I thought my mom had to be the best mom ever, just ever. She always let me know that I was special and dear to her. (Sophie)

Many subsequent siblings spoke of relationships in their extended families or communities that were vital sources of support and that encouraged their development and growth. Kenneth and Mary, both subsequent children, identified their grandfathers as primary sources of love and care.

I dearly loved my grandfather. He would visit in the summers and help paint the house. I remember sitting outside and hanging out with him. That's one of my really good memories. I remember him more than I do my parents. (Kenneth)

My grandfather was a honey. He probably helped make up for the deficiencies I had in terms of parenting and a father figure. I lived with him for three years. I wish that he was still alive. (Mary)

Janet, born after a deceased brother, relied on a community of caring adults for the nurturance that she needed as a child.

One of the things that helped me was that I grew up with loving neighbors and a church community. I knew that I was loved, and I loved the people back. I had a lot of mom-like figures. I knew that I was the light of my grandfather's world, I had caring teachers in high school, and an elderly couple that was there for me. I found my emotional support and identity outside the home. (Janet)

Susan, who was born after the death of a sister, believes that her bond to her pets and her overall affinity with animals allowed her to survive. She chose not to have children and views her pets as her children. As an adult she went on to train animals, demonstrating the ongoing significance of animals in her life.

Ollie was my dog, and my relationship with him was truly the first uncomplicated relationship I ever had. I knew he was a dog and related to him as a dog, but he had no judgment. There were no complications. With him I was truly able to be an authentic child. (Susan)

Conclusion

The loss of a child ripples through a family, leaving a lasting mark upon all members. Children who are born after the death of a sibling inherit a painful loss and a complex role, but many are also remarkably adaptive. Those who can form a positive bond with at least one loving adult, inside or outside of their immediate family circle, generally fare best. Even one healthy attachment can provide them with a critical steppingstone, allowing them to feel accepted and loved while heightening their resilience and self-esteem.

Many subsequent children identify themselves as flexible survivors. When they recognize silver linings in their lived experience, without negating difficulties, they may be able to reframe their life stories and find pieces of healing. Their acknowledgment of strengths gained within their subsequent child role may allow them to identify and accept the many layers of their experience and the coexistence of suffering and resilience. Their discoveries of silver linings and opportunities for healing do not erase their painful or burdensome subsequent sibling histories, but they can foster growth, self-discovery, and empowerment.

21

Words of Wisdom

As they were interviewed, many participants shared that they had never talked so openly about their experiences or met another person with a subsequent child background. Their loss histories were often unspoken because they rarely had organic opportunities to discuss them, and the significance and impact of their sibling's death were often overlooked. Many subsequent children had words of advice and care for others in the same role and a deep desire to connect and share wisdom. Some expressed curiosity about the responses of other participants. They verbalized eagerness to read the research findings, as they were unsure how their feelings and experiences might compare. They frequently demonstrated a hope to prevent distress for future subsequent children and a desire to educate parents and families about the possible negative repercussions of being born after loss. In addition to the advice shared for subsequent children, words of guidance for bereaved parents were provided, both by subsequent children and by some of the bereaved parents who were interviewed.

Seeking Answers

Many subsequent children, like Michael, Edwin, and Dana, reinforce the importance of having adequate information. They encouraged other subsequent siblings to seek knowledge about their sibling and their sibling's death, and to get answers to any questions that they harbor.

Ask questions, while you still have the opportunity. If you feel like there is a mysterious event that happened that no one is talking about, ask questions and get answers while your parents are still alive, to get that closure. Because once your parents are gone, and the other people who were there when your sibling died are gone, you won't have the chance anymore. (Michael)

Without having more information about [your deceased sibling], it might be hard to live your life. It might be good to know. (Edwin)

Try to find out as much as you can. It is part of you, part of your history. Maybe I am giving myself advice. (Dana)

Others, like Jenna and Bal, elaborated upon the deep value in understanding their history and the significance of their loss.

It's important to understand all of this, because when you are a child, your personality really gets formed. (Jenna)

Sibling loss is important [for subsequent children] because it impacts you as your personality is developing, and those values are contributed to you right from the beginning. You carry them for your life and pass them on to the next generation. (Bal)

Andrew, who was born after his three-year-old brother drowned, shared the positive perspective that he gained from his loss and his brother's story. He encouraged other subsequent children to pursue information.

> *Try to learn as much as possible about your sibling, no matter what age they were. In my case, something really positive came up through discussing my brother. It helps to have a sense of respect for your deceased sibling, similar to the respect that you have for your elders. There are so many things that we could take for granted. My [deceased] brother gave me an appreciation of life.* (Andrew)

Advice for Parents of Subsequent Children

Several participants offered advice for bereaved parents who have a subsequent child. Karen, who was born after a deceased brother, grew up in a family that avoided all discussion of loss. They did not engage in any rituals to remember and honor her brother, and his death was a taboo topic. She shared her detrimental experience, and she encouraged grieving parents to engage in open communication and thoughtful commemorations for their deceased child.

> *Parents should never hide the death of their child from the sibling who is born after. Or leave a child out if there is any type of death in the family. I was born after my brother died, and then my dad died when I was really young. When my dad died, my mom sent me to the neighbor's house, and I spent two days there. They thought it was the right thing to do but removing a child from the grieving process is actually the worst thing to do. I started having nightmares about everyone else in my family dying, because I lost my brother and then my dad, and no one really talked to me about it. It would have been better if my [deceased] brother had been talked about. We could have said a little prayer for him at the table. Or brought a little token to his grave once a year. My family tried to protect me by not talking about him, but I wish we could have talked about him and remembered him.* (Karen)

Likewise, Tanya and Angelo, both subsequent children, grew up with parents who did not discuss their deceased siblings. They yearned for information and a shared grieving process. In their advice for bereaved parents, they stressed the importance of open dialogue.

If your child asks you [about their deceased sibling], explain it to your child. That's the best thing you can do. Leave the lines of communication open. (Tanya)

People should talk about it. [Subsequent children] should be able to ask questions that they need to ask. Parents should tell them everything. (Angelo)

Paulina, who was born after a deceased brother, agreed that communication is paramount.

It is important to talk about the deceased child. It should not be a taboo subject in the family for kids. (Paulina)

In addition to advising open discussion, many subsequent siblings provided feedback about how best to talk about the deceased child in the family. Tanya urged age-appropriate conversations that align with the family's spiritual beliefs, while Jane provided a reminder to avoid dwelling upon the loss.

Let [your subsequent child] know about their deceased sibling in a very clear way, and in a way that fits whatever your religious affiliation and spiritual affiliation may be. And it's got to be age appropriate for the child. (Tanya)

If you want to have another child, by all means have one. I think that's important. But in terms of raising the [subsequent] child, I would say it's important to talk about the loss. Talk about it, but don't dwell on it. (Jane)

Alan, born after a deceased sister, reflected upon the complexity of discussing and commemorating the loss of a child within a family. Cultural, personal, and spiritual influences inform each family's needs and practice. He thoughtfully encouraged grieving families to communicate in a way that is fitting for them.

I would say to talk about it, but I don't think there is just one way. Find what's right for you. (Alan)

Tanya reiterated the value of open communication in grieving families, pointing out that she and other subsequent children rarely have the opportunity to discuss their deceased sibling and their experience of loss.

It wasn't like you could go to somebody and say hey, I had a brother or sister who died before I was born. It's just not the kind of thing that kids have an outlet to go talk to other kids about. (Tanya)

Dierdre was born after a brother died of sudden infant death syndrome. She urged bereaved parents to get their own support and to be self-aware, with a goal of minimizing detrimental impacts of their grief upon their subsequent children.

My advice for parents is to work things through, so when you have a [subsequent] baby you don't keep thinking that this one is going to die too. Work it out before you have another kid, because some [bereaved] parents make a decision to have another kid and want it, but then freak out. That's not good. Counseling can help. (Dierdre)

In some cases, subsequent siblings used strong words or expressed anger in their advice for parents. Like Marisol and Pierre, they may carry frustration and sorrow about the toll and negative repercussions of parental grief.

Parents should go treat their issues and their grief. They are not the issues of the child who is born after. They can mention [the deceased child], but I find that when people harp on something too long it becomes a problem. To take their experience and to put it as part of their [subsequent child's] upbringing is sick. Parents should try to deal with it, and not put it on the [subsequent] child. (Marisol)

Don't throw guilt or baggage on the new kid. Baggage hurts. The more you lay on them, the more they have to carry around. (Pierre)

Despite the difficult ramifications of their sibling's death, such as replacement dynamics, familial pressures, and disrupted attachment experiences, it is conflictual for most subsequent children to feel angry at their bereaved parents. They have been tasked, in spoken and unspoken ways, to care for their parents and to avoid upsetting them. Most subsequent children feel immense empathy for their parents' grief. As they grow and evolve, many subsequent children may need to own and accept contradictory feelings toward their parents of anger and love, resentment and empathy. The ability to recognize and accept polarities in one's feelings and experiences is a sign of integration and health.

Words from Bereaved Parents

Several bereaved parents, like Agnes, shared advice for others who have lost a child. They recommended talking about one's grief and seeking support.

I think the one thing that helped me was that I wasn't afraid to talk about it. I feel like I did heal a little bit faster from telling the story. It helped me go through the grieving process. (Agnes)

Caroline, a bereaved mom, shared that she felt immense gratitude for her living children, despite struggling with her terrible loss. Her journal, which documented the trajectory of her grief but also recorded the stories of her surviving children, is an example of the healthy and healing way that she integrated the loss into her life story. She kept her deceased child close, but also continued to live and to treasure her living family members. Her story provides a healthy model of balance after loss.

> *It took me many, many years to come to terms with the whole thing, but I was so thankful to get two living children. One lovely gift that [my deceased child] Sebastian granted me was a journal. I started journaling as a way to measure my progress through the grief, and I just never stopped. The journal now has all the fun stories of my living children growing up. They are the greatest blessing of my life.* (Caroline)

Various parents, like Kate, commented upon the growth that they experienced because of their loss and urged others to be aware of silver linings.

> *I don't know that I would be the same person had I not lost Matthew. I might have a false sense of control. I think I'm a better person. I think I'm much more sensitive. I think I have a lot more compassion. I think I'm more present in all my relationships with people.* (Kate)

Ann, a bereaved mother with a subsequent child, highlighted the importance of open communication and advocacy, because outsiders are initially unaware of a family's history of loss.

> *When your child starts daycare, caregivers will need to be more sensitive to you and your child. They're not going to know that your family has gone through things, and you will need to tell them. You will need a relationship with them in order to feel safe leaving your baby.* (Ann)

Jayne reinforced the importance of letting subsequent children know, from the very beginning, about their deceased sibling.

She also believes that her subsequent child had an awareness of the deceased child, because they shared the same womb.

> *Charlotte [my subsequent baby] already knows Frank [her deceased brother]. She is the closest person to him because she shared the same space in the uterus.* (Jayne)

Perspective Finding

Some subsequent children advised seeking positives within the difficult and unwanted experiences of loss. Martin compared the experiences of subsequent children and bereaved parents and urged perspective taking. His message may be a double-edged sword for many. Perspective is helpful and can promote resilience, but it is also vital not to minimize or disenfranchise the experiences of subsequent children.

> *I would say that if it was difficult for you, just try to imagine how it was for your parents. I'm not a parent, but I can only imagine that's as bad as it gets. Burying your child must be the worst possible feeling. So if you find it to be some kind of stumbling block, just think about how your parents went on. How they continued to go to work and brush their teeth, everything every day, that says something about the human spirit.* (Martin)

Bal, who was born after a deceased brother, spoke of the perspective of gratitude that sometimes emerges after challenge and loss.

> *I think that loss always makes people in families come together and that's a good thing that comes out of something bad. It makes you realize the value of what you have rather than what you don't.* (Bal)

Remembering the Gifts

Several subsequent children, like Jenna, Margie, and Charlotte, encouraged others to use the skills acquired in their role to make the world a better place. Many also recommended finding meaning and purpose in accomplishing good deeds in the deceased sibling's name.

> *You can use your experience to help others. I just had a friend who had a stillbirth. She really went off the deep end. I used my family experience and background to talk to her about it.* (Jenna)

> *There are always blessings in hardships. Now I'm an includer. I don't like to see people left out. I do think that is part of who I became.* (Margie)

> *I really like to help others who are grieving or going through something really hard. I seek out people who need help. We call it Sabastian [my deceased brother's] legacy and say that he lives on through us.* (Charlotte)

Building Family Connection

Natalie, who was born after her three-year-old sister drowned, commented upon the importance of living in the present and of forming bonds and positive memories with family members who are still alive.

> *I think we should all have rituals as a family, with the family who is still here. Like not just holidays. More everyday types of rituals that could bring the family closer together. Maybe like a game night, or family vacations. Little everyday things, to have more fun together.* (Natalie)

Growth and Self-Care

Many subsequent children, like Daniel and Sally, underscored the value of gaining support, engaging in self-care, and building self-awareness.

> *If something comes up, and feelings hit you or something, or becomes in focus, I'd say not to deny it and not to ignore it. Please deal with your feelings. Don't hide them or push them down. Get the help you need. You need to cry, you need to be angry, you need to be hurt, you need to feel whatever the feeling is. (Daniel)*

> *My advice is to deal with it. Get therapy. If addiction is a problem, go to a twelve-step program. For me, a twelve-step program gave me the stability and support that I needed. (Sally)*

Author Kristina Schellinski, who is a subsequent child herself, states that some subsequent siblings will greatly benefit from heightening self-awareness, perhaps in therapy, to fully embody and access their true sense of self. She believes that not all subsequent children serve in a replacement role, but that those who experience replacement dynamics often struggle to form an authentic identity. She thinks that one of the most important tasks for subsequent children is individuation, or the formation of an authentic self, and that subsequent children often need to explore unconscious content and engage in therapeutic work in order to individuate.

"The question arises: 'Who am I really?' . . . Consciously encountering content that has remained unconscious for a long time can help to free a replacement child from being tied to the destiny of a dead other, and lead to a rediscovery of the inalienable life force, the self."[1]

Sarah: Illustrations of Meaning Making

Like Kristina, I believe that many of us need to explore our subsequent child roles and histories in order to fully understand who we are. There is much that we cannot control or change. As we revisit our histories and reconstruct meaning, we may forge new understanding and feel empowered and transformed as the authors of our own stories.

As an art therapist, I often turn to a creative process to make meaning. Themes connecting to my deceased sister and my role as a subsequent child sometimes organically appear in my artwork. I will share a few examples to demonstrate their scope and to illustrate that, for many of us, meaning making is an ongoing process throughout our lives. I was in my forties when I wrote the following piece, but it was the first time that I allowed myself to take ownership of my relationship to my sister. I surprised myself as I wrote with emotion and playfulness, reimagining my sister outside the lines of my family's closely guarded narrative.

What I Never Told You

Only silence has stretched between us, warm and flat as the grass on your tomb. You were six when you died and a little girl, so I was never mad at you, even though Mom always said that you were perfect, and you were everyone's favorite.

It occurs to me now that you never asked for that legacy, and that actually, you have nothing to do with it. It makes me happy to imagine you rebelling against your angelic reputation. Maybe we could have gotten into a lot of trouble together. I'd love to see how you would have proved Mom wrong. Domestic, married, home with kids? Surely you would have done the opposite. Maybe you would have been the cool big sister with gorgeous floral tattoos, bohemian perhaps, you would have lived in New York City before I got there and introduced me to all of your theater friends. I would have slept on your patchy velvet couch and heard all about your latest lovers and auditions. We would have stayed up late, lighting candles and draping scarves over the lamp shades for ambiance, while we ordered Afghan food from your huge folder of take-out menus. Maybe you would have been a vegetarian and dating the handsome dog walker who cared for your rescued greyhound named Stella.

Or you could have been a dynamo. Traveling the world with some important job, living out of a suitcase, trying to make the planet a better place. You'd smell like airports and expensive shampoo, and wear clothing that was always pressed, never a stain or a wrinkle. You'd call me from Tokyo; you would have still made time for me, I'm sure of it, and we'd giggle about my latest misadventures and make a plan to meet up in an improbable place. You'd outtalk the best of talkers and be one of those people who get things done.

I don't want to idealize you either, so I need to think of your flaws. You and I would have hurt each other sometimes, even the best of sisters do. Maybe you'd be a little selfish or you'd forget me sometimes, and I'd be the kid sister waiting for your call. Maybe you would have stolen my favorite T-shirt from my closet and never returned it, used my towel, or you could have been critical and cutting at times. You'll need some annoying habits, like always running late or interrupting and being a bad listener. I hope you would have been flawed in tons of ways but that I could have counted on you, and known that you had my back, just as I would have had yours.

What I never told you? I never said how deeply sad I am that you aren't here. That I am sorry and sad that you only had six short years to live, six short spins around the sun, such a short and unfinished dance. You didn't get to do many things. Like hang out with me. I really needed you, the cool and kind sister who would have been my ally, surely it would have been so.

Art Explorations

I created a series of story quilts while in quarantine during the COVID-19 pandemic. One of them features two girls. After sewing in the figures, I was surprised to recognize them as myself and my deceased sister, and to realize that some of my old losses were being rekindled by the many losses of the pandemic. I was initially unclear about which figure represented each of us and knew that our interchangeable identities and facelessness pointed to my experiences of replacement. One, a pink head and shoulders with striped hair, is placed in the foreground like an observer, while the other walks with the Empire State building behind her. I added Stella, the imaginary and wished-for greyhound, and a scattering of pink roses to represent the many flowers left on my sister's grave. I soon realized that I am the walking figure, whose placement in New York City, my beloved former home, is of significance. It is the location of my young adulthood, where I independently forged my professional life and carved out core pieces of my identity. While the figures are in different planes and do not interact, the quilt provided me with a space for a gentle coexistence with my deceased sister. In claiming the figure in movement, with outstretched arms and a complete body, as myself, I claimed my own aliveness and power.

Finally, I'll share a self-portrait. I made a series of painted envelopes during the pandemic, using ripped junk mail as my canvases. They became representations of my fluctuating moods, worries, and feelings of loss. One day, after creating another colorful and chaotic envelope, I glued it down to a larger piece of paper and added a figure who stands back to observe. I immediately recognized myself. She is in silhouette, which hints at a shadow of loss, but she is strong and clearly defined. She seems to look toward the envelope like a figure might study a painting at a museum. Her painted colors align with the tones of the envelope, but she is separate, refusing to be overwhelmed or entrapped by the envelope's chaos. As my self-portrait, I understand that she is marked and colored by her background of loss, but that she is not defined by it.

As subsequent children make meaning of the past, they can simultaneously look toward the future and begin authoring their next chapters. Their sibling's death and family's journey of loss will always be a part of who they become. My hope and wish for all of them is to weave an empowered and colorful life narrative, that holds the loss and its repercussions, but also gives weight to their strengths, inner truths, and authentic selves. They are the writers of their own expansive stories.

Notes

Preface

1   Vollmann, S. (2014). A legacy of loss: Stories of replacement dynamics and the subsequent child. *Omega: Journal of Death and Dying*, 69(3), 219–47.

2   O'Leary, J., Warland, J., and Parker, L. (2011). Prenatal parenthood. *Journal of Prenatal Educators*, 20:4.

Chapter 1

1   Cain, A.C., and Cain, B.S. (1964). On replacing a child. *Journal of American Academy of Child Psychiatry*, 3, 443–56.

2   Vollmann, S. (2014). A legacy of loss: Stories of replacement dynamics and the subsequent child. *Omega: Journal of Death and Dying*, 69(3), 219–47.

3   Cain, A.C., and Cain, B.S. (1964). On replacing a child. *Journal of American Academy of Child Psychiatry*, 3, 445.

4   Reid, M. (1992). Joshua – Life after death. The replacement child. *Journal of Child Psychotherapy*, 18(2), 109–38; O'Leary, J.M., Gaziano, C., and Thorwick, C. (2006). Born after loss: The invisible child in adulthood. *Journal of Prenatal and Perinatal Psychology and Health*, 21(1), 3–23; Sabbadini, A. (1988). The replacement child. *Contemporary Psychoanalysis*, 24(4), 528–47.

5   Anisfeld, L., and Richards, A.D. (2000). The replacement child: Variations on a theme in history and psychoanalysis. *Psychoanalytic Study of the Child*, 55, 301–18; Kogan, I. (2003). On being a dead, beloved child. *The Psychoanalytic Quarterly*, 72, 726–66.

6   Grout, L., and Romanoff, B. (2000). The myth of the replacement child: Parents' stories and practices after perinatal death. *Death Studies*, 24(2), 93–113; Wheeler, S.R. (2000). A loss of innocence and a gain in vulnerability: Subsequent pregnancy after a loss. *Illness, Crisis and Loss*, 8(3), 310–26.

7   Grout, L., and Romanoff, B. (2000). The myth of the replacement child: Parents' stories and practices after perinatal death. *Death Studies*, 24(2), 111.

Chapter 2

1   Neimeyer, R.A. (Ed.). (2001). *Meaning reconstruction and the experience of loss*. Washington, DC: American Psychological Association.

2   Cacciatore, J., and Flint, M. (2012). Mediating grief: Postmortem ritualization after child death. *Journal of Loss & Trauma*, 17(2), 158–72.

3   Doka, K. J. (2008). Disenfranchised grief in historical and cultural perspective. In M. S. Stroebe, R. O. Hansson, H. Schut, and W. Stroebe (Eds.), *Handbook of bereavement research and practice: Advances in theory and intervention* (pp. 223–40). Washington, DC: American Psychological Association.

4   O'Leary, J., and Warland, J. (2013). Untold stories of infant loss: The importance of contact with the baby for bereaved parents. *Journal of Family Nursing*, 19(3), 1–24.

5   Levang, E. (1998). *When men grieve: Why men grieve differently and how you can help*. Minneapolis, MN: Fairview Press, 58.

Chapter 3

1   Van den Bergh, B.R.H., van den Heuvel, M.I., Lahti, M., Braeken, M., et al. (2020). Prenatal developmental origins of behavior and mental health: The influence of maternal stress in pregnancy. *Neuroscience & Biobehavioral Reviews*, 117, 26–64.

2   O'Murchu, D. (2004). *Quantum theology: Spiritual implications of the new physics*. New York: The Crossroad Publishing Company, 84.

3   O'Leary, J., and Thorwick, C. (2008). Attachment to the unborn child and parental representation of pregnancy following perinatal loss. *Attachment: New Directions in Psychotherapy and Relational Psychoanalysis*, 2(3), 292–320.

4   O'Leary, J., and Warland, J. (2016). *Meeting the needs of parents pregnant and parenting after perinatal loss*. London: Routledge Publishing.
5   Côté-Arsenault, D., and Donato, K. (2011). Emotional cushioning in pregnancy after perinatal loss. *Journal of Reproductive and Infant Psychology*, 29(1), 81–92.
6   Knight, M. (1997). *Love letters*. Travis City, MI: Single Eye Publishing.
7   O'Leary, J., and Warland, J. (2016). Offering a therapeutic educational support group. In J. O'Leary and J. Warland (Eds.), *Meeting the Needs of Parents Pregnant and Parenting after Perinatal Loss* (pp. 156–71). London: Routledge Publishing.
8   O'Leary, J.M., and Henke, L. (2017). Therapeutic educational support for families pregnant after loss: A continued bond/attachment perspective. *Journal of Psychotherapy: Special Section*, 3(54).

Chapter 4

1   Bowlby, J. (1982). *Attachment and loss* (second edition). New York: Basic Books.
2   Trout, M. (2021). *Four decades in infant mental health: This hallowed ground*. Newcastle Upon Tyne: Cambridge Scholars Publishing.
3   Ainsworth, M.D.S. (1979). Infant-mother attachment. *American Psychologist*, 34, 932–37.
4   Erikson, E.H. (1950). *Childhood and society*. New York: Norton.
5   Fraiberg, S., Adelson, E., and Shapiro, V. (1975). Ghosts in the nursery: A psychoanalytic approach to the problem of impaired infant-mother relationships. *Journal of American Academy of Child Psychiatry*, 14, 387–421.
6   Markin, R. (2018). "Ghosts" in the womb: A mentalizing approach to understanding and treating prenatal attachment disturbances during pregnancies after loss. *Psychotherapy*, 55(3), 275–88.
7   O'Leary, J., and Gaziano, C. (2011). The experience of adult siblings born after loss. *Attachment*, 5(3), 246–72.
8   Knight, M. (1997). *Love letters*. Travis City, MI: Single Eye Publishing.

9   O'Leary, J., and Warland, J. (2016). *Meeting the needs of parents pregnant and parenting after perinatal loss.* London: Routledge Publishing.

Chapter 5

1   Cain, A.C., and Cain, B.S. (1964). On replacing a child. *Journal of American Academy of Child Psychiatry,* 3, 443–56.
2   Vollmann, S. (2014). A legacy of loss: Stories of replacement dynamics and the subsequent child. *Omega: Journal of Death and Dying,* 69(3), 219–47.
3   Shellinski, K. (2019). *Individuation for adult replacement children: Ways of coming into being.* London: Routledge.

Chapter 6

1   Powell, M. (1995). Sudden infant death syndrome: The subsequent child. *British Journal of Social Work,* 25(2), 227–40.
2   Grout, L., and Romanoff, B. (2000). The myth of the replacement child: Parents' stories and practices after perinatal death. *Death Studies,* 24(2), 93–113.
3   Vollmann, S. (2014). A legacy of loss: Stories of replacement dynamics and the subsequent child. *Omega: Journal of Death and Dying,* 69(3), 219–47.
4   Burnett, F. H. (1886). *Little Lord Fauntleroy.* New York: Charles Scribner's Sons.

Chapter 7

1   Attig, T. (2011). *How we grieve: Relearning the world,* second edition. New York: Oxford University Press.
2   Neimeyer, R.A. (Ed.). (2001). *Meaning reconstruction and the experience of loss.* Washington, DC: American Psychological Association.

Chapter 9

1   O'Leary, J., and Gaziano, C. (2011). Sibling grief after perinatal loss. *Journal of Pre and Perinatal Psychology & Health,* 25(3), 173–93.

2   Jonas-Simpson C., Steele, R., Granek, L., Davies, B., and O'Leary, J. (2014). Always with me: Understanding experiences of bereaved children whose baby sibling died. *Death Studies*, 39(1–5), 242–51.

3   Howard Sharp, K.M., Russell, C., Keim, M., Barrera, M., Gilmer, M.J., Foster Akard, T., Compas, B.E., Fairclough, D.L., Davies, B., Hogan, N., Young-Saleme, T., Vannatta, K., and Gerhardt, C.A. (2018). Grief and growth in bereaved siblings: Interactions between different sources of social support. *School Psychology Quarterly*, 33(3), 363–71.

4   Wegner, M. (2015). *Embracing Laura: The grief and healing following the death of an infant twin.* Morrisville, NC: Lulu Publishing Services, 7.

5   O'Leary, J. (2007). Pregnancy and infant loss: Supporting parents and their children. *Zero to Three*, 27(6), 42–49.

6   Wegner, M. (2015). *Embracing Laura: The grief and healing following the death of an infant twin.* Morrisville, NC: Lulu Publishing Services, 14.

7   Limbo, R., and Kobler, K. (2009). Will our baby be alive again? Supporting parents of young children when a baby dies. *Nursing for Women's Health*, 13(4): 302–11.

Chapter 10

1   Rosen, G. (1982). Replacement children: Expanding the concept. *Journal of Developmental and Behavioral Pediatrics*, 3(4), 239–40.

Chapter 11

1   Hayes, J. (2016). Praising the dead: On the motivational tendency and psychological function of eulogizing the deceased. *Motivation and Emotion*, 40, 375–88.

Chapter 14

1   Cain, A.C., and Cain, B.S. (1964). On replacing a child. *Journal of American Academy of Child Psychiatry*, 3, 443–56.

Chapter 17

1   Klass, D., Silverman, P.R., and Nickman, S.L. (Eds.). (1996). *Continuing bonds: New understandings of grief*. London: Taylor & Francis.
2   Freud, S. (1917). Mourning and melancholia. In *The Standard Edition of the Complete Psychological Works of Sigmund Freud, Volume XIV (1914–1916): On the History of the Psycho-Analytic Movement, Papers on Metapsychology and Other Works* (pp. 237–58). https://pep-web.org/browse/document/SE .014.0000A?page=PR0005.

Chapter 18

1   Silverman, P.R., Nickman, S., and Worden, J.W. (1992). Detachment revisited: The child's reconstruction of a dead parent. *American Journal of Orthopsychiatry*, 62(4), 496.
2   Anisfeld, L., and Richards, A.D. (2000). The replacement child: Variations on a theme in history and psychoanalysis. *Psychoanalytic Study of the Child*, 55, 301–18.
3   Bergmann M.S., and Jucovey, M.E. (1990). *Generations of the Holocaust*. New York: Columbia University Press.
4   Shoshan, T. (1989). Mourning and longing from generation to generation. *American Journal of Psychotherapy*, 43, 193–207.
5   Kellermann, N.P.F. (2001). Transmission of holocaust trauma— an integrative view. *Psychiatry*, 64(3), 256–67.
6   Lieberman, S. (1979). A transgenerational theory. *Journal of Family Therapy*, (1)3, 347–60.
7   Hirsch, M. (2012). *The generation of postmemory: Writing and visual culture after the Holocaust*. New York: Columbia University Press, p. 5.

Chapter 21

1   Schellinski, K. (2019). *Individuation for adult replacement children: Ways of coming into being*. London: Routledge, p. 42.

Bibliography

Ainsworth, Mary S. "Infant–Mother Attachment." *American Psychologist* 34, no. 10 (1979): 932–37.

Anisfeld, L., and A.D. Richards. "The Replacement Child. Variations on a Theme in History and Psychoanalysis." *The Psychoanalytic Study of the Child* 55 (2000): 301–18.

Anisfeld, Leon, and Arnold D. Richards. "The Replacement Child: Variations on a Theme in History and Psychoanalysis." *The Psychoanalytic Study of the Child* 55, no. 1 (January 2000): 301–18.

Attig, Thomas. *How We Grieve: Relearning the World*. Oxford: Oxford University Press, 1996.

Bowlby, John. *Attachment and Loss. 3: Loss: Sadness and Depression*. London: Penguin Books, 1991.

Burnett, Frances Hodgson. "Little Lord Fauntleroy, by Frances Hodgson Burnett." January 16, 2006. Accessed April 19, 2024. https://www.gutenberg.org/files/479/479-h/479-h.htm.

Cacciatore, Joanne, and Melissa Flint. "Mediating Grief: Postmortem Ritualization After Child Death." *Journal of Loss and Trauma* 17, no. 2 (March 2012): 158–72.

Cain, Albert C., and Barbara S. Cain. "On Replacing a Child." *Journal of the American Academy of Child Psychiatry* 3, no. 3 (July 1964): 443–56.

Doka, Kenneth J. "Disenfranchised Grief in Historical and Cultural Perspective." In *Handbook of Bereavement Research and Practice: Advances in Theory and Intervention*, edited by Margaret S. Stroebe, Robert O. Hansson, Henk Schut, and Wolfgang Stroebe, 223–40. Washington, DC: American Psychological Association, 2008.

Erikson, Erik H. *Childhood and Society*. New York: W. W. Norton & Co., 1950.

Fraiberg, S., E. Adelson, and V. Shapiro. "Ghosts in the Nursery. A Psychoanalytic Approach to the Problems of Impaired Infant-Mother
Relationships." *Journal of the American Academy of Child Psychiatry* 14, no. 3 (1975): 387–421.

Freud, S. "Mourning and Melancholia." In *The Standard Edition of the
Complete Psychological Works of Sigmund Freud, Volume XIV
(1914-1916): On the History of the Psycho-Analytic Movement,
Papers on Metapsychology and Other Works.* London: The Hogart
Press, 1917.

Gaziano, Cecilie. "Sibling Grief After Perinatal Loss." *Journal of Prenatal & Perinatal Psychology & Health* 25, no. 3 (2011): 173–93.

Grout, L.A., and B.D. Romanoff. "The Myth of the Replacement Child:
Parents' Stories and Practices After Perinatal Death." *Death Studies*
24, no. 2 (March 2000): 93–113.

Hayes, Joseph. "Praising the Dead: On the Motivational Tendency and
Psychological Function of Eulogizing the Deceased." *Motivation
and Emotion* 40, no. 3 (June 2016): 375–88.

Hirsch, Marianne. *The Generation of Postmemory: Writing and Visual
Culture After the Holocaust.* New York: Columbia University
Press, 2012.

Howard Sharp, Katianne M., Claire Russell, Madelaine Keim, Maru
Barrera, Mary Jo Gilmer, Terrah Foster Akard, Bruce E. Compas,
et al. "Grief and Growth in Bereaved Siblings: Interactions between
Different Sources of Social Support." *School Psychology Quarterly*
33, no. 3 (September 2018): 363–71.

Jonas-Simpson, Christine, Rose Steele, Leeat Granek, Betty Davies, and
Joann O'Leary. "Always With Me: Understanding Experiences of
Bereaved Children Whose Baby Sibling Died." *Death Studies* 39,
no. 4 (April 21, 2015): 242–51.

Kellermann, N. P. "Transmission of Holocaust Trauma: An Integrative
View." *Psychiatry* 64, no. 3 (2001): 256–67.

Klass, Dennis (Ed.). *Continuing Bonds: New Understandings of Grief.*
Philadelphia, PA: Taylor & Francis, 1996.

Knight, Mary. *Love Letters Before Birth and Beyond.* First edition. Bal-
timore, MD: Single Eye Pub, 1997.

Kogan, Ilany. "On Being a Dead, Beloved Child." *The Psychoanalytic
Quarterly* 72, no. 3 (July 2003): 727–66.

Levang, Elizabeth. *When Men Grieve: Why Men Grieve Differently and
How You Can Help.* Minneapolis, MN: Fairview Press, 1998.

Lieberman, Stuart. "A Transgenerational Theory." *Journal of Family Therapy* 1, no. 3 (1979): 347–60.

Limbo, Rana, and Kathie Kobler. "Will Our Baby Be Alive Again? Supporting Parents of Young Children When a Baby Dies." *Nursing for Women's Health* 13, no. 4 (August 2009): 302–11.

Markin, Rayna D. "'Ghosts' in the Womb: A Mentalizing Approach to Understanding and Treating Prenatal Attachment Disturbances during Pregnancies after Loss." *Psychotherapy* 55, no. 3 (September 2018): 275–88.

Menninger, W. Walter. "Generations of the Holocaust—Edited by Martine S. Bergmann and Milton E. Jucovy; Basic Books, New York City, 1982." *Psychiatric Services* 34, no. 10 (October 1983): 970–71.

Murchu, Diarmuid. *Quantum Theology: Spiritual Implications of the New Physics.* Chestnut Ridge, NY: Crossroad, 2004.

Neimeyer, Robert A. *Meaning Reconstruction & the Experience of Loss.* Washington, DC: American Psychological Association, 2001.

O'Leary, J., C. Gaziano, and C. Thorwick. "Born after Loss: The Invisible Child in Adulthood." *Journal of Prenatal and Perinatal Psychology and Health* 21, no. 1 (2006): 3–23.

O'Leary, Joann. "Subsequent Pregnancy: Healing to Attach after Perinatal Loss." *BMC Pregnancy and Childbirth* 15, no. 1 (April 15, 2015): A15.

O'Leary, Joann M. "Pregnancy and Infant Loss: Supporting Parents and Their Children." *Zero to Three* 27, no. 6 (July 2007): 42–49.

O'Leary, Joann M., and Lindsey Henke. "Therapeutic Educational Support for Families Pregnant after Loss (PAL): A Continued Bond/Attachment Perspective." *Psychotherapy* 54, no. 4 (December 2017): 386–93.

O'Leary, Joann, and Jane Warland. *Meeting the Needs of Parents Pregnant and Parenting After Perinatal Loss.* London: Routledge, 2016.

O'Leary, Joann, and Jane Warland. "Untold Stories of Infant Loss: The Importance of Contact With the Baby for Bereaved Parents." *Journal of Family Nursing* 19, no. 3 (August 2013): 324–47.

O'Leary, Joann, Jane Warland, and Lynnda Parker. "Prenatal Parenthood." *The Journal of Perinatal Education* 20, no. 4 (January 2011): 218–20.

Powell, Maria. "Sudden Infant Death Syndrome: The Subsequent Child." *The British Journal of Social Work* 25, no. 2 (April 1995): 227–40.

Reid, Marguerite. "Joshua - Life after Death. the Replacement Child." *Journal of Child Psychotherapy* 18, no. 2 (July 1992): 109–38.

Rosen, Gerald. "Replacement Children: Expanding the Concept." *Journal of Developmental & Behavioral Pediatrics* 3, no. 4 (December 1982): 239–40.

Sabbadini, Andrea. "The Replacement Child." *Contemporary Psychoanalysis* 24, no. 4 (October 1988): 528–47.

Schellinski, Kristina E. *Individuation for Adult Replacement Children: Ways of Coming into Being*. London: Routledge, 2019.

Shoshan, Tamar. "Mourning and Longing from Generation to Generation." *American Journal of Psychotherapy* 43, no. 2 (April 1989): 193–207.

Silverman, Phyllis R., Steven Nickman, and J. William Worden. "Detachment Revisited: The Child's Reconstruction of a Dead Parent." *American Journal of Orthopsychiatry* 62, no. 4 (1992): 494–503.

Stroebe, Margaret S., Robert O. Hansson, Henk Schut, and Wolfgang Stroebe (Eds). *Handbook of Bereavement Research and Practice: Advances in Theory and Intervention*. Washington, DC: American Psychological Association, 2008.

Trout, Michael. *Four Decades in Infant Mental Health: This Hallowed Ground*. Newcastle Upon Tyne, UK: Cambridge Scholars Publishing, 2021.

Van Den Bergh, Bea R.H., Marion I. Van Den Heuvel, Marius Lahti, Marijke Braeken, Susanne R. De Rooij, Sonja Entringer, Dirk Hoyer, et al. "Prenatal Developmental Origins of Behavior and Mental Health: The Influence of Maternal Stress in Pregnancy." *Neuroscience & Biobehavioral Reviews* 117 (October 2020): 26–64.

Vollmann, Sarah Reed. "A Legacy of Loss: Stories of Replacement Dynamics and the Subsequent Child." *OMEGA - Journal of Death and Dying* 69, no. 3 (November 2014): 219–47.

Wegner, Martha. *Embracing Laura: The Grief and Healing Following the Death of an Infant Twin*. Omaha, NE: Centering Corporation, 1998.

Wheeler, Sara Rich. "A Loss of Innocence and a Gain in Vulnerability: Subsequent Pregnancy after a Loss." *Illness, Crisis & Loss* 8, no. 3 (July 2000): 310–26.

Index

About the Authors

Sarah Vollmann, MPS, ATR-BC, LICSW, is a registered, board-certified art therapist and a licensed independent clinical social worker. She maintains a private practice with a focus upon grief and traumatic loss, and she is a faculty member of the Portland Institute for Loss and Transition. Sarah is also the lead counselor at Buckingham Browne & Nichols School. She is associate director of the Young Widowhood Project, and she is earning her doctorate in social work at Tulane University. A member of the Artful Grief team of art therapists, Sarah works with military families facing suicide bereavement and traumatic loss. Her international art therapy concentration includes work with The Red Pencil. Sarah has published articles and book chapters on grief and loss, including a research article entitled "A Legacy of Loss: Stories of Replacement Dynamics and the Subsequent Child" (2014). Her interest in the transgenerational transmission of loss has additionally led to some work and upcoming research in Rwanda with second-generation survivors of the genocide. She presents both nationally and internationally on art therapy, grief, and bereavement.

Joann O'Leary began her career as a licensed practical nurse in a neonatal intensive care unit, then a birth to five special education program. After her MPH, she moved into a hospital setting working with families within a high-risk perinatal center. Her PhD is in family education. Her area of focus, research, and writing is on pregnancy and parenting after the loss of a baby and how the loss impacts not only the parents but siblings alive at the time of the loss of a baby, as well as those (children and adults) who were born after the loss. She has taught courses at the university level for over thirty years with a focus on prenatal parenting and unexpected outcomes of pregnancy, including the impact on children. She has facilitated support groups for bereaved families for over thirty-five years. She has published over fifty-seven articles and is the author of *Meeting the Needs of Parents Pregnant and Parenting after Loss* (2016) and *Different Baby, Different Story: Pregnancy and Parenting after Loss* (2020). She has also authored two book chapters on pregnancy after loss.